Demanding the Impossible?

Human Nature and Politics in Nineteenth-Century Social Anarchism

David Morland

CASSELL
London and Washington

To Liane

Cassell
Wellington House
125 Strand
London WC2R 0BB

PO Box 605
Herndon VA, 20172

First published 1997

British Library Cataloguing-in-Publication Data
A catalogue record for this book is available from the British Library.

Library of Congress Cataloging-in-Publication Data

Morland, David.

Demanding the impossible?: human nature and politics in nineteenth-century social anarchism/David Morland.

p. cm.

Includes bibliographical references and index.

ISBN 0–304–33685–8. — ISBN 0–304–33687–4 (pbk.)

1. Anarchism. 2. Social psychology. 3. Kropotkin, Petr Alekseevich, kniaz, 1842–1921. 4. Proudhon, P.-J. (Pierre-Joseph), 1809–1865. 5. Bakunin, Mikhail Aleksandrovich, 1814–1876.

I. Title.

HX833.M647 1997

320.5'7' 09034—dc21   97–1672
                                                               CIP

ISBN 0 304 33685 8 (hardback)
      0 304 33687 4 (paperback)

Designed and typeset by Ben Cracknell Studios

Printed and bound in Great Britain by Biddles Ltd, Guildford and King's Lynn

Contents

Preface

Traditionally, anarchists are seen to possess an optimistic conception of human nature, an optimism essential to the success of their vision of a stateless society. By illustrating that social anarchism employs a conception of human nature that assumes the existence of both egoism and sociability, this book endeavours both to correct common misapprehensions about its conception of human nature and to reveal the true nature of the relationship between that conception of human nature and social anarchism's ideal of a future society.

The concept of human nature is critical to arguments about what is wrong with society and how those wrongs should be put right. It is a descriptive and evaluative formula that justifies social change, or the maintenance of the status quo if deemed appropriate. Consequently, any ideology is the more convincing if its conception of human nature is commensurate with its political prescriptions. If a conception of human nature has elements within it that jeopardize the success of its recommendations for change, then the persuasive capacity of its host ideology is seriously undermined.

This is the case with social anarchism. This work will demonstrate that the social anarchists' conception of human nature is fundamentally incompatible with their self-incurred obligation of establishing a future stateless society. Given this discrepancy the feasibility of their preferred society looks increasingly improbable on two counts. First, there is little in their conception of human nature that merits profound faith in the eventual realization of an anarchist society. And secondly, even if that society came about the assumptions of imperfection and egoism inherent in their conception of human nature render the maintenance of order, without recourse to something akin to a state, unsustainable.

The task of revealing this discrepancy is one that I approached with some ambivalence. I have deep sympathies for much of what anarchism has to offer, but am conscious of the need to understand one's own weaknesses in an essentially normative set of considerations, which is the battle of ideologies. Recognition of an ideology's weak spots helps fortify it for the inevitable criticism that will come its way. This much anarchists of all hues should acknowledge. For that I am grateful to some of my fellow sympathizers who have tolerated my scepticism and explicit criticism of anarchism. Perhaps that is the ultimate testament to the value that anarchists place on freedom.

Acknowledgements

This book is the end result of my doctoral research, which I undertook as a part-time student at the University of York. Whilst the work has undergone a series of changes since then, its basic argument remains the same. Because of that I am indebted to my supervisor, Peter Nicholson, for his perspicuous comments and analysis and for correcting the numerous errors of style, interpretation and factual accuracy that permeated earlier drafts. Similarly, I owe a debt of gratitude to John Crump, whose assistance in helping me come to terms with the overall project was invaluable.

I should like to thank my former colleagues at the University of Sunderland, Peter Hayes, Mike Jones and Peter Rowell, for their comments on this work. I am also deeply indebted to my former colleague at the University of Northumbria, John Armitage, for his thoughtful and telling advice on a number of sections. I should also like to thank Steve Millett and Jon Purkis for the benefit of their proofreading and analytical skills when asked to read various chapters.

For easing the financial difficulties of this research as a part-time student I owe many thanks to my parents. And finally, but most of all, I should like to thank my partner, Liane Brierley, for helping me edit much of what I have written, and for her understanding and forbearance which enabled me to complete this project when I should have been devoting far more attention to my parental responsibilities.

Introduction

Political ideologies are complex and compelling phenomena. They have, in recent years, been subject to a resurgence of interest and analysis, particularly but not exclusively within academia. It is in the nature of political ideologies that they may rest in slumber for lengthy periods of time before erupting onto the political stage, disgorging fundamental changes in social and political institutions whilst simultaneously triggering an introspective analysis of their concepts and values. This book is about one ideology in particular, anarchism; an ideology that is becoming increasingly important as a source of inspiration to those who feel that the democratic practices of contemporary society have little, if anything, to commend them. Disenchanted with parliamentary politics many people, like those who protest against new road-building, are now employing tactics, such as direct action, that have long been at the heart of the anarchist activist creed, and are incorporating some of anarchism's most basic principles when moulding their own ideological clay.

Despite the renewed interest in anarchist ideas and arguments, there is little point in simply resurrecting the works of long-dead theorists and treating them as revolutionary gospels that encapsulate permanent truths. Whilst much of what past anarchist thinkers said is still seminally important and relevant, the errors and inconsistencies in these works cannot be ignored. Part of the problem is that some of these faults remain undetected, or are dismissed as insignificant. It is my intention to illustrate what I consider to be the most fundamental inconsistency in anarchist ideology, a theoretical disparity that has to be addressed if anarchists are to produce a coherent argument that can form the basis of their attempts not only to persuade the people that their cause is just and right but that it is feasible also.

Anarchism and Human Nature

As James Joll has remarked, there are at least three different ways of looking at anarchism.[1] Anarchism may be seen as a political ideology – a collection of ideas about social organization and social change.

Alternatively, it may be regarded as a political movement that endeavours to transform a political revolution into a social revolution that is consistent in both means and ends. Further still, anarchism may be perceived as a temperament that inspires and engages in revolution as an act in itself. Although this work covers all three perspectives, it deals principally with the first. In particular, it is concerned with the relationship between human nature and politics in anarchist ideology.

As an ideology anarchism should be understood as a collection of concepts, principles and assumptions that go together to form a world view. But this is a partial or biased vantage point. As Robert Eccleshall observes, ideologies provide the linguistic and conceptual material through 'which people clarify and justify their actions as they pursue divergent interests'.[2] Political ideologies afford an interpretation of the past and the present and offer a set of political recommendations for a future society. Ideologies are therefore in the business of interpreting history and of winning converts to their cause. And, inevitably, political ideologies, including anarchism, are concerned with defining conceptions of human nature and establishing courses of action in light of their results.

There are, of course, many definitions of anarchism. Most of these correspond to divergent theories of economic organization, such as mutualism, collectivism and communism. Mutualism is most closely associated with Pierre-Joseph Proudhon. Essentially, mutualism is premised on individuals entering into self-assumed obligations with one another expressed through the notion of a free contract. The individual, who is the basic unit of Proudhon's programme, retains possession of the instruments of labour. Proudhon operates a labour theory of value, and goods are exchanged accordingly, either directly for other products of the same value or for labour notes which are issued by a People's Bank. Michael Bakunin coined the term collectivism. Whereas Proudhon envisaged individuals or groups of individuals as the building blocks of economic organization, Bakunin regarded associations of producers as the primary economic organs. Here, private property is restricted to individual labour, and Bakunin assumes that associations of workers control the land and the means of production, which are held in common. The other distinguishing feature of collectivism is its labour proviso. Under collectivism the principle of distributive justice is as follows: From each according to their ability, to each according to their deeds. Communist-anarchism achieved its intellectual culmination in the works of Peter Kropotkin.

Communism assumes the common ownership not only of the means of production but of the products of labour too. Therefore, it is the commune rather than associations of workers which forms the basic unit of society; and the principle of distributive justice here consists of the more familiar adage: From each according to their ability, to each according to their needs.

For the purposes of this analysis all of the above categories and theorists are incorporated under the label of social anarchism, which constitutes the investigative remit of this work. Defining social anarchism is not easy. Perhaps it is best summarized as a broad belief in a society underpinned by a spirit of solidarity, a society perceived as an organic whole within which individual freedom is mediated through some notion of communal individuality. This contrasts starkly with individualist anarchism, which is largely the product of American writers like Josiah Warren, Lysander Spooner, Benjamin Tucker and Murray Rothbard. Individualist anarchism is the stream of anarchist thought that approximates most closely to classical liberalism. It is best conceived as a theory of an atomistic society of sovereign individuals whose relationships with one another are framed within the context of the economic market. Individual sovereignty is considered inviolable, and all functions now carried out by the state would be brokered through the market.

The term anarchism may be defined in a number of ways, but the concept of human nature is subject to interminable dispute. Indeed, it is what political philosophers refer to as an essentially contested concept: that is, there is no universal agreement about the meaning of human nature. Broadly speaking, the controversy centres on whether human nature should be thought of as something innate to the entire species of Homo Sapiens or whether it ought to be viewed as a reflection of particular environmental circumstances. Human nature, it is argued, either is universal and something that is inherent in all of us, or is socially constructed within a given human and social environment. However, this division is seldom maintained with any thoroughness. Political ideologies, including social anarchism, often rely on a conception of human nature that draws on both dimensions of this argument.

Besides the debate over what constitutes human nature, a debate to which there may be no satisfactory resolution, conceptions of human nature may be subjected to various forms of analysis. Graeme Duncan has outlined three different kinds of approach.[3] The first involves the collation of evidence, sociological or historical, for example, to challenge the feasibility of the argument under examination. A second approach concerns itself with the consequences that arise from a conception of human nature, thereby offering judgment on its practical or tangible outcome. The third method of inspection concentrates on whether the conception of human nature is consistent with the remainder of the ideology or wider political theory.

The Argument of this Book

The argument of this book is an analytical exercise constrained within the parameters of the third approach adumbrated above. It is definitely not an attempt to elaborate a definition of human nature itself. Given the essential contestability of the concept of human nature, such an exercise is probably futile. Rather it is an analysis of the conception of human nature employed by anarchist writers in their broader political ideology, and of whether their notion of human nature is commensurate with the other elements of the ideology when all are taken together.

The book endeavours to uncover some of the strengths together with one of, if not the, major weakness of this often misunderstood ideology. To that end this work embarks on an analytical investigation of the conception of human nature that is integral to anarchist ideology. By 'anarchist ideology' I refer, here and throughout the remainder of the book, to the ideology of social anarchism. Accordingly, this work does not attempt to examine the writings and philosophy of individualist anarchism. Rather, it concentrates on the writings of the three giants of nineteenth-century European social anarchism, Proudhon, Bakunin and Kropotkin, and attempts to reveal what it is about their conception of human nature that unites them, and, more importantly, why it is that their ideological narrative ultimately fails. Herbert Read, the influential art critic and anarchist, once argued that the 'task of the anarchist philosopher is not to prove the imminence of a Golden Age, but to justify the value of believing in its possibility'.[4] To accomplish that task the social anarchists of the nineteenth century have to conceive of human nature in such a way that will not only explain why anarchy is desirable, but how it is possible. In other words, their conception of human nature has to be strong enough to bear the weight imposed by their goal of a future stateless society.

It is precisely at this juncture that anarchism is most frequently misrepresented. To illustrate this I should like to present the reader with two recent examples, although other instances of such misapprehension permeate past academic writings, such as those of David Apter and Andrew Gamble.[5] My first contemporary example is located in a work by Ian Adams. In his book *Political Ideology Today*, Adams argues that anarchism rests 'upon certain basic assumptions about human nature and its relation to society', one of which is: 'Humanity is essentially good, but is corrupted by government.'[6] This may be true of Jean-Jacques Rousseau, but it is neither an accurate nor a comprehensive assessment of the role played by the concept of human nature in anarchist ideology. A similar error of perception emerges in another recent work on ideologies by Andrew Heywood. In his *Political Ideologies: An Introduction*, Heywood contends that the core of anarchism is founded on 'an unashamed utopianism, a belief in the natural goodness, or at least potential goodness, of humankind. Social order arises naturally and spontaneously; it does not require the machinery of "law and order". This is why anarchist conclusions have been reached by political thinkers who possess an essentially optimistic view of human nature.'[7]

It is the design of this work to furnish an alternative and more accurate perspective concerning anarchists and their conception of human nature. Anarchism is not inspired by 'an unashamed utopianism', at least not in the manner that Heywood believes, nor is it the ideological outcome of those working with 'an essentially optimistic view of human nature'. To be fair to Heywood, he does go on to say that 'anarchists have seldom asserted that people are "naturally good" . . . [more willingly they see human nature as 'plastic'] . . . fashioned by environmental factors rather than any innate "goodness" or "badness"'.[8] But even in this qualified interpretation, Heywood is only partly right. Whilst anarchists certainly rely on 'environmental factors' to establish the groundwork for their belief that human nature is capable of providing a strong enough basis for anarchy to become a realistic alternative to state-led exploitation and domination, this is only one element in the anarchists' ideological conception of human nature. Parallel to the contextual or environmental element there is a given or inherent constituent that is incontrovertibly characterized as 'badness'. Sociability and egoism are opposite sides of the same coin. Heywood and others, among them Adams and Gamble, are simply mistaken in asserting that anarchists are the proprietors of an essentially optimistic view of human nature. It would be more accurate to suggest that social anarchists erect their ideological narrative upon a double-barrelled conception of human nature. Human nature, for the social anarchists, is composed of both sociability and egoism (which correspond rather loosely to what Heywood and others term 'goodness' and 'badness'). All three anarchists under examination in this work acknowledge that they employ a notion of human nature that follows this basic paradigm. Differing as they do in other parts of their ideological argument, Proudhon, Bakunin and Kropotkin definitely share a substantial measure of common ground when mapping out their conception of human nature.

This is not to suggest that each anarchist's conception of human nature is identical in all respects. There are variations on the common theme, and these will become apparent as this analysis unfolds. That these distinctions exist simply reflects the fact that no political ideology can claim to be entirely coherent. Some ideologies may be more consistent than others, but all are subject to tensions, if not blatant contradictions, occasioned by differing members of the ideological canon proceeding in opposite directions to one another. Anarchism is no exception to this. Unfortunately, commentators like Heywood simply ignore the susceptibility of ideologies to incoherence. Charges of romanticism are levelled against anarchism just as frequently as those of utopianism.[9] What is more important, perceptions of utopianism and romanticism seem to lead to an erroneous assumption that anarchists adopt an optimistic position when expounding a conception of human nature. I intend to demonstrate that such assumptions are misplaced. However, the crucial factor here is that analysts appear to be drawn into such conclusions for the sake of preserving the consistency or integrity of their own argument, whilst simultaneously imposing upon the theorist or ideology a degree of coherence that does not exist. In that sense, Heywood and Adams may be attributing or constructing a coherent argument that does not stand up to serious investigation. A more detailed exploration of the conception of human nature employed by the social anarchists advises greater caution. The point that some interpreters seem to miss is that, in elucidating a vision of the good life, anarchists have advanced a series of proposals that are tinged with an air of realism and prudence fuelled by what is, at times, a particularly honest, if not brutally pessimistic, account of the darker side of human nature. Precisely because of this realism, social anarchism can afford to be neither excessively romantic nor utopian.

The central question of this work, then, is whether the social anarchists, in elaborating both a revolutionary methodology and a post-revolutionary society, remain true to the teachings of their conception of human nature? When examining this question it will become apparent that a concept of human nature is an integral part of any ideology and, as such, is partly responsible for staking out the boundaries of the possibilities that avail themselves to political theory. Social anarchism, as found in the writings of Proudhon, Bakunin and Kropotkin, embraces a vision of the good life despite its protestations to the contrary. But in any ideology the prospect of an ideal society demands corroboration or justification from the other elements of that ideology. The concept of human nature often fulfils this role, for human nature is frequently utilized as a sanction to praise or condemn social visions. If the social anarchists propagate a vision of a future society that exceeds the capabilities of their conception of human nature, then their ideological narrative can only be judged as utopian and incoherent.

The major argument of this text is that anarchism, because of its conception of human nature, cannot escape that judgment. Despite its vision of a harmonious, non-hierarchical, egalitarian and just society, its emphasis on egoism as an undeniable and lasting component within human nature renders its struggle to release itself from the grip of the state futile. That is, because social anarchism embodies a conception of human nature that comprises both sociability and egoism, in which both are enduring elements, it is exceedingly difficult if not impossible to rescue the ideology without performing some form of radical surgery. In other words, the anarchist conception of human nature results in a political theory that fails to meet its self-incurred obligation of a stateless society. Consequently, anarchists' demands for a stateless future exceed what their conception of human nature will permit, thereby jeopardizing the validity of the label of anarchism if not the status of the ideology itself.

The Organization of this Book

Assessment of any political ideology will always be open to accusations of subjectivism, and this work is no exception. Even though the focus of concern here is social anarchism, some readers may dispute the selection of anarchists placed under study. Why, it might be asked, is there no consideration of William Godwin, commonly regarded as one of anarchism's most thoughtful proponents? There are, to my mind, two reasons for his absence. First, Godwin is most properly a philosophical anarchist.[10] For that reason alone Godwin does not really belong under the category of social anarchism. He is, however, excluded from consideration on another count. Whilst examining the anarchist writers included under the label of social anarchism, this work concentrates on those anarchists that belong to the movement of nineteenth-century anarchism. By studying what I designate as the principal nineteenth-century social anarchists, my argument endeavours to uncover the nature of the relationship between conceptions of human nature and politics in anarchist writings in the most representative authors of anarchism when the movement itself was at its revolutionary zenith. This is not to devalue the achievements of Godwin or more contemporary anarchists in any way. Rather it is simply to acknowledge two things. First, unlike most, if not all other political ideologies, anarchism may be regarded as an ideology with two separate progenitors. That is, anarchism may be seen as the logical outcome of both liberalism and socialism. The second point concerns the nature of anarchism itself. As Martin Miller has commented, the 'anarchist movement did not really develop until the middle of the nineteenth century and did not produce its brilliant theorists until that time'.[11] The inclusion of Godwin into this work, focusing as it does on social anarchists, would not recommend itself. Whilst Godwin's *Political Justice* (1793) may have been published close to the nineteenth century, he belongs to this tradition neither in terms of chronology nor philosophy.

With that in mind this work commences with an analysis of the ideology of anarchism and the concept of human nature. To illustrate how central the concept of human nature is to the wider ideology of social anarchism, the writings of the major nineteenth-century social anarchists are scrutinized. In particular, their respective conceptions of human nature will be revealed and examined in light of what each theorist has to say concerning the organization of a future society. Of key importance here is how, and how easily, their notion of human nature fits into their ideological vision, a prescriptive vision which embodies a set of principles for establishing a future anarchy.

Notes

1. J. Joll, 'Anarchism: A Living Tradition', in David E. Apter and James Joll (eds), *Anarchism Today*, (Macmillan, London, 1971) p. 213.
2. R. Eccleshall, V. Geoghegan, *et.al*, *Political Ideologies: An Introduction*, (Unwin Hyman, London, 1984) p. 23.
3. G. Duncan, 'Political Theory and Human Nature', in I. Forbes and S. Smith (eds), *Politics and Human Nature*, (Pinter, London, 1983) p. 15.

4. H. Read, *Anarchy and Order*, (Faber & Faber, London, 1954) p. 14.

5. See, for example, D.E. Apter, 'The Old Anarchism and the New: Some Comments', in Apter and Joll, *op. cit.*, pp. 1 and 3. Andrew Gamble is another who misjudges the anarchists' conception of human nature. See his *An Introduction to Modern Social and Political Thought*, (Macmillan, London, 1981) pp. 109–10.

6. I. Adams, *Political Ideology Today*, (Manchester University Press, Manchester, 1993) p. 172.

7. A. Heywood, *Political Ideologies: An Introduction*, (Macmillan, London, 1992) p. 198. In a similar vein Adams, *op. cit.*, pp. 174–5, argues that anarchism involves a tremendous act of faith and is largely a romantic hankering after the values of social solidarity which are irreconcilable with the contemporary world.

8. Heywood, *op. cit.*, pp. 205–6.

9. See, for example, D. Miller, *Anarchism*, (Dent, London, 1984) pp. 175–6. Martin Miller contends that anarchists favoured 'a primitive, simplistic, somewhat romantic culture based on the fulfilment of need'. See M.A. Miller, *Selected Writings on Anarchism and Revolution. P.A. Kropotkin*, (MIT Press, Boston, 1970) p. 5.

10. As David Miller has argued, philosophical anarchism is unlike individualist or social anarchism because it lacks both a true social vision for the future and, consequently, any tangible strategy for radical change. It is simply an 'attitude, a way of responding to authority.' See D. Miller, *op. cit.*, p. 16. A contemporary account of philosophical anarchism is R.P. Wolff, *In Defense of Anarchism*, (Harper Torchbooks, New York, 1976).

11. See M.A. Miller, *op. cit.*, p. 2.

2

Anarchism and Human Nature

All political ideologies are protean in nature. Of all the major ideologies of the western world none are without discord or disunity, either in terms of theory or practice. Consequently, the task of discussing ideologies is, as Bhikhu Parekh highlights, 'an exceedingly hazardous enterprise'.[1] Ideologies often harbour a number of divergent facets or strands under their architectural umbrella. Each strand may adopt radically opposed views on certain issues. Such divisions do not only embrace tactics but stem from the most basic assumptions that constitute the very foundation of an ideology. One such example is the transformation of liberalism at the close of the nineteenth century. At the heart of liberalism is the concept of liberty. Yet it was precisely a dispute over what liberty meant that, for some commentators like Isaiah Berlin, the liberal philosopher, distinguishes the old liberalism from the new.[2] More recently, the British Conservative Party has been engaged in an introspective analysis over its approach to European integration, with questions of sovereignty and national identity foremost in the minds of many Eurosceptics. Occasionally, it is not the ends which are in dispute but the means. Differences of opinion on how to achieve socialism have resulted in multifarious tactics and a multiplicity of parties. It is hardly surprising, then, that the message of ideologies is distorted and abused by their political rivals.

Perhaps, though, there is a more serious problem when discussing ideologies. It has less to do with making political capital at the expense of one's rivals, and rather more to do with a lack of comprehension in the first place. If we are honest enough, we all employ ideological labels wrongly sometimes. This may be born out of passion rather than rational analysis. Many a time was Margaret Thatcher, the former leader of the British Conservative Party, accused of fascism, both by those who knew what the term meant and by those who undoubtedly did not. Alternatively, and more importantly as far as this analysis is concerned, people talk, often with a self-assumed authority, about ideologies of which they know little if anything. This is usually the stuff of taproom arguments, but is evident in academic debate too. The danger that should be avoided here is one of filling in the blanks inappropriately. Political ideologies are complex phenomena. Understanding how their various cross-currents and multiple assumptions fit together should not be underestimated. It behoves us, therefore, to take care when completing the ideological crossword. Presenting a rough sketch of an ideology is well within the capabilities of many, but presenting an accurate representation of an ideology is a more tricky matter. It is the task of this chapter to outline the difficulties that face us when confronting anarchism and to provide some possible strategies, if not solutions, to them.

Defining Anarchy: Some Conceptual and Methodological Difficulties

As Lisa Newton notes, almost 'every point of view other than support of the existing nation-state can be found somewhere within [the anarchist tradition.]'[3] Anarchism is not a particularly consistent ideology. Moreover, given the sheer diversity if not disparateness of the opinions within anarchism, one has to question whether anarchism is an ideology at all. The risk of establishing a set of definitive parameters within which one can assign a collection of theorists that do not belong together is a very real one. Traditionally, the unifying theme of anarchism is taken to be 'a rejection and criticism of all state authority and of the power and coercion that combine to make up the machinery of government'.[4] But even this is contested by some. For instance, in his essay 'What is Anarchism?' John P. Clark asserts that there is no one central defining characteristic that distinguishes anarchism from other social theories.[5] Such a judgment may be deeply subjective, but may also be indicative of the fact that ideologies are seldom coherent constructs. Ideologies in general are distilled from a number of sources, each carrying its own distinctive flavour that results in a melding of the fine with the coarse, the banal with the astute. Indeed it should be obvious to anyone with more than a passing interest in the study of ideologies that no one ideology is a mutually exclusive body of political ideas. Ideologies readily share ideas and arguments, because, as Andrew Vincent notes, there is an 'overlapping of ideological continuums'.[6]

This cross-fertilization of ideological arguments and assumptions leads us into an even deeper and more elusive problem. It is a danger that is inherent in all writings on ideology, and is self-manufactured. For when consciously endeavouring to provide a definitive and disinterested account or judgment of a particular ideology it is difficult not to submit one's own ideological perspective as an account of the facts or truth. The quest for a non-ideological account of an ideology may never be fully realizable. One can only attempt to be as impartial as possible. Firstly, though, for an analysis of anarchism to proceed it must first be defined. One of the most usual procedures for advancing a definition of anarchism is to commence the discussion by way of an etymological investigation of the word itself. That is the way adopted by the Italian anarchist Errico Malatesta, and it is also the strategy adhered to by more contemporary authors. One of the most recent examples is Alan Carter's 'Some Notes on "Anarchism"'. As Carter explains, the word 'anarchy' is derived from the Greek and means literally 'without government'. Moreover, 'anarchy is a stateless society. It is a society where one group does not have power over another group (with possible exceptions, such as children or mental defectives).'[7] Besides the etymological perspective there is also a historical reference to take into account. During the formative years of the Athenian democracy there were nine magistrates called archons. After Solon, the Athenian statesman, instituted constitutional reforms party strife erupted which eventually resulted in tyranny. Little is actually known about the strife, but as Bury reports it is known that it 'took the form of a struggle for the archonship, and two years are noted in which, in consequence of this struggle, no archons were elected, hence called years of *anarchy*'.[8] Historically speaking, then, anarchy describes not an absence of government, but an absence specifically of one type of public official.

One of the first things to note is that because anarchy designates a society without government, in an etymological sense, this does not translate into a society in chaos. As Carter insists, and rightly so, without rule does not mean without rules or without structure. The format of this structure, however, is unparalleled in its importance to the well-being of anarchy. For the structure 'both should be empowering to those within it and should not lead to a centralisation of power or decision-making'. When spelt out, this argument entails that anarchists 'prefer a system where there is no centralized and/or authoritarian government, where no one has a monopoly of force, where no group exercises power over another group, and where decision-making is as widely dispersed as possible'.[9] Despite these noble sentiments, anarchism struggles to sustain its cherished principles. Because of its assumption of an innate egoism in human nature none of the social anarchists under examination here can claim to have entirely eradicated all forms or mechanisms of government. Indicatively, there is little evidence to suggest that anarchists have entirely forsaken familiar measures in an effort to establish social order. Indeed, the writings of both Proudhon and Bakunin provide room for the inclusion of some form of residual government as a mechanism for settling disputes. Moreover, Bakunin's *Revolutionary Catechism* (1866) incorporates into its federal political matrix a fully-fledged legislative and judicial structure.[10] Anarchist societies, both in practice and in theory, are never likely to match a set of criteria which stipulates that there is to be no division of political labour nor any institutions that enable that to occur. Consequently, it is not clear, as Carter stipulates, that anarchy is a stateless society.

One of the faults of Carter's analysis is that he is inadvertently drawn into a grave error of judgment. In accusing statists of 'erroneously conflat[ing] an absence of government with an absence of order', Carter is guilty of the very sin he denounces by confusing an absence of state with an absence of power.[11] To be more precise, whilst Carter does seem to acknowledge that power will exist in one form or another in an anarchist future he does not appear to be cognizant that power will still be exercised by one group over another, possibly through means of force. His concern is merely to avoid the conclusion that power is concentrated in the hands of one group within society. Whilst such concerns are admirable and lie at the heart of the anarchist critique of contemporary political society, Carter offers nothing that can obviate the judgment that a certain section of society may remain subject to the power of another. In other words, what materializes from Carter's analysis is an anxiety over the form rather than the substance of power itself.

Attempts to define power are notoriously problematic, but if an appraisal of the term 'anarchism' is to be discharged a delineation of the concept has to be advanced. A convenient starting-point is Michael Taylor's work, *Community, Anarchy and Liberty*, in which the author develops a notion of power that owes much to rational choice theory.[12] Whatever the strengths or weaknesses of this kind of reasoning, Taylor produces an argument of some merit. Power, he relates, is essentially the ability one has to alter the alternatives that face individuals when choosing between one course of action or another. In this sense, the ability to offer a reward or enunciate a credible threat are instances of power, because both affect the available alternatives that face an individual when deciding upon a particular course of action.[13] But power is not just about rewards or threats. Within a context of interdependent decision-making, power, as Taylor observes, becomes available through the strategic position of one group over another.

That is, power is made available to those who, by virtue of their position, are able 'to bring about outcomes relatively favourable to themselves and unfavourable to the others', by deciding on one course of action on the presupposition that others will also choose that course of action when presented with the alternatives.[14] It is not without justification, then, that Taylor can pronounce that the classical anarchists like Proudhon, Bakunin and Kropotkin were unable to elaborate models of political and social organization that 'would not, and could not, entail the complete disappearance or equality of power, or coercion, or authority'.[15] It is in this spirit that Harold Barclay writes that anarchists do not 'deny power; on the contrary, in anarchist theory this is a central issue for all human societies and the limiting of power is a constant concern'.[16]

If anarchy is not about the elimination of all forms of power, authority and coercion, the question of definition remains unanswered. Of course, it could be maintained that an anarchist society is nevertheless a stateless society, despite the fact that power, authority and coercion are resident features of that society. Even if legislative, judicial and governmental configurations constitute a part of that society, this does not necessarily equate that society with a state. Like so many other concepts within politics, the state is defined as a matter of degree rather than kind. It is where a particular level in the development of political societies is reached; a stage at which one can detect that a concentration of organized force is employed by a group or section of society to enforce the decisions that have been made by that group throughout the rest of that society. This is the hallmark of the state, and this is what anarchists hope to evade. It might be argued that to define anarchy in this manner, as a society in which forms of power, coercion and authority remain, rebuts the usual proclivity to dissociate anarchism from statist ideologies. The argument tends to run as follows. With the possible exception of ecologism and feminism, all other major ideologies revolve around the state. That is, they may be located somewhere along the continuum of the left–right political spectrum. Their position on that scale confirms their 'statist' origins and nature. Anarchism, however, cannot be correctly characterized as either left or right because it is not amenable to the rationale behind such denotations. If anything defines anarchism and differentiates it from other political doctrines it has to be something similar to Malatesta's definition: anarchy is 'the condition of the people who live without a constituted authority, without government'.[17] But to define anarchy after the manner of Malatesta is to offer nothing more than tautology. It is almost meaningless. And it would seem that our analysis has come full circle; it is back where it started with an interpretation that has progressed little beyond the inaugural etymological departure-point.

By construing anarchism as an anti-state ideology as opposed to a non-statist ideology, by which is meant a complete dissolution of the state, perhaps more is afforded than greater meaning alone. By characterizing anarchism as anti-state one also eludes the necessity of imposing a 'hard core' identity upon the ideology. As such, the interpretation alleviates the problematical nature of elaborating a definition of the ideology itself. It does this in at least three respects. First, having carried over the concerns of the argument surrounding human nature, that human nature can only outline the possibilities of politics, the explication of anarchist ideology as anti-state rather than non-state leaves sufficient possibilities for the individual adherents of the ideology to differ in their rendition of that ideology. Second, in retreating from a limited or particularly tight definition of the core of an ideology, which may be tendered as the basis for examination, one escapes the discontent that is likely to arise concerning which thinkers are purported to be the actual proprietors of that tradition. Accordingly, there is minimal room for objection that the three thinkers under consideration here, Proudhon, Bakunin and Kropotkin, are not truly representative of the anarchist tradition. All three offer sharp and telling arguments against the state. But judgment must be reserved as to whether they are non-statist, in completely rejecting every aspect of the state, until their respective arguments have been analysed according to the possibilities released by their conception of human nature.

The third area in which the problems of definition can be eroded is that which corresponds to the danger of imposing a measure of coherence that does not exist. As Quentin Skinner has informed us, if the rationale for the investigation of a body of work is conceived as the elaboration of a particular theme, it becomes dangerously easy for the interpreter to discover a coherent message that is actually not present. The problems are compounded when endeavouring to maintain the proper or original tone and emphasis of the work upon translation into the interpreter's own argument.[18] It is a difficulty that confronts one quite forcefully when researching anarchist writings, especially those of Proudhon and Bakunin, both of whom are commonly regarded as inconsistent writers and inherently paradoxical. But in contending that anarchist ideology, because of the innate relationship it shares with human nature, can only hope to adumbrate the possibilities available to anarchists, opportunities for imposing coherence where it cannot be otherwise found are perforce reduced. The alternative of working under the assumption that anarchists have to be non-statists, that they repudiate all aspects of the state, may blind the interpreter to anything other than what he or she perceives as a consistent message about rejection of the state.

In thinking of anarchism as an exploration of the possibilities in the development of anti-state social and political structures, which are subject to the demarcation implied by its conception of human nature, there is one objection that presents itself almost immediately and has to be dealt with before proceeding any further. It is that in classifying anarchism as anti-state rather than non-state, one leaves the definition open to the charge that anarchism can no longer be distinguished from liberalism. After all, liberals generally desire a reduction in state interference in the private realm. This is a goal which is, in part, inspired by their conception of human nature, and which, in turn, motivates their arguments against unwarranted state incursions. Liberals and anarchists share many areas of concern. Not only are both distrustful of the state, each cherishes liberty and individuality. Both are highly suspicious of an excessive concentration of political authority and view with scepticism the development of institutionalized bureaucracies that strengthen the stranglehold on power that is held by centralized governments. Where they begin to diverge is in the liberal belief that government has to be constitutional government. As John Gray has observed, the essence of a liberal political order is that 'it must contain constitutional constraints on the arbitrary exercise of governmental authority'.[19] Thus liberalism need not concern itself with democracy so long as it meets the requirements of constitutional constraints.

Anarchism, however, is concerned with creating a more democratic society, albeit a drive for democracy that is animated more by participation than a system of representation. More importantly, anarchists have usually been regarded as rebuffing a political or social order that is dependent upon a constitutional agreement. As Peter Marshall remarks, anarchism

> goes beyond the liberal justification of law to establish rights, to protect freedom and to solve disputes. Where liberals rely on the rule of law established through parliament and political parties, the anarchists argue that such institutions are not the

bulwark but the grave of genuine freedom. They see no need for the government to defend society against external threat or internal dissension. They do not want to limit the powers of the State, but to dissolve them altogether.[20]

The concept of the rule of law, so cherished by liberal thinkers as the benchmark of their philosophy, is, for anarchism, another example of one of the many mechanisms that are employed by the state to ensure the continued dominance of one group over another group. One of the central questions of this work, however, is whether Marshall's claim about total dissolution of state power is accurate?

Perceptions of Anarchism

Anarchism, as a political noun, is much misunderstood and is often subject to misuse and abuse. It has on occasion been applied as a pejorative label to malign political rivals. This was the sense in which Vladimir Ilyich Ulyanov, more widely known as Lenin, the first leader of the Soviet Union, used it when he described anarchism as 'bourgeois individualism in reverse'.[21] It is, today, frequently employed in media bulletins as an adjective to summarize events that occur outside the prescriptions of law and order. And as Anthony Arblaster once commented, the term anarchist is 'a label the simple use of which is enough, it is evidently assumed, to discredit the labelled effectively in the eyes of the general public'.[22] The term anarchism has had a troubled past and is still beset by difficulties in the present period. In the eyes of some contemporary commentators anarchism is a romantic, pre-industrial ideology that is not quite able to detach itself fully from its agrarian or peasant roots.[23] To others, it is a 'naïve' political doctrine or 'puerile utopia' that offers little of value to the modern world aside from its appropriateness as a critical yardstick against which to measure the excesses of the state.[24] In essence, both criticisms are historical in context and both receive some corroboration, even if only of an anecdotal nature, in contemporary society. Scholarly attitudes are, of course, amplified by occasional critics who tend to reinforce the popular fiction of anarchism as an outdated ideology that bears little relationship to events in the real world. The terms anarchism and anarchist are more often than not sneered at by the general public, if not for their assumed utopian impracticality then for their association with violence.

The very word 'anarchism' is difficult to pin down. Anarchist ideology has no *magnum opus* to afford easy access to the uninitiated. Consequently, its theoretical writings are often inconsistent and sometimes less than remarkable. Much of this is due to the very nature of anarchism. As an ideology it is an active creed. E.H. Carr once argued that anarchism 'is no mere vision of a golden age in the past or in the future. It is a creed of active rebellion against the State, which it seeks to destroy, if necessary by force.'[25] Many groups have been, by their very nature, inclined towards activism. The Diggers, in England during the middle of the seventeenth century, and the Enragés, during the French Revolution, are just two such groups. Both were involved in direct action of one form or another, and both were distrustful of the authority of the state.[26] More lately, Michael Bakunin has been widely regarded as the principal architect of the international anarchist movement; but the apogee of anarchist activism did not arrive until the end of the nineteenth century, with the concept of propaganda by the deed, as expounded by, amongst others, the Italian anarchists Carlo Cafiero and Errico Malatesta.[27] None of this, however, signifies a consensus on the best form of action to take. William Godwin, the eighteenth-century English novelist and anarchist, believed that change should be brought about through a process of gradual reform rather than revolution. Education was the key to this reform, reinforced by rational argument to alter public opinion. Proudhon spent some time engaged in parliamentary politics before urging abstention from this kind of activity, whilst suggesting that the working class ought to emancipate itself through the construction of self-managed economic institutions, such as a People's Bank. Others, such as the Russian author Leo Tolstoy and the Indian political leader Mahatma Gandhi, both categorized as anarchists by many scholars, were firm advocates of non-violent civil disobedience.

The sheer diversity of positions within anarchism has often been used as evidence to argue that there is no coherence to or indeed no tradition of anarchism. One version of this is to be found in a recent text by Ball and Dagger.[28] Working from the assumption that any 'ideology is a fairly coherent and comprehensive set of ideas that explains and evaluates social conditions, helps people understand their place in society, and provides a programme for social and political action', they proceed to argue that because anarchism assumes 'so many forms' and is 'entwined with so many different ideologies' it is better not to regard anarchism as a distinct ideology at all.[29] Even sympathetic commentators like David Miller have questioned anarchism as an ideology on this score.[30] Likewise, Noam Chomsky has argued that there are 'too many styles of anarchist thought and action . . . to try to encompass all of these conflicting tendencies in some general theory or ideology'.[31] Vicissitudes of theory and practice, it has to be said, do not necessarily preclude the imposition of some wider definitive structure within which one could place a variety of thinkers and label them anarchist. The very fact that we do label them anarchist indicates that they belong to a certain tradition of political thought. Moreover, much the same could be said about socialism. As an identifiable ideology socialism contains almost innumerable variants that are sometimes implacably opposed to one another. Nevertheless, this does not undermine the standing of socialism as a particular strand of political thought that is recognizable. The same is true of anarchism.

Differences of position are largely dependent on the selection of criteria. What is of importance here is the identification of the common bond that unites anarchists and marks them off as an intelligible body of political ideologists. Generally speaking, anarchism has been overwhelmingly characterized as a series of negative assertions or arguments; that is, anarchism is often portrayed as an ideology erected on a succession of criticisms directed against the state, the church, economic exploitation, educational institutions, and so on. Objections levelled at the state are particularly telling. Hostility towards it and demands for its abolition appear to be the benchmark for the identification of anarchists. Critiques of this nature are of primary importance when drafting the parameters or boundaries against which various figures are classified as either non-anarchist or anarchist, and further what type of anarchist. It is, however, all too easy to emphasize the critical modes of anarchist thought at the expense of any exploration of the benefits anarchists feel they can offer. Indeed, part of the problem is that anarchists themselves have, supposedly, seldom been willing to discuss the future organization of society. Anarchists, according to Malatesta,

> are no more prophets than anyone else; and if we claimed to be able to give an official solution to all the problems that will arise in the course of the daily life of a future society, then what we meant by the abolition of government would be curious to say the least. For we would be declaring ourselves the government and would be prescribing, as do the religious legislators, a universal code for present and future generations. . . . After all,

a programme which is concerned with the bases of the social structure, cannot do otherwise than suggest a method.[32]

Unfortunately, this so-called method often amounts to little else than high-sounding and vague ideals concerning social action.

Before attempting to trace the common bond that unites anarchists, it will be worth returning to examine the basis of the doubts associated with anarchism, for such an analysis should help reveal some of the misconceptions that surround anarchism as a political ideology. It is a common belief that anarchism has little to offer the contemporary world. If taken alone, such an argument would not represent an insurmountable obstacle. However, the magnitude of the hesitancy that traditionally accompanies discussions on anarchism is increased by two conceptual issues, issues that pervade the popular imagination and some academic considerations as well. The first is to do with the image anarchism inherited at the end of the nineteenth century, with which it remains associated. The picture is that of the anarchist as an armed insurgent. This vision of the anarchist as a clandestine terrorist lingers in the memory and has been solidified in novels like Joseph Conrad's *The Secret Agent* (1907). As Peter Marshall writes, 'the very word "anarchist" continues to evoke a shiver of anxiety among the respectable and well-off'.[33] And yet, most anarchists have little if anything to do with violence. For some, Tolstoy and Gandhi being the most famous, anarchism means pacifism. In this manifestation anarchists repudiate physical violence completely, even when it is used against them. The state is the incarnation of brutality which must be opposed by non-violent actions such as strikes, demonstrations, civil disobedience and similar tactics. Only by adopting non-violent means, argue the pacifists, can we ever hope to achieve a non-violent society. This is not to say that anarchists have never been implicated in violence. Even celebrated anarchists, such as the Lithuanian Alexander Berkman, have been involved in assassination attempts. Berkman, in conjunction with the Russian anarchist Emma Goldman, both of whom were living in the United States at the time, had planned the assassination of Henry Clay Frick, a manager at a Carnegie steel plant. Carnegie is alleged to have ordered gunmen to shoot strikers at the plant in Homestead.[34] Whilst Berkman's assassination attempt failed, he was given a 22-year prison sentence for his endeavours. More recently, anarchist groups like Class War participated in the Poll Tax riots in London during 1990. Most, however, seem content to agitate within social and political movements: the trade unions, green, women's or peace groups, for example.[35]

Human Nature and Anarchism

The second conceptual issue, which forms the crux of this investigation, is that of human nature. The popularly accepted incredulity about the viability of anarchism as a rationale for the organization of future society is not based only on historical argument. Rather, this commonly accepted disbelief has to do with the largely sceptical appraisal of human nature that abounds amidst the popular imagination. Human nature is invoked time and again in everyday conversation as evidence for and against competing ideologies. As Christopher Berry has remarked, '"human nature" has a prominent place in the repertoire of explanations and justifications that is embedded in popular consciousness. It is this consciousness that is largely responsible for the perceptions people have of their society and it is these perceptions that directly affect their political beliefs and actions.'[36] It is, perhaps, something that anarchists may be blissfully unaware of. The point is articulated succinctly by Marshall. 'Anarchists,' he notes, 'are confident that the natural solidarity of interests and the advantages of a free and communal life will be enough to maintain social order, and with the principal causes of strife – imposed authority and unequal property – eradicated, social harmony will prevail.'[37]

Without due caution one may be led too easily to the supposition that anarchists do have an overly optimistic conception of human nature. My argument is that anarchists themselves have a rather different approach. George Woodcock has sometimes concluded that certain anarchists, Proudhon in particular, have propounded an optimistic conception of human nature.[38] But a more accurate view is presented by David Miller, for instance, who insists that Proudhon was fairly 'pessimistic about human nature'.[39] Differences of opinion are endemic in the business of interpretation, but as April Carter has noted, it is 'an over-simplification to say that anarchists believe men are always naturally co-operative and peaceable'.[40] In general, anarchists exercise a rather cautious assessment of human nature. Miller illustrates this in a comparison of anarchism with Marxism. Focusing on the differences between means and ends, Miller suggests that it is the anarchists who are more cognizant of the possibility of humankind's 'domineering and exploitative instincts' overshadowing any wider or long-term goals. Put simply, this is because the anarchists possess 'a stronger sense of the imperfections of human nature'.[41] Woodcock explains more fully how the potential for confusion arises. It is true to say, like Marshall above, that anarchists believe human beings are capable of living in a society that lacks the array of compulsive and punitive measures that accompany capitalism. Nevertheless, this ought to be tempered by a recognition that humankind also has the ability to perform wrongs. Thus Woodcock reflects that anarchists 'may not believe that man is naturally good, but they believe very fervently that man is naturally social'.[42]

The point is well made, but underestimates the extent to which anarchists argue the converse. It is not just that anarchists do not believe that humans are naturally good; at times they stress that, given the opportunity, humans can be positively evil. Proudhon, in particular, assumes so. Humankind, he contends, knows how to do 'evil with all the characteristics of a nature deliberately maleficent, and all the more wicked because, when it so wishes, it knows how to do good gratuitously also and is capable of self-sacrifice'.[43] According to Proudhon's understanding of human nature, environmental factors may not be as cogent or as influential as first thought. This also seems to be the implication of Miller's point about 'the imperfections of human nature' above.

It is imperative, then, that one appreciates that the social anarchists' conception of human nature rests on the twin pillars of egoism and sociability. This is significant for two reasons. The first is that not all commentators grasp a full understanding of the message imparted by anarchists about human nature. Vincent's analysis, for instance, provides a telling example of the way in which the anarchists' position is distorted.[44] For, whilst he notes with some perception that the broad division between individualist and social anarchists corresponds to two competing conceptions of human nature that start at different locations, he argues that within such positions there is a level of differentiation that obscures any visible common ground. This is both inaccurate and simplistic. It may be true to say that there is 'enormous diversity' on the subject of human nature within anarchism. But much the same could be said about liberalism, socialism or conservatism. That does not mean that there is an absence of some definitive agreement or consensus on the concept of human nature upon which anarchist political ideology is built. All ideologies are subject to diversity, both in principles and programmes.

The second reason is that failure to appreciate the double-sided conception of human nature means that a true understanding of anarchist political ideology cannot be attained. This latter point is, quintessentially, an acknowledgement of the argument that only by identifying a theorist's conception of human nature is one able to unearth the character of the other dependent parts of that theorist's ideology. One may argue much further than this, by suggesting that the concept of human nature not only assists in the identification of an ideology but constitutes part of the bedrock upon which the other component parts of the ideology are constructed. Within political ideologies the concept of human nature may be utilized as a tool to determine how society ought to be. Accordingly, ideologies have the capacity to distinguish between how society is at present and how it should be in the future, based on their conception of human nature. However, this relationship is not without its difficulties. By ascribing to human nature an ability to depict the finer details of how society ought to be, one may be burdening human nature with a task that lies beyond its constituent capacity. That is, a conception of human nature cannot and hence does not delimit the precise kind of society that will emerge from its prescriptive function. Both liberalism and socialism, for example, pay heed to humankind's rationality in their respective conceptions of human nature. Yet both proceed to develop differing theories of politics which owe their identity, in part, to a commonly accepted attribute of human nature. Rationality, for the liberal, constitutes the basis of an individual's ability to reason; to make judgments about the consequences of actions and to lead, therefore, a life in which liberty and individuality are the highest ends. Indeed it was a belief in the power of reason that led to the Enlightenment's rejection of faith and superstition. Socialists, on the other hand, derive a radically different outcome from the assumption of rationality in human nature. Having rejected the existence of capitalism on grounds of alienation, which is itself a factor in their account of human nature, they use the capacity of rationality in humankind to overcome the chaos of capitalist production for profit by implementing some form of central or rational planning mechanism to distribute goods according to an accepted principle of social justice.

That human nature cannot determine political theory and, correspondingly, cannot impel a vision of the good life in any one particular direction, does not entirely nullify an association between a conception of human nature and a vision of the future. But it does redefine the role that the concept of human nature occupies within an ideology. Instead of depicting in fine detail how future society will look, a conception of human nature can only offer a rough sketch of how that society might begin to develop. It informs us of the contours of possibility, rather than providing cartographic accuracy about the social and political patterns that ought to exist in the future. Just as a notion of human nature does not determine any one future society so a particular conception of human nature does not determine any one programmatic method. As Parekh elucidates, no one 'doctrine is *necessarily* entailed by a metaphysical system, and nor does a political doctrine *necessarily* presuppose a particular metaphysical system'.[45] There are no rigid parameters that force ideologies into a narrow conduit travelling in one direction only. Just as socialists have differed over whether to take the parliamentary or revolutionary road to a socialist society, so anarchists have proffered a number of competing strategies to secure progression into anarchy.

Despite these uncertainties it would be foolish to suggest that an ideological narrative is not interwoven with threads of consistency. Roger Eatwell, for instance, has recently acknowledged that programmatic ambiguity does not belie the inherent consistency of ideologies. He remarks that, even though there may be much variation of programmatic strategy,

> the crucial point is that it is hard to imagine someone supporting such a set of formal arrangements without, implicitly or overtly, holding related arguments. Concepts such as the 'rule of law', or 'checks and balances' are clearly related to a view of human nature, and/or to some knowledge of history.[46]

Without some form of association between their component parts political ideologies would be entirely characterless. One would be indistinguishable from another. Indeed it would be absurd if ideologies were not supported by some type of interrelational matrix, as it is this framework which helps mould the features and dimensions of the ideology itself. There has to be then, some degree of interconnectedness among the elements of an ideology, otherwise these evolving traditions of political thought would disintegrate amidst the highly competitive political environment of which they are an integral part. They would fail to meet the requirements both of their epistemological status and their sociological dimensions. In other words, without some modicum of coherent structural bonding ideologies would neither be vindicated in advocating the validity of their arguments nor be able to offer a convincing portrayal of social events, and thereby attract converts.

The real difficulty lies in determining exactly how much may be demanded from a conception of human nature. The place of human nature within any given ideology is not in question. But that says little about the kind of claim that is actually being made by the statement that ideologies are grounded on ideas of human nature. What is it that is being claimed here? How is human nature defined within this context? It is, of course, extremely difficult to provide clear answers for one very simple reason. That is, human nature is what is commonly referred to as an essentially contestable concept. What is at stake is the authenticity of the epistemology through which human nature is defined. In other words, there appear to be two procedures for laying claim to what is a supposedly truthful account of human nature. Either human nature is taken to be a construct of one's social context, or it is held to possess certain transcendent, universal elements. That is, either human nature is viewed as a product of the environment of which it is a part, or it is seen as something which is immanent. It is either contextual or universal. In so far as it is contextual or shaped by society, it is difficult to perceive how a concept of human nature could actually be employed to judge that society. The implication of this is that society and more particularly the political organization of society may only be judged against a concept of human nature that is considered to be universal.[47] But this, in turn, presents another problem. To begin with, the difficulty of locating the essence of human nature is immense and should not be underestimated. And even if it is possible to identify the fundamental, transcendent component(s) of human nature, the incontrovertible facts or essence of human nature, it does not automatically follow that human nature can yield a prescription about how society ought to be. As Raymond Plant has remarked, 'in so far as the theory of human nature is factual in content it cannot yield any conclusion about the morally desirable form of human organization'.[48] The dilemma is created by the 'is/ought' or 'fact/value' distinction. Conversely, in so far as a conception of human nature is not factual but rather evaluative then it may be said to be capable of supporting moral arguments about social and political reform. But again, that still leaves an unanswered question: in what will that conception of human nature be grounded?

Alternatively, one might argue that the discussion has hitherto been labouring under a false dichotomy, the division of the contextual and the universal elements of human nature. Whilst some theorists may lean more heavily to one rather than the other, it is seldom the case that ideologies encompass one and completely exclude any reference to the other. Conservatism, for example, is commonly held to be indebted to a contextualist conception of human nature, with its emphasis on the individual's gradual acquisition of culture as a major element that forges his or her personal identity.[49] Conservatives are deeply suspicious of talking about human beings in the abstract. Nonetheless, despite this perception that the context or environment in which an individual finds him or herself is vital to an understanding of what goes to make up that person, the conservative may equally accentuate the influence of a universal concept like original sin or the limited capacity of humanity's power of reason. Likewise, liberalism is often regarded as exhibiting a universalist conception of human nature. Reason or rationality is the hallmark of humankind, according to the liberal, but even here due credit is given to the character-forming basis of circumstance.[50] In fact, if it were not for the ability of the environment to impress an identity on people's minds then the whole liberal impulse of the Enlightenment would have been an irrelevant exercise in the triumph of reason over faith and superstition. Conceptions of human nature, then, often combine both contextualist and universalist elements. Nevertheless, the problem remains of how to evade recourse to some wider philosophy for substantiating the basis of one's preferences about human nature. For even if it is accepted that a conception of human nature owes its origins to both contextualist and universal aspects, to both factual and evaluative accounts, some wider philosophy is a prerequisite for the purpose of justification. Moreover, it may be argued that a concept of human nature could never be entirely factual. A basic appreciation of the arguments surrounding the philosophy of science reveals that answers are often determined by what one assumes are the relevant questions to ask. Similarly, categorizing the appropriate questions is itself a reflection of an antecedent theoretical position. Thus, the identification of so-called transcendent or universal elements within a conception of human nature will in itself be the result of some prior philosophical perspective about how important those factors are and where they may be found. Even the empirical classification of the constituent parts of human nature is dependent upon an essentially normative starting-point. Seemingly, the philosophical basis of an ideology is imperative not only for the type of inquiry it embarks upon, but for the possibilities of politics that constitute its conclusion. The concept of human nature is not the sole font of ideological genesis. Both the philosophical basis of an ideology (in social anarchism its philosophy of history) and its related conception of human nature are responsible for drafting the boundaries of what is taken to be possible in politics.

Consequently, there are two traits that emerge from this analysis of the role of the concept of human nature in ideologies. The first is that although human nature remains a core characteristic of any ideology, it should not always be considered the most vital part of the ideology's structural matrix. It shares its formative role with the philosophy that underpins the ideology, and which may be the lifeblood of the concept of human nature itself. The exact balance between the two parts may vary across competing ideologies, but the significant fact is that the two are somehow locked together in an endeavour to stake out the boundaries of the possible. This is particularly true of social anarchism. This latter point is also the foundation of the second feature of human nature. That is, human nature ought to be regarded as a concept that is only capable of predefining what an ideology *may* achieve through political action. In serving both to describe how things are now and to prescribe what is desirable in the future, human nature can only offer general guidelines for the latter. As Ball and Dagger remark, 'each ideology's notion of human nature sets the limit of what it considers to be politically possible'.[51] Human nature is not involved in delimiting the fine detail of future societies. It cannot perform such a task because it is itself reliant upon an overarching normative theory about the nature of the world of which it is just one part. Whilst human nature is an analytical concept that is heavily value-laden, it is also a concept that helps predefine the boundaries of political theory, marking out what is and what is not possible. The question we have to address now is whether the social anarchists' conception of human nature permits them to establish a future stateless society. In other words, are their assumptions about human nature consistent with the political prescriptions it is supposed to yield? The investigation begins by way of the writings of Proudhon.

Notes

1. B. Parekh, *The Concept of Socialism*, (Croom Helm, London, 1975) p. 1.
2. See I. Berlin, 'Two Concepts of Liberty', in his *Four Essays on Liberty*, (Oxford University Press, Oxford, 1969).
3. L. Newton, 'The Profoundest Respect for Law', in J.R. Pennock and J.W. Chapman (eds), *Anarchism, NOMOS XIX*, (New York University Press, New York, 1978) p. 164.
4. J. Jennings, 'Anarchism', in R. Eatwell and A. Wright (eds), *Contemporary Political Ideologies*, (Pinter, London, 1993) p. 128.
5. J.P. Clark, 'What is Anarchism?' in Pennock and Chapman, *op. cit.*, p. 4.

6. A. Vincent, *Modern Political Ideologies*, (Blackwell, Oxford, 1992) p. 17. A contemporaneous work on political ideologies enunciates an almost identical argument about overlap. See A. Heywood, *Political Ideologies: An Introduction*, (Macmillan, London, 1992) p. 11. In the same work, at p. 195, Heywood describes anarchism as 'a point of overlap between two very different political ideologies, liberalism and socialism.'

7. Alan Carter, 'Some Notes on "Anarchism"', *Anarchist Studies*, 1, 2, (1993) p. 141.

8. J.B. Bury, *A History of Greece*, (Macmillan, London, 1963) p. 188.

9. This and the previous quotation are from Alan Carter, *op. cit.*, pp. 143 and 144.

10. For more exact details on how Bakunin weaves these legislative and judicial constructs into his federal framework, see M. Bakunin, 'Revolutionary Catechism', in S. Dolgoff (ed.), *Bakunin on Anarchy*, (Allen & Unwin, London, 1973) pp. 83–4.

11. The quotation is drawn from Alan Carter, *op. cit.*, p. 141.

12. Rational choice theory is prominent in some forms of economic analysis. See, for example, A. Sen, *Choice, Welfare and Measurement*, (Blackwell, Oxford, 1982), or R.M. Hogarth and M.W. Reder (eds), *Rational Choice: The Contrast between Economics and Psychology*, (University of Chicago Press, 1986). For a more politically oriented essay, see Albert Weale, 'Politics as Collective Choice', in A. Leftwich (ed.), *What is Politics? The Activity and its Study*, (Blackwell, Oxford, 1984), pp. 46–61.

13. See, for example, M. Taylor, *Community, Anarchy and Liberty*, (Cambridge University Press, Cambridge, 1982) pp. 11–13.

14. Ibid., p. 13.

15. Ibid., p. 11. As Taylor defines them, and they are definitions I have no objection to, coercion is employed to make credible threats that bring about compliance, and authority is acceptance and acquiescence in the face of advice or command because such measures are believed to carry convincing reasons that justify their initial origin.

16. H. Barclay, *People Without Government: An Anthropology of Anarchy*, (Kahn & Averill, London, 1990) p. 21.

17. E. Malatesta, *Anarchy*, (Freedom Press, London, 1974) p. 11.

18. For a more detailed discussion of the potential dangers of constructing coherence without a valid foundation in the text or texts, see Q. Skinner, 'Meaning and Understanding in the History of Ideas', in J. Tully (ed.), *Meaning and Context: Quentin Skinner and his Critics*, (Polity Press, Cambridge, 1988) pp. 38–43.

19. J. Gray, *Liberalism*, (Open University Press, Milton Keynes, 1986) p. 74.

20. P. Marshall, *Demanding the Impossible: A History of Anarchism*, (HarperCollins, London, 1992) p. 640.

21. V.I. Lenin, 'Anarchism and Socialism', in K. Marx, F. Engels and V.I. Lenin, *Anarchism and Anarcho-Syndicalism*, (Progress Publishers, Moscow, 1972) p. 185.

22. A. Arblaster, 'The Relevance of Anarchism', in R. Miliband and J. Saville (eds), *The Socialist Register*, (The Merlin Press, London, 1971) p. 157.

23. See, for example, D. Miller, *Anarchism*, (Dent, London, 1984) pp. 175–6. Details of Miller's accusation that Kropotkin is pre-industrial appear in his earlier article 'The Neglected (II): Kropotkin',

Government and Opposition, 18 (1983) pp. 334ff. Martin Miller contends that anarchists favoured 'a primitive, simplistic, somewhat romantic culture based on the fulfilment of need.' See M.A. Miller, *Selected Writings on Anarchism and Revolution: P.A. Kropotkin,* (MIT Press, Boston, 1970) p. 5.

24. One proponent of this view is L. Kolakowski, 'For brotherhood or for destruction', *Times Literary Supplement* (04/01/1985) pp. 3–4.

25. E.H. Carr, *Studies in Revolution,* (Macmillan, London, 1950) p. 47. It has to be said that Carr is referring in particular to nineteenth-century anarchism; but as this work focuses on the three major figures of nineteenth-century anarchism the citation seems appropriate.

26. Marshall, *op. cit.,* pp. 96–103 has a useful but brief survey of the Digger movement. G. Woodcock, *Anarchism: A History of Libertarian Ideas and Movements,* (Penguin, Harmondsworth, 1975) pp. 51–5 offers some insight into the development of the Enragés during their year of agitation, 1793. Other activist movements that could be incorporated under the broad umbrella of anarchism include the anarcho-syndicalists and the situationists.

27. A brief exposition of the Italian anarchists is provided in chapter 28 of Marshall, *op. cit.* A more detailed assessment of Malatesta is offered by V. Richards (ed.), *Errico Malatesta: His Life and Ideas,* (Freedom Press, London, 1977). A brief but useful discussion of propaganda by the deed may be found in D. Miller, *op. cit.,* pp. 98–101.

28. T. Ball and R. Dagger, *Political Ideologies and the Democratic Ideal,* (HarperCollins, New York, 1991).

29. Ibid., pp. 8 and 18. April Carter, *The Political Theory of Anarchism,* (Routledge & Kegan Paul, London, 1971) p. 60 also refers to 'the inherent diversity of the anarchist tradition'.

30. D. Miller, *op. cit.,* p. 3.

31. See his 'Introduction' to D. Guérin, *Anarchism: From Theory to Practice,* (Monthly Review Press, New York, 1970) p. vii. This view is contested by Guérin (p. 4) himself who believes 'anarchism presents a fairly homogeneous body of ideas.'

32. E. Malatesta, *op. cit.,* pp. 44–5. A similar argument may be found in E. Goldman, *Anarchism and Other Essays,* (Dover, New York, 1969) pp. 43–4 and 63. Herbert Read advances a fundamental philosophical reason for the abstention from creating blueprints. See H. Read, 'Existentialism, Marxism and Anarchism', in his *Anarchy and Order: Essays in Politics,* (Faber & Faber, London, 1954) p. 148.

33. Marshall, *op. cit.,* p. 630.

34. Andrew Carnegie was a Scottish steel magnate whose family had emigrated to America in 1848. Carnegie's business was the largest steel and iron works in America.

35. Apart from *op. cit.,* p. 638, support for this picture of a general non-violent methodology comes also from R. Sylvan, 'Anarchism', in R.E. Goodin and P. Pettit (eds), *A Companion to Contemporary Political Philosophy,* (Blackwell, Oxford, 1993) p. 217.

36. C.J. Berry, *Human Nature,* (Macmillan, London, 1986) p. x.

37. Marshall, *op. cit.,* p. 629.

38. G. Woodcock, *Pierre-Joseph Proudhon: A Biography,* (Black Rose Books, Montréal, 1987)

p. 172. This may be true of some anarchists, but it is not a valid criticism when it comes to Kropotkin. Kropotkin was fully aware that some of the major objections toward anarchism stemmed from perceptions about human nature. See P. Kropotkin, *The Conquest of Bread*, (Elephant Editions, London, 1985) p. 17.

- 39. D. Miller, *op. cit.*, p. 69.
40. April Carter, *op. cit.*, p. 16.
41. D. Miller, *op. cit.*, p. 93.
42. Woodcock, *op. cit.*, p. 19.
43. P-J. Proudhon, *System of Economical Contradictions or The Philosophy of Misery* vol.1 (Arno Press, New York, 1972) p. 410.
44. Vincent, *op. cit.*, p. 126.
45. Parekh, *op. cit.*, p. 3.
46. R. Eatwell, 'Ideologies: Approaches and Trends', in Eatwell and Wright, *op. cit.*, p. 7.
47. For a more comprehensive debate on this issue see Berry, *op. cit.*.
48. R. Plant, *Modern Political Thought*, (Blackwell, Oxford, 1991) p. 70.
49. For an insightful essay on the contextualist dimension of the conservatives' conception of human nature, see C. Berry, 'Conservatism and Human Nature', in I. Forbes and S. Smith (eds), *Politics and Human Nature*, (Pinter, London, 1983) pp. 53–67.
50. See, for example, Paul Smart's essay 'Mill and Human Nature', in Forbes and Smith, *op. cit.*, pp. 36–52.
51. Ball and Dagger, *op. cit.*, p. 13.

3

Proudhon: The Politics of Federalism

It seems appropriate to commence the substantive analysis of individual anarchist thinkers with Proudhon as he was the first person both to describe himself as an anarchist and to employ the term anarchism to furnish a definition of a particular kind of society. For that reason alone, Proudhon's pedigree as the real father of nineteenth-century social anarchism is incontestable.[1] However, labelling oneself an anarchist is not in itself proof that the label is accurately applied. What did Proudhon mean by anarchism? In Proudhon's words, anarchism is

> a form of government or constitution in which the public and private conscience, formed by the development of science and right, is sufficient by itself for the maintenance of order and the guarantee of all liberties, and where consequently the principle of authority, police, institutions, the means of prevention or repression, bureaucracy, taxation, etc., are reduced to their simplest expression.[2]

Proudhon admits that the idea of anarchic government sounds 'absurd' (if not a little paradoxical, for which his works are renowned), but he is keen to stress that 'the idea of anarchy is quite as rational and concrete as any other. What it means is that political functions have been reduced to industrial functions, and that social order arises from nothing but transactions and exchanges.'[3] In general terms, the partnership between state and political authority has been eroded (Proudhon was not in favour of revolution) to reveal a free federation of autonomous units that are bound to one another by contract.

To understand how Proudhon arrives at this definition of anarchy some appreciation of his conception of human nature is required. It is Proudhon's notion of human nature that provides the foundation for his opinion that only a contract can be the basis of a fair and free transaction between individuals or groups without the diminution of autonomy that occurs in political relationships established within the state. Whilst proffering an occasionally compelling argument in favour of contract, Proudhon's vision of the good life, which is dependent upon transactions and exchanges, ultimately fails because his conception of human nature precludes it. Proudhon's account of human nature assumes the existence of a permanent egoism that scuppers the possibility of a future social order without recourse to some form of political authority to keep it in check. By examining his conception of human nature in conjunction with his writings on politics it will become clear that Proudhon is obliged to concede that some kind of state is indispensable in future society. In other words, Proudhon's anarchist ideological narrative ultimately fails because his account of human nature renders his vista of a desirable social future impossible.

The Parameters of Human Nature

The basis of Proudhon's argument about anarchy begins with the relationship between individuals and their society. In one of his earlier works, *De la Création de l'Ordre dans l'Humanité* (1843), Proudhon is keen to emphasize the social nature of humankind. One of Proudhon's lesser known texts, *De la Création* is best remembered because of his endorsement of Fourier's notion of the 'Serial Law' which imparted 'a lasting effect on Proudhon's philosophical and social beliefs'.[4] It is this that underpins Proudhon's observations on human nature in *De la Création*. The 'Serial Law' can best be explained as the law of the relationships in which various phenomena and natural objects react to one another. It is this law that facilitates the classification of social and natural phenomena, under investigation, into series. Each thing is a member of a series, including the individual in society. The individual is a single unit within the serial order of society; this is what Proudhon took from Fourier. And it is by being a part of the serial order that 'man's personality finds function and fulfilment'.[5]

Under the 'Serial Law' all individuals belong to a serial order, society. Human beings are social creatures. 'Nature has made men sociable', Proudhon writes in his later text *System of Economical Contradictions* (1846).[6] It is within this social matrix that humans fulfil themselves, for each individual has the capacity and opportunity to exercise 'reciprocal action and reaction on the group's development'.[7] As Proudhon made clear in his later works, this capacity for free will or control over one's actions is fundamental to his whole philosophy. Human beings are creatures capable of consciously acting on the world around them. And such thinking emerges strongly in his assertion that it is the workers who should control the production process; for it is this capacity for active participation in the workers' associations that serves as the bedrock for future society.[8]

Like later anarchists, Proudhon is cognizant of the evolutionary inheritance that accompanies humankind. Proudhon attributes the recognition of this fact to Aristotle, who defined human beings as rational and social animals.[9] The importance of Aristotle's definition, for Proudhon, is that it acknowledges 'man's essential quality – animality'.[10] Humans are, then, social animals, or animals living in society. There are, however, important differences that divide humans from other animals, and it is important to come to an understanding of what these are in order to facilitate a more comprehensive insight into Proudhon's conception of human nature. The significant factors that separate humans from other animals are to be found in humankind's ability to communicate and the reflection humans engage in as a result of this. As Proudhon puts it, the human animal

> communicates with his fellows through the mind, before he is united with them in heart; so that with him love is born of intelligence . . . [whereas] animals live side by side without any intelligent intercourse or intimate communication, – all doing the same things, having nothing to learn or to remember; they see, feel, and come in contact with each other, but never penetrate each other. Man continually exchanges with man ideas and feelings, products and services. Every discovery and act in society is necessary to him. . . . Man would not be man were it not for society, and society is supported by the balance and harmony of the powers which compose it.[11]

Some of Proudhon's conclusions may now be considered rather inaccurate or outdated, (one has only to conduct a minimum of research into almost any species of sea mammal, for example, to recognize that its levels of communication may be complex and profound), but he had not the benefit of contemporary research to inform him otherwise. His basic proposition, like that of Marx later, is that the 'labours which animals perform, whether alone or in society, are exact reproductions of their character'.[12] Thus 'brute beasts obey the laws that govern them without knowing it, while man's life is ordered only as the result of knowledge and deliberation, and if I may put it in this way, only because he elaborates his own laws'.[13] In other words, animals are what they do; in Marxian terminology, animals fail to make their own life activity an object of their own consciousness or will.

Just as the sociality of human nature leads to a recognizable difference between human beings and other animals it also results in egoism, one of the two fundamental components of Proudhon's conception of human nature. Humankind's intellectual abilities, which facilitate communication and comparison, result in moral depravity. In one particularly telling passage toward the end of his 'First Memoir' in *What is Property?* (1840), Proudhon describes the intimate ties that bind humankind's intellect to its own downfall. Thus he comments that

> man acquires skill only by observation and experiment. He reflects, then, since to observe and experiment is to reflect; he reasons, since he cannot help reasoning. In reflecting he becomes deluded; in reasoning he makes mistakes, and, thinking himself right, persists in them. He is wedded to his opinions; he esteems himself and despises others. Consequently, he isolates himself; for he could not submit to the majority without renouncing his will and his reason, – that is, without disowning himself, which is impossible. And this isolation, this intellectual egoism, this individuality of opinion, lasts until the truth is demonstrated to him by observation and experience.[14]

Having detailed the relationship between the intellectual capacities of humanity and its ability to err, Proudhon is convinced that 'moral evil' is descended from 'our power of reflection'. Humanity's yoke stems from and is defined by its capacity for rationality. 'The mother of poverty, crime, insurrection, and war was inequality of conditions, which was the daughter of property, which was born of selfishness, which was engendered by private opinion, which descended in a direct line from the autocracy of reason.'[15]

Humanity's essential animality dictates that humans are social beings. 'Man by his nature and his instinct,' writes Proudhon, 'is predestined to society; but his personality, ever varying, is adverse to it.'[16] Despite the social nature of human beings, egoism constantly opposes its social counterpart. It may be true, as Proudhon observes, that the 'human is born a social being, – that is, he seeks equality and justice in all his relations, but he loves independence and praise'.[17] Following Rousseau, Proudhon cites egoism as an integral part of our nature. Unlike Rousseau, Proudhon locates the cause of wickedness in egoism and believes individuals are unwilling to attribute the cause of this wickedness to their own nature, preferring instead to blame others. According to Proudhon, there can be little doubt that egoism, if left to its own devices, will bring about the ruin of humanity. The truth of this is to be found in the acknowledgement that laws are necessary to contain it. Why then, asks Proudhon, 'has preventive, repressive, and coercive legislation always been necessary to set a limit to liberty? For that is the accusing fact, which it is impossible to deny: everywhere the law has grown out of abuse; everywhere the legislator has found himself forced to make man powerless to harm, which is synonymous with muzzling a lion or infibulating a boar.'[18] This emphasis on egoism and the measures that have been necessary to contain it suggest that there is a need for some kind of authority to settle matters of arbitration, a need which Proudhon concedes in his later work on federalism.[19] It is in this sense that David Miller furnishes an accurate assessment of Proudhon's general position on human nature. Referring to the writings of both Proudhon and Bakunin, Miller explains that both thinkers 'had some appreciation of the complexity of human motivation . . . [but that] Proudhon was the more pessimistic about human nature. Like Rousseau, he believed that the primitive ingredients of the human character were egoism and sympathy, with egoism by far the stronger impulse.'[20]

It is hard to resist the conclusion that Proudhon's account of human nature was influenced by Rousseau. Nevertheless, there are certain differences, one of which is that Proudhon does not consider humans to be essentially good. Nor does he believe it just to apportion the blame of humanity's wrongdoings at the door of social institutions. It is not that, in Proudhon's eyes, human beings are wholly bad. Rather they have the capacity for both good and evil. 'Man,' he writes,

> has, of himself and without any necessity, made the contradiction of society so many instruments of harm; through his egoism civilisation has become a war of surprises and ambushes; he lies, he steals, he murders, when not compelled to do so, without provocation, without excuse. In short, he does evil with all the characteristics of a nature deliberately maleficent, and all the more wicked because, when it so wishes, it knows how to do good gratuitously also and is capable of self-sacrifice.[21]

It would be an error to forget that in this, as in other aspects of human nature, humans are like other animals. As 'we are good, loving, tender, just, so we are passionate, greedy, lewd and vindictive; that is, we are like the beasts'.[22] Appreciating the complexities of human nature, Proudhon requests that someone 'explain this mystery of a manifold and discordant being, capable at once of the highest virtues and the most frightful crimes'.[23] There are, then, two sides to human nature. Egoism and love, he claims, are 'the two faces of our nature, ever adverse, ever in course of reconciliation, but never entirely reconciled. In a word, as individualism is the primordial fact of humanity, so association is its complementary term.'[24]

Sharing Rousseau's belief that pity is fundamental to the human constitution, Proudhon, in particular, pictures it as a kind of attraction that humans feel towards beings which are similar to themselves. And in conjunction with reason, pity produces a sense of justice which is manifested by way of an individual's cognizance of the equal standing of mutual personalities. A sense of benevolence certainly exists in Proudhon's writings on humans, but it is impossible not to concede that human nature, as far as Proudhon is concerned, is marked by an irrefutable inherent egocentrism. This does not mean that human nature bears a finality that cannot be obviated, at least not in a religious or metaphysical sense. Proudhon may be inclined toward uncovering the depravity of human nature, but when repudiating Rousseau's arguments in favour of the essential goodness of humankind he simultaneously pours scorn on theories of original sin, whether the fable be Eve's apple or Pandora's box. 'The ancients,' as he puts it, 'accused the individual man; Rousseau accuses the collective man: at bottom, it is always the same proposition, an absurd proposition.'[25] This is a rather peculiar point, simply because Proudhon's intentions are decidedly vague. It appears that his pairing of the doctrine of original sin with Rousseau's theory of the essential goodness of humanity is designed to illustrate that 'Rousseau's formula, precisely because it was an opposition, was a step forward'.[26] The step forward was an advance against the idea, encapsulated in the concept of original sin, that the origin of evil in the world may be found in humankind.

The important point here, though, is that the doctrine of original sin is essentially and symbolically correct to Proudhon. Given the evidence, as Proudhon sees it, of the everlasting battle in human nature between good and evil

the dogma of the fall is not simply the expression of a special or transitory state of human reason and mortality: it is the spontaneous confession, in symbolic phrase, of this fact as astonishing as it is indestructible, the culpability, the inclination to evil, of our race. . . . Religion in giving this idea concrete and dramatic form, has indeed gone back of history and beyond the limits of the world for that which is essential and immanent in our soul; this, on its part, was but an intellectual mirage; it was not mistaken as to the essentiality and permanence of the fact.[27]

In opposition to Rousseau, then, Proudhon discredits any notion that human nature can be changed by merely altering social institutions. Indeed any reading between the lines of what Proudhon has to say concerning human nature leaves one with the distinct impression that human nature is almost incorrigible.[28] I say 'almost incorrigible' for the simple reason that, whilst there are occasions when Proudhon portrays human nature as 'constant and unalterable', there are others when he indicates that humankind not only is capable of moral and social progress, but is actually engaged in that process. There is, of course, no point in disguising the fact that, even in his more optimistic modes, Proudhon's writings are characterized chiefly by a cautious approach to any discussion concerning human nature.[29] To Proudhon, humanity's inherent faults are obvious. Indeed it is this confidence in the erring ways of humanity that leads him to ask such questions as: 'Do we not know that man is frail and fickle, that his heart is full of delusions, and that his lips are a distillery of falsehood?'[30] Faint praise indeed!

The Dichotomy of Human Nature

Proudhon's pessimism is partially offset by a cautious optimism. As we have seen, any notion of original sin is absurd for Proudhon. The concept bears a finality that he finds unacceptable. Humanity's predicament is neither without hope nor the prospect of improvement.

> Mankind makes continual progress toward truth, and light ever triumphs over darkness. Our disease is not, then, absolutely incurable, and the theory of the theologians is worse than inadequate; it is ridiculous, since it is reducible to this tautology: 'Man errs, because he errs.' While the true statement is this: 'Man errs, because he learns.'[31]

The concept of original sin, conceived as an indelible stamp upon human nature, is at odds with Proudhon's conception of self-assertive freedom. Human action is creative action. But that is not to say that human actions are without limit or determination. All actions are performed within the context of a natural and a social world. These worlds have laws which may mould the scope and purpose of human actions and, in consequence, may influence the outcome of those actions. As Harbold has suggested, Proudhon's conception of freedom dictates that only in the light of experience 'can men learn what in the exercise of their freedom they may become'.[32] Humanity, then, is learning, it is moving toward the truth now. The individual is becoming increasingly social. Social by instinct, humans are 'becoming social by reflection and choice'.[33] Seemingly, dark skies are illuminated by a brighter future ahead. Writing in his *General Idea of the Revolution* (1851), Proudhon remarks that good is already beginning to subjugate evil. 'Usually good and evil, pleasure and pain, are inextricably entangled in human dealing. Nevertheless, despite continual oscillations, the good seems to prevail over the evil, and, taking it altogether, there is marked progress toward the better, as far as we can see.'[34] And as Proudhon argues, who is to say that humanity has not already embarked on this process of reform?

In fact it is humankind's immanent sociability that ought to serve as the basis of our actions, according to Proudhon. Sociability is comprised of three elements, or degrees, as Proudhon terms them. The first is sympathy. Like other animals, humans are motivated by a 'sympathetic attraction' toward others. It is this which causes individuals to associate; thus 'every living creature, when deprived of the society of animals of its species, seeks companionship in its solitude'.[35] Sympathy is 'a sort of magnetism awakened in us by the contemplation of a being similar to ourselves, but which never goes beyond the person who feels it; it may be reciprocated, but not communicated. Love, benevolence, pity, sympathy, call it what you will, there is nothing in it which deserves esteem – nothing which lifts man above the beast.'[36] Being the first degree of sociability, sympathy serves as the motor force for justice, the second degree of sociability. According to Proudhon, justice in humankind is fuelled 'by an internal attraction towards his fellow, by a secret sympathy which causes him to love, congratulate and condole; so that, to resist this attraction, his will must struggle against his nature'.[37] Justice, says Proudhon, 'may be defined as the *recognition of the equality between another's personality and our own*'.[38] Whilst other animals may experience this sentiment of justice, only human beings have focused the general sentiment into a narrowly defined concept. If any adage can be invoked to convey the quintessence of justice, Proudhon believes it is that which was inspired by Kant: '*Do unto others that which you would that others should do unto you; do not unto others that which you would not that others should do unto you.*'[39] This second degree of sociability, justice, is a product of 'our reflective and reasoning powers'.[40] And as sympathy acts as the driving force for justice, so justice provides the basis for the third and final degree of sociability, equity.

Possessing intelligence and rationality, individuals find themselves in a position to be able to determine between right and wrong actions. Individuals, as Proudhon contends, are forced to consider the consequences of their actions.

> It is our reason which teaches us that the selfish man, the robber, the murderer – in a word, the traitor to society – sins against Nature, and is guilty with respect to others and himself, when he does wrong wilfully. Finally, it is our social sentiment on the one hand, and our reason on the other, which cause us to think that beings such as we should take the responsibility of their acts.[41]

Sympathy, the first degree of sociability, is the attraction felt by human beings for each other, courtesy of their sentient powers. 'Justice is this same attraction, accompanied by thought and knowledge.'[42] Equity, likewise, is dependent upon justice. All three degrees of sociability are inextricably interdependent. And it is an individual's knowledge of what is right and what is wrong that leads that person to a recognition of his or her duties. Thus equity, which comprises friendship, generosity and gratitude, defined by Proudhon as the admiration or esteem of a superior power, renders 'it at once our duty and our pleasure to aid the weak who have need of us, and to make them our equals; to pay to the strong a just tribute of gratitude and honour, without enslaving ourselves to them; to cherish our neighbours, friends and equals, for that which we receive from them, even by right of exchange'.[43] As justice amounts to a combination of our social instinct and reflection, so equity is a combination of justice and taste which is manifested in urbanity or politeness. It is in this manner that humanity's 'social nature becoming *justice* through reflection, *equity* through the classification of capacities, and having *liberty* for its formula, is the true basis of morality, – the principle and regulator of all our actions'.[44] Human nature whilst often egocentric, is, simultaneously, fundamentally social. In elucidating a contextualist view of human nature, Proudhon has developed a conception of human nature that cannot be understood if divorced from its social context. Human beings are social animals, therefore human nature will be social nature.

The evidence of Proudhon's writings suggests that his conception of human nature possesses the requisite capacities to allow humankind to engage, to some degree, in a process of moral and social improvement. Just how far this process can be taken is difficult to estimate. Proudhon undoubtedly advances a predominantly pessimistic attitude toward human nature, but he does leave room for moral advance. There are some compelling reasons for believing that progress can be made, but there is less optimism for thinking that progress can be charted on a continuous upward curve. As Proudhon acknowledged in his *Confessions of a Revolutionary* (1849), the philosophical method of studying history reveals 'that there is no inevitability in particular events and that these may vary infinitely according to the individual wills that cause them to happen'.[45]

According to Peter Marshall's interpretation of Proudhon, progress appears inevitable.[46] But if social improvement is dependent upon the moral improvement of the individual progress may be somewhat hindered. Moral improvement occurs within definite limits. As Vincent notes, Proudhon

> did believe that some inroads into the social ill-effects of man's egoistic impulses could be made, but no amount of education or reform would overcome entirely what he considered to be man's inherent depravity. There could be moral improvement, yes; but complete moral triumph, decidedly not. . . . Virtuous man was a moral asymptote which could be approached but which would forever elude man's grasp.[47]

The reasons for this are not immediately visible. At times Proudhon talks as if humans are capable of perfection. In his *General Idea of the Revolution,* for example, Proudhon writes encouragingly about the human individual as a 'sexual and social being, endowed with reason, love and conscience, capable of learning by experience, of perfecting himself by reflection, and of earning his living by work', whilst in the same text he also refers to 'the imperfection of our nature'.[48] The plain fact, as Proudhon admits in a later work, is that: 'We are born perfectible, but we shall never be perfect.'[49] To my mind, this unresolvable tension hinges upon his belief that humankind is everything; that any attempt to define human nature borders on the ineffable and leads to bewilderment when confronted by the complexities of that which we seek to investigate. In Proudhon's words:

Man, an abridgement of the universe, sums up and syncretises in his person all the potentialities of being . . . [man] is at once spirit and matter, spontaneity and reflection, mechanism and life, angel and brute. He is venomous like the viper, sanguinary like the tiger, gluttonous like the hog, obscene like the ape; and devoted like the dog, generous like the horse, industrious like the bee, monogamic like the dove, sociable like the beaver and sheep. And in addition he is man, – that is, reasonable and free, susceptible of education and improvement.[50]

The only tangible fact to emerge, as Proudhon sees it, is that whilst 'the contradictions of political economy may be solved; the essential contradiction of our being never will be'.[51]

One fact that does emerge from Proudhon's investigation of the intricacies of human nature is that the concept utilized in his ideological narrative is far more realistic than one might first care to imagine. It may be argued that his emphasis on egoism is grossly exaggerated, but such considerations are not of major importance. The psychological accuracy of Proudhon's concept of egoism does not carry a great deal of weight. Its importance lies in its pivotal role as a foundation for his general political ideology; here is the source of its theoretical imperativeness. Reflecting humanity's harsh if not brutish nature, egoism defends Proudhon from assertions of utopian dreaming by dismissing any suggestion that amelioration of social conditions may be brought about by moral argument alone. Future social institutions will have to take into account this aspect of human nature.

As has been demonstrated, however, egoism is offset by sociability. If individuals are egoistic, then they may be just and equitable also. But Proudhon's portrait of human nature is not as black and white as this simple division suggests. Egoism may lead to wickedness and humanity's ruin, but sociability does not equate with some quality that might be labelled goodness. Proudhon's conception of human nature is a little more complex than that. In a manner similar to Rousseau before him, Proudhon weaves into his conception of humankind's social nature a capacity for conflict. Integral to human nature is intellect, and it is this which provides the basis for egoism. The power of reason in human nature leads not only to communication, but also comparison with others; which, in turn, leads to a love of praise. In order to gain this praise individuals must first win the acceptance of others. And in agreeing to abide by a set of social norms individuals win the approval of others. However,

Proudhon also recognized that humans behave as they do due to socialization. Social norms, which are a part of the wider social morality that presides over the society in which an individual lives, are gradually assimilated. This does not mean that individuals are subjugated to the whims of social conventions; far from it. As Proudhon acknowledges, each individual has a conscience and 'conscience grants men a right to judge that is prior to society's conventional existence'.[52] In effect, individuals are free; and free-will provides the means for them to disobey social norms and even their own consciences.

Accordingly, both egoism and sociability may warrant some form of social restraint. Humanity's social nature simultaneously provides a basis for social criticism and creates an obstacle in the way of anarchy. Egoism, which arises from the social nature of human nature, is an ineradicable feature of human nature for Proudhon; as is sociability. As such, individuals may be quarrelsome, aggressive, greedy or wicked. Alternatively, their actions may be characterized by love, compassion and concern for others. Because of the multifarious dimensions of Proudhon's conception of human nature, future society will have to be prepared to accommodate the rough with the smooth. Changes in social practices and social organization may encourage the development of a new social morality, but there is no level of social and political transformation that will completely curtail the exercise of egoism. This much Proudhon makes clear. The question we have to begin to address now is whether Proudhon's realistic analysis of human nature renders it possible for him to abandon dependence on an authority structure that resembles the state?

The State and the Suffocation of Liberty

Having argued that Proudhon's conception of human nature is delicately balanced between a rather sour pessimism and a cautious optimism, I now want to suggest that his view of the state is similarly ambivalent. Although this section is designed to provide an assessment of Proudhon's attitude toward the state it will only be when we have considered his notion of federal politics that I will finally be able to persuade the reader that Proudhon's theory of anarchist government fails to release itself completely from a dependence upon the state. What I intend to investigate here is the ambivalence exuded in Proudhon's writings on the state. For whilst there is no dearth of denunciation of the state in Proudhon's writings, his invective sometimes conceals his quiet acknowledgement of that same thing. It is this ambiguous attitude that arouses the suspicion that his political ideology relies on the state.

That Proudhon disliked the state intensely is irrefutable. The death of his brother, Jean-Etienne, during military service, unquestionably influenced Proudhon's position. Nonetheless, there is hard evidence that his dissatisfaction with the state and government was already apparent before the death of his sibling. After returning home to Besançon to aid his parents upon his brother's call to military service, Proudhon was offered the task of editing *L'Impartial,* a local newspaper, by Just Muiron. In reply to Muiron, Proudhon wrote: 'Why should we not profess publicly an absolute pyrrhonism towards all ministers, past, present and future? Why should we not invite the population to make themselves capable of managing their own affairs and of preparing the way for a confederation of peoples?'[53] Such thoughts bear witness to the beginnings of Proudhon's hostility toward the state and his encouragement of people to manage their own affairs without dependence on either government or state. It was in all likelihood, though, the death of his brother that consolidated these sentiments into something more solid. From then on his animosity toward the entity we call the state was marked by a bitter invective. Writing in his *General Idea of the Revolution,* Proudhon characterized the state as a 'fictitious being, without intelligence, without passion, without morality'.[54] His analysis in *What is Property?* is hardly less scathing; for whilst the state may take many different forms, be it despotism, monarchy, aristocracy or democracy, one thing is certain, it always represents 'tyranny'.[55] Moreover, as he stipulates in his *Confessions of a Revolutionary:* 'All men are equal and free: society, by nature and destination, is therefore autonomous and ungovernable . . . [so] Whoever puts his hand on me to govern me is an usurper and a tyrant; I declare him my enemy.'[56] Proudhon's abhorrence of state and government is unmistakable and perhaps without equal. Nowhere is this demonstrated with more vigour and passion than in his classic denunciation of government, in his *General Idea of the Revolution.*

> To be GOVERNED is to be kept in sight, inspected, spied upon, directed, law-driven, numbered, enrolled, indoctrinated, preached at, controlled, estimated, valued, censured, commanded, by creatures who have neither the right, nor the wisdom, nor the virtue to do so . . . To be GOVERNED is to be at every operation, at every transaction, noted, registered, enrolled, taxed, stamped,

measured, numbered, assessed, licensed, authorised, admonished, forbidden, reformed, corrected, punished. It is, under pretext of public utility, and in the name of the general interest, to be placed under contribution, trained, ransomed, exploited, monopolised, extorted, squeezed, mystified, robbed; then, at the slightest resistance, the first word of complaint, to be repressed, fined, despised, harassed, tracked, abused, clubbed, disarmed, choked, imprisoned, judged, condemned, shot, deported, sacrificed, sold, betrayed; and, to crown all, mocked, ridiculed, outraged, dishonoured. That is government; that is its justice; that is its morality.[57]

Proudhon's objections to the state are dependent on more than his personal experiences, however. No matter how painful the death of his brother proved to be, it has already been shown that Proudhon was thinking seriously about the possibility of life without government before Jean-Etienne's demise. The basis of his protestations toward the state is ultimately dependent upon his conception of human nature. Indeed one should note that Proudhon also considers human nature to be partly responsible for the genesis of the state. There are two things that appear to be accountable for the rise of the state. The first is human nature. The second is the family, or more particularly the relationship of the child to the father. To take the latter first, it seemed plain to Proudhon that 'the principle of authority and government has its source in the dominating attitude of the family'.[58] Authority and government are like hand and glove to Proudhon, and both spring from the family. It is 'family customs' and the 'domestic experience' that typifies family life that lead Proudhon to categorize the family as 'the embryo of the State'.[59] Headed invariably by a male, families provided the authority structure that was replicated in the state. 'The first states', he notes, 'were generally families or tribes governed by their natural leader – husband, father, patriarch, finally a king.'[60] Whether Proudhon's analysis applies equally to modern states is open to doubt. And as Richard Vernon has noted, given Proudhon's assessment of the nature of authority he has either to deny that there is any significant difference between pre-modern and modern states, that is, those founded upon the personal authority of a monarch and those states based 'upon formal norms of legality', or to surrender the explanatory power of his original analysis.[61]

However uneasily Proudhon's original analysis may lie in conjunction with the development of modern states, the important element of Proudhon's thinking under consideration here is the relationship of the state to human nature. That human nature is partly responsible for the development of the state is accounted for by the fact, according to Proudhon, that humankind naturally follows a chief or leader. All social animals, he observes, follow a chief by instinct, and humankind is no exception. 'Man (naturally a social being) naturally follows a chief. Originally, the chief is the father, the patriarch, the elder; in other words, the good and wise man, whose functions, consequently, are exclusively of a reflective and intellectual nature.'[62] Possessing an innate instinct to follow a leader, human nature, for Proudhon, supplied the necessary material for ambitious leaders to work on.

The crucial aspect of the relationship between human nature and the state may only be unearthed by focusing on Proudhon's conception of liberty, which is fundamental to his notion of human nature and the well-being of the individual. Its importance for Proudhon may be gauged from his rather panegyrical pronouncement that liberty is 'the original condition of man'. To forsake liberty, he writes, 'is to renounce the nature of man; after that, how could we perform the acts of man?' It is of little wonder that Proudhon considers liberty to be 'inviolable'.[63] It is in this vein that Proudhon develops a concept of negative liberty; liberty that is maintained by an absence of restraints other than the law, which is designed to provide the requisite conditions for a like liberty for all. It may not be clear how easily this argument sits with the former suggestion that humans naturally follow a chief or leader, but it seems that Proudhon has to think of liberty in this way. If this were not the case, then Proudhon's vision of a mutualist society based on free contracts could hardly be imaginable. Contracts that are freely entered into remove the external constraints that may restrict an individual's freedom. The only constraint upon the individual is that of the self-incurred obligation that arises from the promise that is integral to the contract. Thus, liberty, being fundamental to human nature, manifested in the form of free association and contract, is 'the only true form of society'.[64]

The problem is that government tends to smother liberty. Established as the 'supreme administrative power' to oversee public utilities and public projects, the 'governmental system', writes Proudhon, 'tends to become more and more complicated, without becoming on that account more efficient or more moral, and without offering any more guaranties to person or property'.[65] Centralization of the governmental system is regarded as an anathema to liberty.

When the Revolution proclaimed liberty of the people, equality before the law, the sovereignty of the people, the subordination of power to the country, it set up two incompatible things, society and government; and it is this incompatibility which has been the cause or the pretext of this overwhelming, liberty-destroying concentration, called CENTRALISATION, which the parliamentary democracy admires and praises, because it is its nature to tend toward despotism.[66]

For the sake of liberty, the true form of human society, the role of the state has to be limited. Liberty cannot survive under the state simply because the state is an instrument of power, and power and liberty are incompatible.

Whilst imperative to Proudhon's conception of human nature, and, therefore, his objections toward the state, liberty also plays a very important role in a further argument against the state. The argument is centred around two concepts: the social contract and political obligation. It is in dealing with these concepts that Proudhon's concerns about human nature being deprived of its fullest expression under the social contract envisaged by Rousseau begin to emerge. His argument, developed principally in the *General Idea of the Revolution,* is that the social contract 'is an agreement of man with man; an agreement from which must result what we call society'.[67] More specifically, the social contract is, essentially, a contract of exchange. In entering into the social contract, an individual enters into an agreement that 'bears only upon exchange'; it deprives that person of neither goods nor property. In its nature it is, remarks Proudhon, 'essentially reciprocal: it imposes no obligation upon the parties, except that which results from their personal promise of reciprocal delivery: it is not subject to any external authority: it alone forms the law between the parties: it awaits their initiative for its execution'.[68] This quality of reciprocity renders the social contract, in its capacity as a contract of exchange, the lifeblood that makes society possible. That is, a society of free men is a society based upon contract and commerce. Indeed commerce may only exist among free men. It is almost as though the act of exchange comprises the core process that constitutes society itself.

So in every exchange, there is a moral obligation that neither of the contracting parties shall gain at the expense of the other; that is, that, to be legitimate and true, commerce must be exempt from all inequality. This is the first condition of commerce. Its second condition is, that it be voluntary; that is, that the parties act freely and openly. I define, then, commerce or exchange as an act of society.[69]

Much of Proudhon's analysis of the social contract stems from his critique of Rousseau, who he claims 'understood nothing of the social contract'.[70] According to Proudhon, Rousseau's understanding was severely handicapped by his failure to see anything but 'the political relations' of the social contract. Thus Proudhon argues that, for Rousseau, 'the social contract is neither an act of reciprocity, nor an act of association. Rousseau takes care not to enter into such considerations. It is an act of appointment of arbiters, chosen by the citizens, without any preliminary agreement.'[71] Whilst the social contract, for Proudhon, is about establishing reciprocal exchange within a free society, Proudhon believes Rousseau's only concern is to create a society founded on government and authority. The crux of the matter, for Proudhon, is that Rousseau has failed to appreciate the true nature of authority. Unable to recognize its intimate connection with the family, Rousseau has, mistakenly, assumed that authority in society can be based upon agreement. Consequently,

> Rousseau did not see that authority, of which the proper sphere is the family, is a mystical principle, anterior and superior to the will of the parties interested, of the father and mother, as well as of the children; that what is true of authority in the family would be equally true of authority in Society ... that, once the theory of a social authority is admitted, it cannot in any case depend upon an agreement; that it is contradictory that they who must obey authority should begin by decreeing it.[72]

Although the nature of this mystical principle remains one of Proudhon's unexplained paradoxical mysteries, it serves as the foundation for an attack on Rousseau's contract as nothing other than a vicious fraud, a fraud which encourages citizens to divest themselves of their sovereignty, and of regions and provinces to surrender to central authority. Outlining its debilitating effects, Proudhon argues that Rousseau's contract, employing universal suffrage and the general will to establish an undivided nation legislating through an undivided assembly, will result in serious consequences for citizen and region alike. Moreover, such problems are exacerbated by the relationship between people and government.

> It is no longer the government that is made for the people; it is the people who are made for government. Power invades

everything, dominates everything, absorbs everything, for ever, for always, without end . . . The citizen has nothing to do but perform his little task in his little corner, drawing his little salary, raising his little family, and relying for the rest on the providence of government.[73]

The centralized power of government and state exerts an increasingly powerful stranglehold over individual citizens, depriving them of liberty and civic participation alike.

The principal means by which liberty is jeopardized under a social contract not based upon equal exchange is through the implementation of universal suffrage. Proudhon's attitude toward universal suffrage is tightly bound to his perception of the social contract and the political obligation that flows from that agreement. He makes it clear, however, that there is general recognition that 'a nation may be oppressed by being led to believe that it is obeying only its own laws. The history of universal suffrage, among all nations, is the history of the restrictions of liberty by and in the name of the multitude.'[74] Rousseau eludes censure here, if only because Proudhon concurs entirely with the conviction that no individual should be forced to obey a law which that individual has not consented to. Yet in a passage that shares some of J.S. Mill's concern over the tyranny of the majority, Proudhon suggests that, despite the reasonableness of his principle, Rousseau erred in his application. 'With suffrage, or the universal vote, it is evident that the law is neither direct nor personal, any more than collective. The law of the majority is not my law, it is the law of force; hence the government based upon it is not my government; it is government by force.'[75] In order to maintain freedom universal suffrage must be abandoned.

That I may remain free; that I may not have to submit to any law but my own, and that I may govern myself, the authority of the suffrage must be renounced: we must give up the vote, as well as representation and monarchy. In a word, everything in the government of society which rests on the divine must be suppressed, and the whole rebuilt upon the human idea of CONTRACT.[76]

There is then, a concern for both positive and negative liberty. Before positive liberty or active participation can be encouraged the liberty of the individual has to be protected from the state. The foundation of active citizenship is a sphere of individual liberty that is, as Proudhon explains, 'inviolable'. To be free as an active citizen the individual must play a full role. According to Proudhon, this cannot be achieved within the parameters of universal suffrage. One way or another the individual is denied the opportunity of exercising and prosecuting the teachings of his or her free will. And if, as Rousseau argues and Proudhon concurs, the individual is forced to obey a law that lacks that individual's consent then that individual cannot be thought of as free. But Proudhon is unable to fulfil his own requirements. His ideological narrative, and the relationship between his conception of human nature and his political prescriptions in particular, is inconsistent. As will be elaborated below, by ascribing to human nature an irrefutable measure of egoism Proudhon is resigned to the permanence of conflict in politics and is forced to concede that the only means to settle such disputes is through the procedure of majority voting. Consequently, it is impossible for Proudhon to evade the criticism that he levels at Rousseau. If the individual is not free, and for Proudhon this cannot be the case where majority voting occurs, then human nature cannot fulfil itself. Restrictions on liberty are restrictions on one's status as a human being. This is the meaning of Proudhon's argument that liberty is essential to humans. To fulfil one's human nature one has to be free to direct one's own life, to obey only one's own will. To be human is to be rational; to order one's own affairs without unnecessary interference from state or government. To satisfy human nature involves leading an active life in the affairs of the community, discharging one's duties, enjoying one's freedom; but active participation requires a sphere of 'inviolable', negative liberty or freedom from constraint. The only way to overcome this, as Proudhon sees it, is by establishing the supremacy of contract.

In rejecting the state (at least for the moment) and its attendant, government, whether direct or representative, Proudhon commits himself to the ideal of contract. Contract, as Crowder has noted, facilitates the development of freedom in two ways. First, by entering into a contract an individual's transactions are as free as can be from interference by the state. Second, and more importantly, when engaged in contract with another an individual's 'dealings express and develop the moral will that constitutes part of his essential human nature'.[77] Emphasis on the notion of contract is imperative to Proudhon because contract is founded on 'the only moral bond which free and equal beings can accept'.[78] Only by establishing a mutualist society on the basis of free contracts are individuals able to maintain their moral autonomy by acting freely. Hence Proudhon argues that by freely entering into an agreement 'with one or more of my fellow citizens for any object whatever, it is clear that my own will is my law; it is I myself, who, in fulfilling my obligation, am my own government'.[79] Indeed it is this idea of contract, together with his dissatisfaction with universal suffrage, that forces Proudhon to question the authenticity of any obligation the state may presume to hold him to. Why, he asks, should he obey the law?

> Who made it? Rousseau teaches in unmistakable terms, that in a government really democratic and free the citizen, in obeying the law, obeys only his own will. But the law has been made without my participation, despite my absolute disapproval, despite the injury which it inflicts upon me. The State does not bargain with me: it gives me nothing in exchange: it simply practises extortion upon me. Where then is the bond of conscience, reason, passion or interest which binds me?[80]

The grounds of Proudhon's remonstration lead him to doubt not only the legitimacy of the state's authority, but whether a contract actually exists at all.

> What relation is there, I ask, between this assembly and me? what guaranty can it offer me? why should I make this enormous, irreparable, sacrifice to its authority, to accept whatever it may be pleased to resolve, as the expression of my will, as the just measure of my rights? And when this assembly, after debates of which I understand nothing, proceeds to impose its decision upon me as law, at the point of a bayonet, I ask, if it is true that I am sovereign, what becomes of my dignity? if I am to consider myself as party to a contract, where is the contract?[81]

Like Rousseau, Proudhon shares little if any faith in the processes of representative government. But contrary to Rousseau, Proudhon is not encouraged by processes of direct legislation. Government, whether direct or indirect, is fundamentally the same; and as far as Proudhon is concerned, 'one is as bad as the other'.[82] Universal suffrage, he contends, cannot adequately serve the interests of the people. An issue or piece of legislation which affects them is, precisely because it affects them, special to them, whereas universal suffrage is only capable of yielding general answers to specific questions. What use are representatives? Individuals ought to negotiate directly for themselves; only in this way, Proudhon warns, will the individual be able to dispense with the 'lottery' that is known as universal suffrage.

Certainly, an element of class antagonism permeates Proudhon's analysis of political obligation. He suggests, quite frankly, that laws and government are biased in favour of the rich. 'Laws! We know what they are, and what they are worth! Spider webs for the rich and powerful, steel chains for the weak and poor, fishing nets in the hands of the Government.'[83] Lamenting the impoverishment of the masses, Proudhon comments on how society 'tends to erect into a political and social dogma the enslavement of the working class and the necessity of its poverty'.[84] That Proudhon's discontent over the notion of political obligation is fuelled, in part, by a recognition of the class disparities across contemporary society is indisputable. However, it seems equally incontrovertible that his dissatisfaction is underscored by a concern for the role assigned to the individual in this process. 'The People,' he suggests, 'have no more voice in the State than they have in the Church: their part is to believe and obey.'[85] Exhibiting sentiments that were echoed in his *The Principle of Federation* (1863), Proudhon's *General Idea of the Revolution* enunciates categorically that the state should not overlook the individual, treating a person as if he or she were the exclusive property of the state to be dealt with as it chooses.

The emphasis here is that individuals, whether alone or as a collective entity known as the people, are perfectly capable of looking after their own affairs without the often ill-judged and oppressive measures of a highly centralized state. It has often been stated, he observes, that the *raison d'être* of the state is to reconcile the so-called 'fatal antagonism of interests' that exists within society.[86] The purpose of government, it is held, is to maintain order; the rub is that this benefits the rich and powerful at the expense of those beneath them. To Proudhon's mind, class privileges simply exacerbate an extant problem, the condescending manner in which the state treats its citizens. Convinced of the people's ability to manage their own affairs, Proudhon announces: 'Let each household, each factory, each association, each municipality, each district, attend to its own police, and administer carefully its own affairs, and the nation will be policed and administered.'[87] Not only is it wrong for the state to underestimate the people's capacities, but it should recognize

> that each citizen in the sphere of his industry, each municipal, district or provincial council within its own territory, is the only natural and legitimate representative of the Sovereign, and that therefore each locality should act directly and by itself in

administering the interests which it includes, and should exercise full sovereignty in relation to them.[88]

The collective entity, or the people, operate through or as an identifiable unit. And whilst it may be inaccurate to term this unit a nation it seems that the unit is the depository of the people's sovereignty in much the same way that the nation became the expression of the people's sovereign power during the French revolution.

In summary, Proudhon's catalogue of complaints against the state amounts to a two-pronged critique. First there is his anxiety that the increasing centralization of political authority leaves individuals deprived of their liberty. Additionally, Proudhon expresses grave fears about the idea of a social contract in the political sense. Autonomy as well as liberty are jeopardized here. Indeed, Proudhon's invective against the state is substantial and often persuasive, but it would be misleading to overlook the fact that Proudhon himself sets precedents for the very existence of the state in human nature. The question that has to be addressed now, is whether Proudhon's solution to the problem of creating a society that will allow each citizen to take an active part in the running of that society's affairs creates a unit that, in defending its members' interests, actually amounts to a state in disguise? The problem that remains is to decide whether, in creating a federal government, Proudhon can justifiably be labelled an anarchist.

The Politics of Federalism

Along with other thinkers under the broad ideological umbrella of anarchism, Proudhon allegedly shies away from any attempt at defining a detailed blueprint for the development of future society. He admits himself that he belongs to no school of thought nor represents any party. His assignment is simply to tell it as it is. 'God forbid that I should set myself up as a prophet, or that I should pretend to have ever invented an idea! I see, I observe, I write.'[89] However, the reader should be aware that Proudhon was not averse to outlining what he believed were the deficiencies of society as he knew it. To this effect he had little trouble in eschewing the oppressive power of political authority. In its place Proudhon championed the cause of federalism, the political framework of his future society. The task that has to be addressed now is to determine whether, in establishing a theory of federal government, Proudhon entirely renounces the state, and if not, where does this leave his concern for increased public participation in the life of the society?

As noted above, the primary reason for Proudhon's apparent rejection of the state and the political authority that accompanies it is his belief that contract is the only moral bond that free individuals (in effect, males only – Proudhon was blatantly sexist) can accept. At first glance this sits quite comfortably with his overt distrust of centralized authority, expressed as early as 1832 in his letter to Muiron. Much of his concern here focused on the authoritarian, centralized conception of politics associated with Robespierre and the community-based theories of Saint-Simon and Fourier, which Proudhon thought represented a threat to individual freedom – sentiments that inspired his later hostility toward communism. Just as, if not more important, though, is the integrity of the individual, so often forsaken or quashed by the state. Summarizing Proudhon's unease with centralized political authority, Vincent contends that Proudhon's misgivings were propelled by a 'dislike of socio-political arrangements which had insufficient respect for the integrity of individuals and groups. He insisted that human dignity required respect for autonomy and that true justice had to be founded on the recognition of liberty and dignity among individuals.'[90] This suspicion of centralized, authoritarian political regimes leads Proudhon to argue that change must be premised on economic reform rather than alterations in the political composition of society. Moreover, if change is to be initiated it should be the workers themselves who take the lead. Writing in his paper *Le Représentant du Peuple,* which first appeared in April 1848, Proudhon had voiced his opinion that 'the proletariat must emancipate itself without the help of the government'.[91] He reinforced his stand against political action in his speech, at the Banquet of the Republic on 15 October 1848, known as the *Toast to the Revolution*, in which he favours direct action. 'The people alone operating on itself without intermediaries, can complete the economic revolution whose foundation was laid in February. The people alone can save civilisation and make humanity advance.'[92]

This might appear strange to some, considering that Proudhon actually served some time as a representative at the Constituent Assembly. Indeed, Proudhon himself was conscious of the irony of his situation. Having denounced universal suffrage and proclaimed himself an anarchist why did he take his seat in the Assembly? I doubt that any universally acceptable answer can be provided, but it does seem that Proudhon was toying with the idea that politics could be utilized in some fashion to further the ends of the working classes. Proudhon was not afraid to engage in politics if he thought it would bring good to the social problems affecting society. Rather than rejecting politics outright, Proudhon approached politics with a measure of caution and suspicion. His personal experiences convinced him of the futility of investing faith in politics. Elected to the Assembly in June 1848, Proudhon was soon disillusioned by the whole experience. His short time there, Woodcock suggests, 'hardened his distrust of political methods, and helped to create the anti-parliamentarianism that marked his last years and was inherited by the anarchist movement in general'.[93] Furthermore, Bonaparte's election in December of the same year is said to have finally convinced Proudhon that nothing was to be gained from political action.[94]

All of this, however, lies in stark contrast to his earlier position of calling for state intervention to aid the miners around Saint-Etienne. After witnessing the appalling conditions that the mine-workers had to endure in the early part of the 1840s, Proudhon, quite openly, 'embraced a programme of state intervention'.[95] Change was to be instituted through a series of reforms, in which the government had a hand. These ideas were reflected in the texts he wrote at that time. In the 'Second Memoir' of his *What is Property?* Proudhon envisages the process in which society changes for the better.

> It is necessary to apply on a large scale the principle of collective production, to give the state eminent domain over all capital, to render each producer responsible . . . and to transform every profession and trade into a public function . . . individual possession will establish itself, without community, under the inspection of the republic, and equality of conditions will no longer depend simply on the will of the citizen.[96]

Whether Proudhon was simply engaging in tactical expediency here is a moot point, which I shall address below. But one unquestionable implication of this line of reasoning is that Proudhon believed the assistance of the state should be used to bring about social transformation. His opinion that the state would have to be involved in any attempt to initiate practical reforms is clear. His message in *De la Création,* published shortly after *What is Property?*, remains unaltered; government is to play an active role in inaugurating and steering socio-economic reforms. 'It is necessary to centralise commerce, agriculture, and industry; to proportion production to needs; to treat with care mineral resources, to support and augment vegetables; [and] it is necessary to regulate the workshop, to police the market, to convert into tax the rent of the capitalist, to REPUBLICANISE . . . PROPERTY.'[97]

This attitude was still present in Proudhon's writings as late as 1848. Vincent has noted with some perception that Proudhon's *Carnets* (1843–64) include proposals for reform that are founded on the management of the economy by the state.[98] By 1849, however, Proudhon's attitude had shifted. No longer was he persuaded that political action could yield useful results. In fact it is open to question whether Proudhon ever truly believed that politics would offer a remedy for the social evils that beset society. It may be true that in some of his earlier works he held the view that the state could be used as a means to realize its own demise, but by 1849 Proudhon had just about washed his hands of state inaugurated and politically orientated social reforms. The most vigorous expression of this attitude appears in his *General Idea of the Revolution,* and he makes it patently obvious that the way forward lies with social economics rather than politics. One has to understand, he implores, that there lies beyond politics a much vaster and much richer domain within which 'our destiny is worked out'. That province is the sphere of social economy.[99] Political reform will be the effect not the means of social reform.

By this time his view of politics was far from favourable. Everyone, he reflects,

> is governed in his choice of party by his passion and his interests; the mind is submitted to the impositions of the will, – there is no knowledge, there is not even a shadow of certainty. In this way, general ignorance produces general tyranny; and while liberty of thought is written in the charter, slavery of thought, under the name of *majority rule,* is decreed by the charter.[100]

By now his ideas are firmly indebted to the superiority of contract and economics over political authority. Hence he writes as if future society should be some loose kind of industrial democracy. 'It is industrial organisation that we will put in place of government. . . . In place of laws, we will put contracts. – No more laws voted by a majority, nor even unanimously; each citizen, each industrial union, makes its own laws. . . . In place of political powers, we will put economic forces.'[101]

The lack of any explanation as to why 'passion' and 'interests' only operate in the political environment and not in industrial unions is an oversight that Proudhon fails to address. Nevertheless, his conviction that reform should be led from below rather than above was reaffirmed in the second edition of *De la Création*, published in 1849, two years before the first appearance of *General Idea of the Revolution*.[102] Indeed, it might be observed that throughout the period of his apparent dependence on political activities to better society Proudhon was merely engaging in expediency. In other words, Proudhon perceived politics as a case of 'as and when'. This explains why his dismissal of universal suffrage was never complete. If elected politicians were blind to or simply turned a deaf ear to his desired social reforms, then Proudhon would rail against it. If, on the other hand, those elected were sympathetic to his programme of reforms then he was quite happy to countenance it. Seemingly, Proudhon bore a permanent suspicion towards politics and political activity, which is why he regarded them as something of a necessary evil. As he wrote with some wit, in his *Carnets*, in 1852, 'to engage in politics is to wash one's hands in shit'.[103]

It was noted above[104] that by 1849 Proudhon had *just about* washed his hands of the state and politics. I say *just about* because, despite his penchant for reforms from below guided by direct action, Proudhon never seems to finally rid himself of a dependency on both state and politics. In the last work to be published before his death, *The Principle of Federation*, Proudhon elaborates some of his most explicit ideas on the future of society. In spite of his convictions that citizens should assume a more active role in the life of society this work reveals that Proudhon's federal society reserves a place for politics and state alike. The problem that confronts Proudhon is nothing less than the permanence of politics. Politics is present in all societies. The reason for this, Proudhon adds, is that each and every society is governed by the relationship of authority and liberty. Political order has been and forever will be subject to two competing principles: authority and liberty. The two are inextricably locked together. 'Authority,' he remarks, 'necessarily presupposes a liberty which recognizes or denies it; in turn liberty, in its political sense, likewise presupposes an authority which confronts it, repressing or tolerating it.' Both are present, to some degree, in all societies; 'no political arrangement is exempt'.[105] Politics feeds on this contest between authority and liberty. It is this which explains the myriad of political controversies. Hence his observation that the 'dualism of authority and liberty supplies the key to all enigmas; without the aid of this primordial explanation, the history of states would be the despair of the mind and the scandal of philosophy'.[106] There is no escape. Regardless of his assertion that 'my whole philosophy is but a perpetuity of reconciliations', Proudhon's principles of authority and liberty are forever in opposition. Complete reconciliation can never be reached. Under Proudhon's dialectical view of reality the only way in which these principles can be realized is through compromise, the essence of politics. In developing his theory of federalism Proudhon came to recognize that politics was necessary; that politics could not simply be reduced to socio-economic relations. The counterbalance to this was that, even if politics is permanent, Proudhon judges that the state, in an increasingly well organized society, would witness a diminution of its own role. 'The state,' he writes, 'in a well organized society, has to reduce itself little by little until it represents nothing.'[107]

Consonant with his preceding works, *The Principle of Federation* makes no bones about documenting the scurrilities that the state has inflicted upon society. It is, he avows, responsible for 'prejudices and abuses of every kind, aristocratic prejudices, bourgeois privilege, ecclesiastical authority, and the people have been oppressed, the mind enslaved; liberty thus remained in a strait-jacket, and civilisation stagnated hopelessly'.[108] Nevertheless, the state still has a role to play. It may be true, as Vernon has highlighted, that the concept 'of the state as an insulated and self-sufficient order is to vanish, and no level of organization, it would appear, is to be distinguished qualitatively from any other'.[109] He continues, however, by submitting the argument that what Proudhon retains from the notion of the state

> is its character as a focus for political life or a vehicle for public sentiment. *Du Principe fédératif* stands squarely in the tradition of 'civic humanism' . . . the tradition springing from Aristotle, Machiavelli, and Montesquieu, which values above all the independence of citizens and their active, responsible participation in the management of their common affairs.[110]

Federalism is more than just a set of political arrangements, it is an approach to life. It is to serve, for want of a better description, as a glasshouse protecting and cultivating the growth of a newly developing civic virtue. In facilitating the development of freedom by the decentralization of political life, federalism provides the political framework within which the people learn to govern themselves by reason. Accordingly, 'the freest and most moral government is that in which powers are best divided, administrative functions best separated, the independence of groups most respected, provincial, cantonal, and municipal authorities best served by the central authority – in a word, federal government'.[111]

Proudhon's federalism is unlike other forms of government. It is, seemingly, non-hierarchical and decentralized. 'Its basic and essential law is this: in a federation, the powers of central authority are specialized and limited and diminish in number, in directness, and in what I may call intensity as the confederation grows by the adhesion of new states.'[112] Federal powers and authority, Proudhon stipulates, should not exceed those and that of the local authorities. Federal authority should be 'a mere delegate and subordinate function'. Within this context Proudhon no longer envisages federalism as a government, rather 'it is an agency created by the states for the joint execution of certain functions which the states abandon, and which thus become federal powers'.[113] The role of the federal state or agency is that of an initiator. Contrary to the practices of centralized unitary states, under federalism the citizen and the local authority are to play a much larger role. It is with this in mind that Proudhon addresses the principal function of the federal authority.

> The state is not an entrepreneur in the public sector, to be confused with the contractors who perform public works. Whether it commands, acts, or supervises, the state is the initiator and ultimate director of change . . . [But] . . . Once a beginning has been made, the machinery established, the state withdraws, leaving the execution of the new task to local authorities and citizens.[114]

Upon recognition that the authoritarian and centralized state threatens the liberty of the citizen, Proudhon hopes that this future federation will encourage the active participation of citizens to resurrect the civic or republican ideal that is smothered by unitary states. Whether monarchy or democracy there is little to choose between when it comes to the freedom of the citizen.

> But what was monarchy? The sovereignty of one man. What is democracy? The sovereignty of the nation, or rather the national majority. But it is, in both cases, the sovereignty of man instead of the sovereignty of the law, the sovereignty of the will instead of the sovereignty of the reason; in one word, the passions instead of justice. Undoubtedly, when a nation passes from the monarchical to the democratic state, there is progress, because in multiplying the sovereigns we increase the opportunities of

the reason to substitute itself for the will; but in reality there is no revolution in the government, since the principle remains the same. Now, we have the proof today that, with the most perfect democracy, we cannot be free.[115]

What he dislikes about democracy is its mass character and what it makes of its citizens, creatures who shun responsibility and freedom, whereas those that reside in a federal state are pleased to accept their responsibilities and work hard to ensure that tyranny does not gain a foothold. As April Carter remarks, 'Proudhon seems to draw on the republican tradition in which democracy is associated with urban mob rule, and the related danger that the masses, lacking the education or the economic independence to sustain civic liberty, will veer towards popular despotism.'[116] His preference is definitely for participatory republics.

> In the Republic every citizen, in doing that which he wants and not doing that which he does not want, participates directly in legislation and government, as he participates in the production and the circulation of wealth. There, every citizen is king, because he has the plenitude of power, he reigns and governs. The Republic is a positive anarchy.[117]

Proudhon's commitment to the liberty of the individual citizen signals a profound regard for the social and political context which would furnish the conditions under which freedom would be permitted to flourish. This aids our understanding of why he adopts the participatory republic, favoured by, amongst others, Aristotle and Rousseau. Indeed, it is when Proudhon considers Rousseau's version of the social contract that he becomes aware that if his idea of contract could be expanded to other groups in society, the '*system of contracts,* substituted for the *system of laws,* would constitute the true government of man and of the citizen; the true sovereignty of the people, the REPUBLIC'.[118] This is so because 'liberty is perfect only when it is guaranteed to all, either by all men taking part in government, or else by their delegating the trust to no one'.[119] Without doubt, Proudhon has assimilated the argument that the liberty of the citizen will flourish most effectively in a society in which the citizen is permitted to engage directly in the organization and management of its affairs.

To achieve this transformation Proudhon expected education and progress to help bridge the gap presented by the deficiencies in human nature. Progress was to be had in the form of new industrial organizations. Association, as mediated through the workshops, would allow Proudhon to avoid any excessive reliance on altruism or authority. By ensuring that the organization of labour was carried out by the workers themselves, and by retaining the driving force of competition, Proudhon was convinced that the vestigial command structures of the unitary state, together with the inadequacies in human nature, could be superseded. Returning control of the productive process to the workers was a central plank of Proudhon's programme. As the citizen deserves greater control over the affairs of his state, so the worker ought to exert his command over industrial and agricultural production. Competition is of cardinal importance to this process, if only because of human nature. As Proudhon puts it: 'Man may love his fellow well enough to die for him; he does not love him well enough to work for him.'[120] Furthermore, 'competition is as essential to labour as division, since it is division itself returning in another form, or rather, raised to its second power; division, I say, no longer, as in the first period of economic evolution, adequate to collective force, and consequently absorbing the personality of the labourer in the workshop, but giving birth to liberty by making each subdivision of labour a sort of sovereignty in which man stands in all his power and independence'.[121] Moreover, modelled on mutuality, or the commitment to reciprocal and equitable exchange, these workers' associations are, for Proudhon, the embryo of the framework under which the federal system will operate.

Education is also to assist in overcoming the evil in human nature. If humanity's inherent egocentrism is to be overcome then education is to be prominent in the restructuring of society. As Proudhon once wrote in the margin of the translation of Ewerbeck's *Christianity, German Philosophy, and Socialism,* 'man is essentially and previous to all education an egoistic creature, ferocious beast, and venomous reptile. . . . He will never *grow tame* [and] is only transformed by education.'[122] Civic virtue is to be fed and watered by education in conjunction with humanity's immanent sense of justice, not a civil religion as in the case of Rousseau. Like Montesquieu and Rousseau before him, Proudhon believes that a republic will only function properly if the 'spirit of society' is fostered and encouraged. Proudhon is searching, then, for something that is capable of stimulating a 'spirit of public virtue'. And in aligning himself to the efficacy of education Proudhon parts company from his predecessors, Montesquieu and

Rousseau, who relied on social and political institutions to encourage this public virtue.

Apparently, Proudhon is fairly optimistic about the future progress of society, if occasionally a little naïve at times. Writing in April 1845 he felt that within a decade France would have been completely transformed and rejuvenated. 'All political apparatus will have been thrown out.'[123] Not surprisingly, on other occasions Proudhon was more sober in his estimation of what could be achieved. When writing his *What is Property?* he was convinced that society was moving towards anarchy. Thus he could predict with some confidence that anarchy 'is the form of government to which we are every day approximating'.[124] Yet by the time he had come to pen *The Principle of Federation,* Proudhon regarded anarchy as a form of government that would never be reached. Because anarchy is one of the four forms of ideal government it will remain forever out of our grasp. Just as monarchy and communism 'can never be realised as absolutely pure types' so democracy and anarchy are 'to remain perpetual desiderata'.[125] The ideal types of government may exist in the form of a concept, but, as Proudhon rationalizes, 'they themselves can never become real'.[126] The rationale behind this conclusion is to be discovered in the relationship between authority and liberty. Destined to remain mutually dependent upon one another, the two principles of liberty and authority will be forced into compromise. Consequently, a compromise between the pure forms of government is inescapable.

The nature of the relationship between liberty and authority affords an intimation as to why Proudhon finds it difficult to rid his political theory of a concept that is very similar to the state. With his not unusual pessimism Proudhon remarks that, because of the ineluctable compromise between liberty and authority 'it is scarcely likely, however far the human race may progress in civilisation, morality and wisdom, that all traces of government and authority will vanish'.[127] It is precisely because of such sentiments that Robert Graham, in a perceptive essay on 'The Role of Contract in Anarchist Ideology', draws the conclusion that when penning *The Principle of Federation* Proudhon had finally accepted that politics could not be 'dissolved in the economic organisation of society'.[128] Fundamentally, *The Principle of Federation* amounts to an exegesis of the political contract that is to supplement the economic contract established in the earlier *General Idea of the Revolution.* The expanded system of contracts envisaged by Proudhon is held together within the federal political matrix. Contracts and agreements may be plentiful in the field of economics, but the various groups in society, be they towns or provinces, will also be party to agreements for political purposes such as the arbitration of disputes. As with the economic contract, the political contract is based on reciprocal obligations that pertain to both parties, in this case the state and the citizen. Furthermore, in order for the political contract to become binding

> the citizen who enters the association must 1) have as much to gain from the state as he sacrifices to it, 2) retain all his liberty, sovereignty, and initiative, except that which he must abandon in order to attain that special object for which the contract is made, and which the state must guarantee. So confirmed and understood, the political contract is what I shall call a *federation.*[129]

Upon association these groups create a federal authority above them, but an authority whose remit is defined and delimited by the contract of association. In Proudhon's mind, this authority or agency operates 'under the strict control of his principals, whose power varies at their pleasure'.[130] However, Proudhon is less certain when it comes to determining whether the units of the federation are completely sovereign and how, in practice, internal and inter-provincial disputes are to be settled. Federalism, for Proudhon, is supposed to be a non-hierarchical and decentralized form of government; but uncertainty arises from a lack of clear argument and ushers us toward a conclusion that even if all runs smoothly in inter-provincial transactions (and that is very unlikely given his own admission for the need to police municipalities)[131] there appears to be no mechanism for guaranteeing free relations within municipalities. With passions and self-interest at the fore in the political arena, Proudhon, rather unwittingly, seems not to have appreciated that human nature may signal the breakdown of political relations not only within but between federal units.

Proudhon accepts that federation, by necessity, entails the right of secession. So if the federal authority acts outside its remit and interferes with the autonomy or internal jurisdiction of a member unit then that unit is fully entitled to secede. The problem is that Proudhon does not leave it at that. In a note discussing the Swiss federation of 1848, Proudhon suggests that in matters that concern the interpretation of the terms of the federal contract the rights of the majority must be respected over those of the minority.[132] Whatever Proudhon may have said later, *The Principle of Federation* leaves little room for avoiding the charge that something like a coercive state is still alive and kicking. Hence Vernon's judgment that

> there are clear hints of, but no explicit defence of or open commitment to, the acceptability of coercion: if authority is to lose its *mystique* in federation, it is nevertheless to retain legitimate coercive power, apparently, and we cannot say that the notion of the state, abstractly conceived, has been entirely abandoned.[133]

Contrary to his predilection for participatory republics, *The Principle of Federation*'s recourse to politics and an ultimate reliance on the principle of majoritarianism leaves Proudhon rather closer to Rousseau than he would care to admit. In what is an admission to a principle fundamental to democracy, majoritarianism, Proudhon throws into doubt his claim to be an anarchist. The claim should be seriously questioned if only because Proudhon's federal political arrangements depend ultimately on some manner of coercion exercised by an authority over and above the member units of the federation.

Aside from the misgivings occasioned by *The Principle of Federation* and notwithstanding the fact that he may, at times, have argued that the state should be used to improve the lot of the working class, one might argue that Proudhon's overall intention was always to see government dissolved in a more rational economic restructuring of society. Moreover, anyone who has read Proudhon's *General Idea of the Revolution* cannot help but recognize the strength of his conviction that underpinned the caustic critique of government *per se*, that is the leitmotif of this text. As David Miller has reminded us, Proudhon essentially levels four charges against the state. These charges are not to be applied selectively, they are what is wrong with each and every state, regardless of the political arrangements of which it may be a part. The state is, then: coercive; punitive; exploitative and destructive.[134] Proudhon's analysis may apparently reinforce the perspective that he was a fierce critic of the state, as he knew it, and therefore defend his pronouncement of faith to anarchism. But to appreciate how Proudhon found it possible to be both critic and patron of the state it is necessary to understand the concept of contract that Proudhon works with. The contract, as he informs us in his *General Idea of the Revolution,* is an agreement or

> act whereby two or several individuals agree to organise among themselves, for a definite purpose and time, that industrial power

which we have called *exchange*; and in consequence have
obligated themselves to each other, and reciprocally guaranteed
a certain amount of services, products, advantages, duties, &c.[135]

Whether designed for economic exchange or political purposes, the
important point to bear in mind is that Proudhon's contract is
inextricably linked to a concept that may be labelled 'self-assumed
obligation'. By entering into a contract in association with others, the
individual, by virtue of co-operating with those that have freely
assumed the obligations imposed by the contract, enlarges the field
of his own actions. Contracts create social relationships of reciprocal
obligation that may help to fulfil an individual's potentialities and
make concrete the benefits to be had out of the community. More
importantly, as Carole Pateman has argued, the concept of self-assumed
obligation is advantageous in facilitating an understanding of how
the individual may be bound by a political obligation yet remain above
the defined political authority.[136] Having entered an agreement for
political purposes within the federation, the various member units,
by virtue of the act of joining together in a political agreement,
constitute a political authority.[137] But this political agreement does not
obligate them to a state over and above them, since it is under their
control; rather they obligate themselves to one another. As Graham
puts it in his review of Pateman's argument, this authority 'is based
on horizontal relationships of obligation between themselves, rather
than on the vertical relationship existing between the individual and
the state'.[138] Thought of in this manner, perhaps self-assumed obligation
provides a buffer between the member units of Proudhon's federation
and a state that thrives on central authority and oppressive power.

Although affording Proudhon's conception of federal politics a
slight respite from accusations that it is statist, the above argument
fails, in my opinion, to absolve him completely. Proudhon's dependence
on the state is systematic, not incidental. That Proudhon cannot be
labelled an anarchist is dependent on three crucial elements of his
ideological narrative. The first element is the economic. Integral to
Proudhon's vision of society is the act of exchange. But since exchange
amounts to the mutual transfer of property it is very difficult to
reconcile Proudhon's notion of the economic contract with his
declaration that property is theft, a proposition that underpins his
moral critique of capitalism.[139] Similarly, his reliance on workers'
associations to mediate reciprocal and equitable exchange within a
federal framework does little to substantiate his claim to be an

anarchist. His belief that returning control of the productive process to the workers would eliminate the need for the state sits uneasily when it is realized that such associations are driven by the force of competition. In admitting the necessity of competition because of human nature, adumbrated above, Proudhon seems to be countenancing one of the pillars of capitalism. Indeed it is highly improbable that by pitting one association against another, even within a federal structure, one is likely to witness the demise of the pursuit of economic self-interest. By transferring control from the capitalist to workers' associations Proudhon hopes, rather optimistically, that the attraction of economic gain will simply evaporate. In fact, Proudhon should have been aware of the weakness of his own argument, as he acknowledges that personal gain is a motivating factor in individual and collective labour. Accordingly, Proudhon argues that society

> labours only with a view to wealth; comfort, happiness, is its only object. Why, then, should that which is true of society not be true of the individual also, since, after all, society is man and entire humanity lives in each man? Why substitute for the immediate object of emulation, which in industry is personal welfare, that far-away and almost metaphysical motive called general welfare, especially when the latter is nothing without the former and can result only from the former?[140]

A society based on the mutual exchange of property may harbour the necessary incentives to work and may provide the requisite buttresses to personal liberty, but it is hardly likely to be free from dispute. By pitching one association against another, competition will create a need for the state, if only to act as referee or arbiter in contractual disputes. Exchange has to be policed, and it cannot be policed by the contracting parties for each will be subject to overriding pressures of self-interest; hence there arises a situation which demands a neutral arbiter – the state.

The second part of Proudhon's ideological narrative that concerns us is the political. Proudhon is willing to admit that the state (although he prefers to call it an agency) does have a role to play under federalism. What he is less willing to concede is that once in place the state may entrench its position rather than withdraw. When considering his discussion of the relationship between authority and liberty this is a rather peculiar conclusion to draw. It is because each and every 'political arrangement' is subject to the inexpiable contest between liberty and authority that Proudhon is forced to acknowledge the inexorable permanency of politics. Proudhon's federal government is the political matrix within which his economic contract is cradled. The point is that politics is permanent because the contest between liberty and authority is endless. This contest gives rise to government and authority. Like disputes in the realm of economics, political altercations require some mechanism that will furnish either resolutions or settlements. That mechanism, as Proudhon admits in *The Principle of Federation*, has its seat in an authority over and above the member units of the federation – an authoritative state.

It is, then, because of the complex intertwining of the economic and the political that Proudhon is powerless to prevent his own dependence on the state. One fundamental reason for this is located in his pessimistic assessment of human nature, the third element that concerns us here. Although Proudhon feels that much could be made of humankind in terms of social and moral progress, the overwhelming experience exuded throughout his writings is one of distrust and scepticism. He admits, for example, that politics is governed by 'passion' and 'interests', yet refuses to acknowledge that the same is true of economics. To my mind, this seems unjustifiable. Whatever the merits or demerits of his consistency, however, the important point is that if politics is susceptible to the egoistic side of human nature then that elicits considerable difficulties for Proudhon. As both human nature and politics are permanent, then there will be a constant and permanent requirement for restraint.

Peter Marshall is one recent commentator who believes that the enduring egoism in Proudhon's conception of human nature does not represent an insuperable problem. But at times it is difficult to reconcile all aspects of Marshall's argument. In Marshall's own interpretation of Proudhon's conception of human nature the individual is seen to be both 'naturally free and selfish. He is capable of self-sacrifice for love and friendship but as a rule selfishly pursues his own interest and pleasure. The result is that left to himself he will inevitably try to gain power over others.'[141] At the same time Marshall believes that humanity's potential for rationality offers an opportunity to overcome the obstacle of egoism in human nature. Citing Proudhon's *Confessions*, Marshall points to the author's argument that 'in society as well as in the individual, reason and reflection always triumph over instinct and spontaneity. This is the characteristic feature of our species and it accounts for the fact that we progress.'[142] Thus Marshall concludes that humans progress to 'a stage where the artificial restrictions of government and law can be done away with'.[143]

Considering that Marshall offers only one reference to sustain his conclusion, this seems a rather weak interpretation. But even if he had presented more evidence there remains the question of how he reconciles the point about rationality with his acknowledgement of the permanence of aggression in Proudhon's conception of human nature. As Marshall concedes, Proudhon 'believed war was rooted in our being'.[144] It is because of this that Proudhon writes, in *War and Peace* (1861), that 'war is an integral part of human life and must endure as long as humanity endures. . . . Let us therefore conclude . . . that war in one form or another is essential to mankind and that it is a vital condition of our social and moral life.'[145] These thoughts echo his earlier concern about the permanence and ubiquity of war. Writing in his *System of Economical Contradictions*, Proudhon reflects how 'man's life is a permanent war, war with want, war with nature, war with his fellows, and consequently war with himself. The theory of a peaceful equality, founded on fraternity and sacrifice, is only a counterfeit of the Catholic doctrine of renunciation of the goods and pleasures of this world, the principle of beggary, the panegyric of misery.'[146]

Marshall recognizes Proudhon's assumption that aggression is an inherent and unchanging component of human nature, but still insists that rationality furnishes 'the key out of the impasse'.[147] The point that Marshall does not seem to understand is the nature of the relationship in which Proudhon ties reflection and egoism together. The evidence that Marshall offers in support of his argument about humanity's progress toward a society without government and law does not truly vindicate his argument. At best it offers a partial account of how Proudhon believes humanity progresses.[148] Marshall would do better to appreciate that in Proudhon's conception of human nature it is humanity's ability for communication, reflection and comparison that result in a disposition for egoism and evil. Harbold is certainly cognizant of this if Marshall is not. Hence his conviction that Proudhon 'found that precisely the same quality in man that enables him to progress also, when corrupted, leads to decadence. This quality is "idealism". . . . Men are always led by an ideal, but their ideals, instead of representing justice, can derive from and represent interests, such as wealth, power and pleasure.'[149] In one way this is a reflection of Proudhon's conception of human nature. Passions and interests are always likely to be involved in politics at a practical level, and

Proudhon recognized this. It is because of this that Proudhon concedes the permanence of politics. Yet, at another level this simply signals a resignation to the way the world is. Proudhon acknowledges that in the course of a lifetime one is often in competition with others; but this is 'both inevitable and desirable'. It 'is inevitable,' he contends,

> because it is impossible for there ever to be complete agreement between two beings who are progressing along the path of knowledge and consciousness but who are not walking in step, between two beings whose viewpoints on all questions are different and whose interests are increasingly opposed. Their meeting will inevitably result in a divergence of opinion, in opposing principles, in polemics and the clash of ideas.
>
> I add on the other hand that this is desirable. It is from divergences of opinion, and the antagonism that this engenders, that a new world, higher than the organic, speculative, effective world, is created. It is the world of social dealings, of law, liberty, politics and morals. But before dealings are possible, strife is inevitable; before the peace treaty there is the duel and war. This is true of each moment of existence.[150]

It is in these times of strife that Proudhon's mutualist society based on contract will be found wanting. As Ritter notes, in the mutualist society Proudhon's 'scheme of bargaining may protect freedom, but it fails to manage conflict, as Proudhon well realised'.[151] Marshall too is aware of this difficulty. In a more sober reflection of Proudhon's conception of human nature (which because of its hard-nosed realism makes it all the more difficult to reconcile with his conclusions outlined earlier), Marshall acknowledges that, given Proudhon's portrayal of human nature as 'aggressive, selfish and domineering, it would seem inevitable that [human beings] would grasp for power in a society without government'.[152] In wanting contracts to replace laws and government Proudhon's contracting parties find themselves under no obligation other than their own personal promises. In light of Proudhon's notion of contract and given 'his pugnacious view of human nature', Marshall writes,

> it is difficult to see why they [Proudhon's contracts] should not degenerate into endless wrangles or dictated settlements. Even if, as he suggests, the contracts are made public, formal and explicit, and public opinion reinforces the purely moral obligation of promises, there is no final certainty that people

will keep their agreements. His resort to a federal authority to solve disputes, and his call for an express oath of fidelity to the rules of contracting show that he was aware of the difficulty, but their introduction would doubtless lead to the reconstitution of the State.[153]

On this occasion Marshall has hit the nail squarely on the head. The mechanism of restraint will be the state. Both humanity's egocentrism and the economic and political disputes that will ensue from this egocentrism have to be restrained. Federal arrangements are not immune. Hence the need for a state. There is one further possibility, though. Throughout his works there is a commitment to cultivate the republican ideals of liberty and participation in the society to which the citizen belongs. By following in the footsteps of this republican tradition, in criticizing the state for not assigning a substantial enough role for the individual, Proudhon may have inadvertently sanctioned the development, not of a single state, but of a multitude of states. His insistence that the individual should play a greater role in society and that each municipality should be sovereign in its own affairs, at the expense of a large and centralized state, may well be interpreted as a recipe for the inauguration of an array of mini-states under the authoritative umbrella of a federal state that will police disputes between its internal districts. Whichever way one looks at it, Proudhon is led to a dependency on the state. The state's *raison d'être* is grounded in human nature and politics.

Notes

1. George Woodcock believes Proudhon's *What is Property?* constituted the very 'foundation on which the whole edifice of nineteenth century anarchist theory was constructed.' See his 'On Proudhon's "What is Property?"' *Anarchy*, 9, 12, (1969) p. 359. James Joll considers Proudhon to be 'the first and most important anarchist philosopher; and later anarchist writers have not added very much to what he said.' See Joll, *The Anarchists*, (Methuen, London, 1979) p. 61.

2. Quoted in E.H. Carr, *Studies in Revolution*, (Macmillan, London, 1950) p. 47.

3. P-J. Proudhon, *The Principle of Federation and the Need to Reconstitute the Party of Revolution*, (University of Toronto Press, Toronto 1979) p. 11.

4. G. Woodcock, *Pierre-Joseph Proudhon: A Biography*, (Black Rose Books, Montréal, 1987) p. 13.

5. Ibid., p. 78.

6. P-J. Proudhon, *System of Economical Contradictions or The Philosophy of Misery Vol. I* (Arno Press, New York, 1972) p. 427.

Throughout his works Proudhon talks of man and men; and his sexism is matched by his racism. The language I employ is designed to remove the prejudices that underpin both Proudhon's language and our own.

7. Woodcock, *op. cit.*, p. 79.

8. What Proudhon meant by 'the workers' is a moot point. Certainly Proudhon had not the experience of large scale industry that later social and political theorists could draw on. Moreover, given Proudhon's peasant background and the scarcity of large industrial concerns during his lifetime it comes as no surprise to note Woodcock's assessment that the 'ideal of the free peasant life was to become a shaping element in Proudhon's social and political thought.' G. Woodcock, *Anarchism*, (Penguin, Harmondsworth, 1975) p. 102. It seems unlikely, then, that when Proudhon referred to 'the workers' he had in mind the industrial proletariat or wage labourer that was central to Marx's analysis of the class system.

9. The absence of any reference to Darwin here can be explained by the fact that Darwin's *Origin of the Species* first appeared in 1859 some 16 years after Proudhon's *De la Création* was originally published. Many of Proudhon's other works were published before the appearance of Darwin's text.

10. P-J. Proudhon, *What is Property?* (William Reeves, London, n.d.) p. 220.

11. Ibid., p. 232.

12. Ibid., p. 242. Cf. K. Marx, *Early Writings*, (Penguin, Harmondsworth, 1975) pp. 328–9.

13. Quoted in S. Edwards (ed.), *Selected Writings of Pierre-Joseph Proudhon*, (Macmillan, London, 1970) p. 239.

14. Proudhon, *op. cit.*, p. 243.

15. Ibid., p. 244.

16. Ibid., p. 242.

17. Ibid., p. 244.

18. Proudhon, *System of Economical Contradictions*, p. 422.

19. This point is detailed in the section below entitled 'The Politics of Federalism'.

20. D. Miller, *Anarchism*, (Dent, London, 1984) p. 69.

21. Proudhon, *System of Economical Contradictions*, p. 410.

22. Proudhon *What is Property?*, p. 223.

23. Proudhon, *op. cit.*, p. 428.

24. Ibid., p. 429.

25. Ibid., p. 404.

26. Ibid.

27. Ibid., p. 430.

28. Marx seemed to think that Proudhon's conception of human nature encapsulated a permanence that was impervious to human history. See his letter to Annekov, dated 28 December 1846, in his *The Poverty of Philosophy*, (Progress, Moscow, n.d.) p. 166. Cf. also P. Marshall, *Demanding the Impossible: A History of Anarchism*, (HarperCollins, London, 1992) p. 248.

29. See, for example, Proudhon, *What is Property?*, p. 31. Cf. also his *General Idea of the Revolution in the Nineteenth Century*, (Pluto Press, London, 1989) p. 140. Similar sentiments are exhibited in his *The Principle of Federation*, p. 28.

30. Proudhon, *What is Property?*, p. 380.

31. Ibid., p. 49.

32. W.H. Harbold, 'Progressive Humanity: In the Philosophy of P-J. Proudhon', *The Review of Politics*, 31, 1, (1969) pp. 33–4.

33. Proudhon, *What is Property?*, p. 246.

34. Proudhon, *General Idea of the Revolution*, p. 41.
35. Proudhon, *What is Property?*, p. 224.
36. Ibid., p. 225. There are obvious parallels here to Rousseau's discussion of pity in his *A Discourse on Inequality*, (Penguin, Harmondsworth, 1968) pp. 99–103.
37. Proudhon, *What is Property?*, p. 222.
38. Ibid., p. 225. Italics in the original.
39. Proudhon, *What is Property?*, p. 50. The emphasis is Proudhon's. In his *General Idea of the Revolution*, Proudhon regards this adage as 'the elementary formula of justice'. (p. 134) It should be noted that Kant rejected this notion in favour of his principle of universalizability.
40. Proudhon, *What is Property?*, p. 223.
41. Ibid. It might be argued that Proudhon does little to endear himself to anarchists or socialists here. Terms such as 'robbery' and 'murder', some may suggest, are loaded, socially dependent terms which are less heinous wrongs than investment (robbery) or war (murder).
42. Ibid., p. 228.
43. Ibid., p. 234. Proudhon does not go as far here as Kropotkin who suggests that mutual aid is integral to the process of evolution.
44. Ibid., p. 268.
45. Quoted in Edwards, *op. cit.*, p. 237.
46. Marshall, *op. cit.*, p. 240.
47. K. Steven Vincent, *Pierre-Joseph Proudhon and the Rise of French Republican Socialism*, (Oxford University Press, Oxford, 1984) p. 123.
48. Proudhon, *General Idea of the Revolution*, pp. 240 and 135.
49. Proudhon, *On Justice in the Revolution and in the Church*. Quoted in Harbold, *op. cit.*, p. 46.
50. Proudhon, *System of Economical Contradictions*, pp. 432–3.
51. Ibid., p. 434.
52. Quoted in A. Ritter, *The Political Thought of Pierre-Joseph Proudhon*, (Princeton University Press, Princeton, 1969) p. 36.
53. Quoted in Woodcock, *Pierre-Joseph Proudhon: A Biography*, p. 21.
54. Proudhon, *General Idea of the Revolution*, p. 208.
55. Proudhon, *What is Property?*, p. 92.
56. Quoted in Woodcock, *op. cit.*, p. 156.
57. Proudhon, *General Idea of the Revolution*, p. 294. As this passage demonstrates, Proudhon often conflates government with state.
58. Ibid., p. 127.
59. Ibid., p. 106.
60. Proudhon, *The Principle of Federation*, p. 9.
61. For a fuller discussion of this point, see Vernon's 'Introduction' to Proudhon's *The Principle of Federation*, p. xviii.
62. Proudhon, *What is Property?*, p. 261. The accuracy of this particular interpretation may be open to question, but it is important to identify that this is what Proudhon believed.
63. Ibid., p. 67.
64. Ibid., p. 272.
65. Proudhon, *General Idea of the Revolution*, p. 242. Proudhon's point about government as the 'supreme administrative power' is made in his *What is Property?*, p. 204.
66. Proudhon, *General Idea of the Revolution*, pp. 71–2. Cf. ibid., p. 26 for Proudhon's opinion that

government represents 'the fiction which makes an end of liberty'.
67. Ibid., p. 112.
68. Ibid., pp. 113–14.
69. Proudhon, *What is Property?*, pp. 41–2.
70. Proudhon, *General Idea of the Revolution*, p. 113.
71. Ibid., p. 115. Proudhon's interpretation is very contentious and, I believe, ultimately wrong.
72. Ibid., p. 136.
73. Proudhon, *The Principle of Federation*, pp. 59-60.
74. Proudhon, *What is Property?*, p. 409n.
75. Proudhon, *General Idea of the Revolution*, p. 205. Presumably, Proudhon's critique is directed toward Rousseau's acknowledgement in Book IV, Chapter 2 of his *Social Contract*, (Penguin, Harmondsworth, 1968) that the general will is found by counting the votes – majoritarianism being inescapably franked with coercion and force. In an earlier passage in the same text, however, Proudhon commends 'the sovereignty of Opinion'. It seems that, whilst Proudhon may share Mill's concern over the tyranny of the majority, his fear of the tyranny of public opinion is less resolute.
76. Proudhon, *op. cit.*, p. 205.
77. G. Crowder, *Classical Anarchism: The Political Thought of Godwin, Proudhon, Bakunin and Kropotkin*, (Oxford University Press, Oxford, 1991) p. 105.
78. Proudhon, *op. cit.*, p. 171.
79. Ibid., p. 205.
80. Ibid., p. 133.
81. Ibid., p. 138.
82. Ibid., p. 149.
83. Ibid., p. 133.
84. Ibid., p. 56.
85. Ibid., p. 137.
86. Ibid., p. 264.
87. Ibid., p. 273.
88. Ibid., p. 276.
89. Ibid., p. 102.
90. Vincent, *op. cit.*, p. 214.
91. Quoted in Woodcock, *Pierre-Joseph Proudhon*, p. 125.
92. Ibid., p. 140.
93. Woodcock, *Anarchism*, p. 117.
94. Woodcock, *Pierre-Joseph Proudhon*, p. 143. Cf. also Joll, *The Anarchists*, p. 56. He notes that, after 1849, Proudhon 'was to turn away from politics and political reforms for good and to develop into a true anarchist.'
95. Vincent, *op. cit.*, p. 88.
96. Quoted in ibid., p. 142. Cf. Proudhon, *What is Property?*, pp. 280–1.
97. Quoted in Vincent, *op. cit.*, p. 143.
98. Ibid., p. 168.
99. This general point and the former citation are from Proudhon, *General Idea of the Revolution*, pp. 45–6.
100. Proudhon, *What is Property?*, p. 110. Emphasis in the original.
101. Proudhon, *General Idea of the Revolution*, pp. 245–6.
102. See Vincent, *op. cit.*, pp. 143–4.
103. Quoted in ibid., p. 208. The translation is my own.
104. See p. 56.
105. Proudhon, *The Principle of Federation*, pp. 6–7.
106. Ibid., p. 26.
107. The quotation is drawn from Proudhon's *Mélanges* in his *Oeuvres Complètes* (Lacroix, Paris, 1868) cited in Vincent, *op. cit.*, p. 285, n. 46. The translation is my own.
108. Proudhon, *The Principle of Federation*, p. 54.
109. Ibid., p. xxv.
110. Ibid. The use of the term 'citizen' here is of some interest. As a political term indicating a member of a state one would think that Proudhon would refrain from using it. But Proudhon seems to employ

the term in a conscious and deliberate fashion.

111. Ibid., p. 72.
112. Ibid., p. 41.
113. Ibid., pp. 40–1n.
114. Ibid., p. 45.
115. Proudhon, *What is Property?*, pp. 55–6.
116. A. Carter, *The Political Theory of Anarchism*, (Routledge & Kegan Paul, London, 1971) p. 72.
117. Quoted in Vincent, *op. cit.*, pp. 169–70.
118. Proudhon, *General Idea of the Revolution*, p. 206. Emphasis in the original.
119. Proudhon, *The Principle of Federation*, p. 13.
120. Proudhon, *System of Economical Contradictions*, p. 235. On the preceding page of that text Proudhon suggests that man is prone to idleness which is only remedied 'when want fills him with anxiety.'
121. Ibid., p. 223.
122. Quoted in Vincent, *op. cit.*, p. 97. Emphasis in original.
123. Quoted in Vincent, *op. cit.*, p. 149.
124. Proudhon, *What is Property?*, p. 264.
125. Proudhon, *The Principle of Federation*, p. 12.
126. Ibid., p. 17.
127. Ibid., p. 20.
128. R. Graham, 'The Role of Contract in Anarchist Ideology', in D. Goodway (ed.), *For Anarchism: History, Theory and Practice*, (Routledge, London, 1989) p. 154.
129. Proudhon, *op. cit.*, p. 38.
130. Ibid., p. 41n.
131. See pp. 33, 53, 57.
132. Proudhon, *op. cit.*, p. 42. It ought to be noted, however, that in his posthumously published *De la Capacité Politique des Classes*
Ouvrières* (1865), Proudhon defended the right of secession as an integral part of any federation. See Graham, *op. cit.*, p. 174, n. 36.
133. Proudhon, *The Principle of Federation*, p. xxii.
134. A more comprehensive discussion can be had from Miller, *op. cit.*, pp. 6–7.
135. Proudhon, *General Idea of the Revolution*, p. 113.
136. A more thorough account of the relevance of Pateman's argument to the concept of contract in anarchist thought may be had from Graham, *op. cit.*, pp. 170–2.
137. See p. 62.
138. Ibid., p. 170.
139. This famous paradox is spelt out in the opening pages of Proudhon's *What is Property?*
140. Proudhon, *System of Economical Contradictions*, p. 225.
141. Marshall, *op. cit.*, p. 248.
142. Edwards, *op. cit.*, p. 243.
143. Marshall, *op. cit.*, p. 249.
144. Ibid., p. 251.
145. Edwards, *op. cit.*, p. 206.
146. Proudhon, *System of Economical Contradictions*, p. 235.
147. Marshall, *op. cit.*, p. 252.
148. Note the discussion above, at pp. 40–1, of justice as a combination of social instinct and reflection. Cf. also the discussion about humankind's abilities of communication and reflection that separate him from other animals (see p. 35), and the part played by reflection in humanity's increasing socialness, p. 38.
149. Harbold, *op. cit.*, pp. 41–2.
150. Edwards, *op. cit.*, p. 205.
151. A. Ritter, 'Proudhon and the Problem of Community', *Review of Politics*, 29, 4, (1967) p. 470.
152. Marshall, *op. cit.*, p. 261.
153. Ibid.

4

Bakunin: Authoritarian Anarchism

Like Proudhon, Bakunin has inherited the mantle of paradox. His work seldom amounts to a coherent theory that reflects a conscious and deliberate effort to render anarchism comprehensible. Rather, his works are rarely more than unedited drafts replete with contradictions and anomalies. Indeed, the only major work of Bakunin's to be published during his lifetime was *Statism and Anarchy* (1873). Although not a systematic theorist, he is undeniably a profound and original thinker.[1] Given Bakunin's proclivity for revolutionary action it is perhaps not surprising that his writings are inconsistent. Bakunin is regarded as the founder of the international anarchist movement, and his writings were individually tailored for different audiences; however, that does not preclude the possibility of a discernible leitmotif.

The difficulty here is that the lack of an identifiable or distinctive body of thought exacerbates the problem of interpretation. Without any obvious guiding thread, Bakunin's works are open to vigorous debate among commentators, hostile and sympathetic alike. It is important to avoid imposing coherence where it plainly does not exist and to strive to maintain the author's original emphasis and meaning.[2] Yet as John Keane has elaborated, history 'is always history as it is narrated, interpreted, explained and judged by particular historians with particular interests and concerns'.[3] The recognition of the problems associated with textual analysis helps to obviate the dangers of fabricating an artificial coherence. It remains the prerogative of the reader to judge whether coherence has been imposed where it was previously lacking. The specific task of this chapter, however, is to identify the connection between Bakunin's conception of human nature and his political theory. It will become evident that there are radical inconsistencies in Bakunin's work, and moreover that they are of a consequence that jeopardizes his standing as an anarchist.

Bakunin on Human Nature and Freedom

In his 'Biographical Sketch' of Bakunin, James Guillaume relates the details of a conversation Bakunin had, whilst on his deathbed, with his friend, the musician Reichel. According to Guillaume, Bakunin is said to have remarked that our entire

> philosophy starts from a false base; it begins always by considering man as an individual, and not as he should be considered – that is, as a being belonging to a collectivity; most of the philosophical (and mistaken) views stemming from this false premise either are led to the conception of a happiness in the clouds, or to a pessimism like that of Schopenhauer and Hartmann.[4]

For Bakunin, traditional philosophy presents an unbalanced picture. Like Proudhon, Bakunin considers humankind to be both individual and social. 'Man,' he remarks, 'is not only the most individual being on earth – he is also the most social being.'[5] There are, then, two innate capacities that are distinctive of humankind: a potential to be egoistic and the facility for sociability. These innate qualities, however, do not extend into the realm of morality. For as far as Bakunin is concerned morality derives from society, from our social traditions and education. In this sense, individuals are a product of their environment. Adopting the contextualist view of human nature, Bakunin, as Godwin did before him, believes that humans are what their environment makes of them. No one, he argues, 'will seriously dispute this opinion, that every child, youth, adult, and even the most mature man, is wholly the product of the environment that nourished and raised him – an inevitable, involuntary, and consequently irresponsible product'.[6] Differences of intelligence or criminality between people, for example, are not '*due to their nature: it is solely the result of the social environment in which they were born and brought up*'.[7] Whilst reflecting Proudhon's awareness of humankind's capacity for evil, Bakunin maintains that such tendencies are strongly reinforced by society. 'Human nature,' he argues, 'is so constituted that the propensity for evil is always intensified by external circumstances, and the morality of the individual depends much more on the conditions of his existence and the environment in which he lives than on his will.'[8]

Herein lies a candid commendation of the contextualist paradigm of human nature. Although initially attracted by German romanticism and idealism, Bakunin later rejected 'his early philosophical idealism and developed a materialist and atheistic view of the world'.[9] As Bakunin wrote in his *The Knouto-Germanic Empire and the Social Revolution* (1871), it is materialism rather than idealism that is right.

'Undoubtedly,' he remarks, 'the idealists are wrong and the materialists are right. Yes, facts come before ideas; yes, the ideal, as Proudhon said, is but the flower, the roots of which lie in the material conditions of existence. Yes, the whole history of humanity, intellectual and moral, political and social, is but the reflection of its economic history.'[10] In Marxian terminology, consciousness is created by society: individuals are a product of their environment. Accordingly, freedom assumes special importance, because freedom is the bedrock upon which the development of an individual's humanity is to be built. And as one's freedom can only be fulfilled in society, so society serves as the matrix within which human nature fulfils its potential. In other words, the individual becomes humanized in society.

Bakunin's high regard for freedom could only have been consolidated by his reading of Hegel and his meeting with Proudhon in early 1844.[11] Indeed his love of freedom constitutes his philosophy of life. As he discloses in his *Confession* (1851), he was inspired by a 'love of freedom and inevitable hatred of all oppression, even more when it fell on others than when it fell on myself. To look for my happiness in the happiness of others, for my own worth in the worth of all those around me, to be free in the freedom of others – that is my whole faith, the aspiration of my whole life.'[12] However, what Bakunin means when he employs the term freedom or liberty is far from certain. Nonetheless, Bakunin's conception of liberty is of crucial importance to his conception of human nature and hence his theory of politics. As Bakunin puts it: 'I am a fanatical lover of Liberty; considering it as the only medium in which can develop intelligence, dignity, and the happiness of man'.[13] Perceived in this manner, Bakunin is referring to a concept of liberty

> which consists in the full development of all the material, intellectual and moral powers which are to be found as faculties latent in everybody, the liberty which recognises no other restrictions than those which are traced for us by the laws of our own nature; so that properly speaking there are no restrictions, since these laws are not imposed on us by some legislator, beside or above us; they are immanent in us, inherent, constituting the very basis of our being, material as well as intellectual and moral.[14]

To be truly free, then, is to remain outside all external restraints and to live according to the laws within us. Freedom, for Bakunin, belongs to that person who 'obeys natural laws because he has *himself* recognised them as such, and not because they have been externally imposed upon him by an extrinsic will whatever, divine or human, collective or individual'.[15] Closer examination of this argument reveals the way in which Bakunin is approaching the concept of freedom. For as Crowder has remarked, Bakunin is utilizing a conception of freedom in its positive sense – in the sense described by the liberal philosopher Isaiah Berlin in his 'Two Concepts of Liberty'. 'I am free,' Berlin writes, 'because, and in so far as, I am autonomous. I obey laws, but I have imposed them on, or found them in, my own uncoerced self. Freedom is obedience, but "obedience to a law which we prescribe to ourselves", and no man can enslave himself.'[16] To ascertain what that law within humankind is, humans require the power of reason. Rationality, therefore, is an important element in human nature. Without it individuals would be unable to determine the natural laws inherent within them. Human reason is the 'criterion of truth'.[17]

˹ It is within this social framework that human nature develops. Employing the power of reason, the individual acts according to laws which that person prescribes to him or herself. But this would be nonsensical if humans were considered as solitary animals, outside society. In a manner reminiscent of Rousseau Bakunin outlines why this is so. Humankind, he notes, 'was born a ferocious beast and a slave, and has gradually humanised and emancipated himself in society, which is necessarily anterior to the birth of his thought, his speech, and his will'.[18] Freedom and, therefore, the development of human nature are things which can only be attained socially. As Bakunin puts it in his *God and the State* (1871), for an individual to be free

> means to be acknowledged and treated as such by all his fellowmen. The liberty of every human individual is only the reflection of his own humanity, or his human right through the conscience of all free men, his brothers and his equals. I can feel free only in the presence of and in relationship with other men. In the presence of an inferior species of animal I am neither free nor a man, because this animal is incapable of conceiving and consequently recognising my humanity. I am not myself free or human until or unless I recognise the freedom and humanity of all my fellowmen.[19]

If liberty is to be won at all then it has 'to be won everywhere'. For an individual is only truly free when all around that individual are also free, because the freedom of others is the 'premise and confirmation' for the freedom of each and all. It is in this sense that

Bakunin's conception of freedom may be considered Hegelian. The fact that liberty has to be everywhere, or omnipresent, and not the privilege of one class suggests that Bakunin is utilizing something like Hegel's argument concerning Master and Slave. An oppressor cannot be said to be truly free because an oppressor is unable to give others the recognition they need to be truly free. And if the oppressor cannot give it to them, then they cannot return it to him. In a society where oppression exists none can be considered to be truly free. It is for that reason that Bakunin perceives a creative role for society. Accordingly, society 'creates the individual freedom of all human beings. Society is the root, the tree, and liberty is its fruit.'[20]

Whilst encouraging the fruition of human nature, Bakunin's emphasis on a concept of positive liberty requires a foundation of negative liberty to support it. That some notion of negative liberty is necessary may be seen on two counts. First, the exercise of positive liberty, or obeying a law which one has prescribed to oneself, would be impossible without the freedom from exposure to some kind of imposed authority, principally the state, which is what continually distinguishes the libertarian from the liberal. Equally important, however, is the need to be free from the unwanted interference of others. Independence from the will of others is a basic prerequisite if reason is to be exercised appropriately.[21] Thus, both negative and positive freedom have their place in Bakunin's overall approach. One complements the other. However, the concept of positive freedom appears to carry more weight, for Bakunin. For, as Marshall states, 'Bakunin remained enough of a Hegelian to see freedom primarily in terms of a state of wholeness in which all duality between the individual and society, between society and nature, is dialectically overcome.' Given the interconnectedness of personal and social freedom, it is not difficult to see why Marshall believes that these freedoms are melded into 'a form of communal individuality',[22] albeit with tensions, paradoxes and ambiguities unresolved.

Prior to Kropotkin's enunciation of anarchism based on an interpretation of the theory of evolution, Bakunin had also acknowledged the concept of evolution. 'Our first ancestors,' he comments, 'our Adams and Eves, were, if not gorillas, very near relatives of theirs.' Indeed, humanity's whole history has as its starting-point animality. The development of humankind, for Bakunin, 'is simply a process of progressive removal from pure animality by way of creating his humanity'.[23] Throughout this process of evolution two basic drives remain: sex and hunger, which other animals share. The two faculties that humans possess in greater measure than other species, though, are the power to think and the desire to rebel. The power to think does not only act as the foundation for the development of freedom within humans; in doing this it also serves to sever the ties between humans and nature. Bakunin perceives the relationship of humanity with nature as one of struggle, and it is humankind's rationality that enables individuals to escape the limitations of the external world, for an individual to become less of a beast and more of a human. Reason allows individuals to modify their basic drives and hence manage their own needs. And it is reason which begets the notion of moral responsibility. With reason bestowing a sense of conscious self-determination, or free will, individuals are responsible for their actions. Evidence for humankind's innate spirit of rebellion is derived from a more metaphysical source. As Proudhon cites the doctrine of the fall as a symbolic but accurate reflection of humankind's inclination toward evil, so Bakunin locates there the genesis of humanity's desire to rebel. 'The lord of the Bible,' he observes,

> had more insight into the nature of man than Auguste Comte and his disciples, who counselled him to be 'reasonable and not attempt the impossible'. To entice man to eat of the forbidden fruit of the tree of knowledge, God had but to command him: 'Thou Shalt Not!' This immoderation, this disobedience, this rebellion of the human spirit against all imposed limits, be it in the name of science, be it in the name of God, constitutes his glory, the source of his power and liberty. By reaching for the impossible, man discovers the possible, and those who limit themselves to what seems possible will never advance a single step.[24]

As the power of reason facilitates the development of humankind's freedom, so humanity's desire to rebel underpins the same concept. Human nature is directly responsible for humankind's freedom. Indeed as Dolgoff suggests, freedom 'is implicit in the social nature of Man'.[25]

Human Nature and Revolutionary Politics

As the investigation of Bakunin's theory of politics unfolds it will become apparent that his desire for freedom underpins much of what he has to say about society and politics. But not all of Bakunin's intellectual energies were directed at enhancing his notion of freedom. His revolutionary strategy, in particular, reverberates with an ominous siren that signals an ambivalence that threatens to eliminate all concern for individual freedoms. For now, though, it is Bakunin's support for freedom against authority that demands attention.

If the free exercise of reason is vital to the development of human nature and the satisfaction of freedom, then individuals must reside in a free society or environment. This, perhaps, is one reason why Bakunin is so enthusiastic in his denunciation of authority in his *Revolutionary Catechism*, published in 1866. His repudiation is quite categoric.

> Absolute rejection of every authority including that which sacrifices freedom for the convenience of the state. Primitive society had no conception of freedom; and as society evolved, before the full awakening of human rationality and freedom, it passed through a stage controlled by human and divine authority. The political and economic structure of society must now be reorganised on the basis of freedom. Henceforth, order in society must result from the greatest possible realisation of individual liberty, as well as of liberty on all levels of social organisation.[26]

The strength of Bakunin's message here should not be understated. For whilst he openly admitted that human nature may be a source of evil so he was sufficiently perceptive to realize that evil may be born from the hierarchical structures of society. Thus Bakunin considers the effects of authority: 'If there is a devil in human history, that devil is the principle of command. It alone, sustained by the ignorance and stupidity of the masses, without which it could not exist, is the source of all the catastrophes, all the crimes, and all the infamies of history.'[27]

Bakunin has no choice but to reach such a conclusion, for in operating a contextualist conception of human nature, in which individuals are a product of their environment, the individual is absolved of total responsibility. There is little danger of Bakunin ever locating the origin of evil solely within human nature, because his analysis of capitalist society renders such a conclusion invalid. But society *per se* is not culpable in this respect. The problem lies with the present mode of social organization. If that can be overturned, then the prospects for individual freedom and social morality become much brighter. It is in this spirit of optimism that Bakunin deliberates on the role of society in the manufacture of the individual. For

> as the crimes and vices infecting present society are due to the evil organisation of society, it is certain that in a society based

on reason, justice, and freedom, on respect for humanity and on complete equality, the good will prevail and the evil will be a morbid exception, which will diminish more and more under the pervasive influence of an enlightened and humanised public opinion.[28]

Aside from Bakunin's identification of the social structures of authority as one of the principal evils in the world, and despite the previous renunciation of 'every authority', he by no means rejects all forms of authority. Bakunin was quite willing to accept the authority of the natural laws that govern and regulate our natural and social worlds. Indeed, as demonstrated above, his argument for freedom is based on the observation of the natural laws within humans. The authority arising from these natural laws was one that each person should obey. In contrast, the authority born of social structures and relationships is approached with more suspicion. He was, for example, willing to countenance the authority of knowledge although he tempers this with a reservation for the individual to reach an independent decision about any particular course of action. His position, then, is not as absolute as it might first have seemed; for as Marshall remarks, Bakunin is 'not against all authority *per se,* but only against imposed external authority'.[29] Such thinking provides the basis for Bakunin's doubt over the universality of scientific authority. His distrust of a ruling scientific élite and the authoritarian dangers that accompany such rule merely confirms his suspicion of imposed authority, whatever its source. Indeed his revolutionary strategy appears to mirror his desire for liberty. It would be contrary to reason and freedom to establish a ruling élite to direct society that by its very nature would undermine both freedom and the propitious development of human nature.

The fact of the matter remains though, if liberty is to flower a revolution is required. The problem of the social question

cannot be resolved either by a preconceived theory or by any isolated system. . . . We need to transform the material and moral conditions of our present-day existence, to overturn, from top to bottom, this decrepit social world which has grown impotent and sterile and incapable of containing or supporting so great a mass of liberty. We must, first, purify our atmosphere and make a complete transformation of our environment, for it corrupts our instincts and our will by constricting our hearts and our minds. The social question thus appears to be first and foremost the question of the complete overturn of society.[30]

Apart from the obvious linkage of human nature with the social environment, it seems that Bakunin is more concerned with revolution than formulating a blueprint for future society. This is hardly surprising, as most other thinkers we label anarchist share a similar reluctance to formulate social blueprints, or at least they purport to. As with Proudhon, however, Bakunin's writings, particularly his *Revolutionary Catechism*, yield some detailed proposals on the constitution of society.

Before examining his more specific plans for future society, which I shall address in the next section, it ought to be noted that Bakunin's desire for liberty demands some form of protection from any possible corrupting effects of the revolutionary process itself. 'Liberty can be created only by liberty,' he argues in his *Statism and Anarchy*, 'by an insurrection of all the people and the voluntary organisation of the workers from below upward.'[31] If the revolution is to be successful the people must emancipate themselves. Vanguard parties and revolutionary dictatorships are a blind alley in which liberty becomes a sacrificial lamb in the quest for political power. As Joll reasons, Bakunin was fully aware of the fact that the methods employed in the revolution would influence the post-revolutionary society. If a free society is the objective then the revolutionary movement has to avoid hierarchical structures and dictatorial procedures.[32] In other words, the means and the ends of the revolution have to be commensurate. Hence Bakunin insists that there should be no dogmatic discipline or hierarchical structure within the revolutionary movement. 'At the moment of action,' he writes,

> in the midst of the struggle, there is a natural division of roles according to the aptitude of each, assessed and judged by the collective whole: some direct and command, others execute orders. But no function must be allowed to petrify or become fixed, and it will not remain irrevocably attached to any one person. Hierarchical order and promotion do not exist, so that the commander of yesterday can become a subordinate tomorrow. No one rises above the others, or if he does rise, it is only to fall back again a moment later, like the waves of the sea for ever returning to the salutary level of equality.[33]

Whilst Bakunin perceives society to be dominated by class struggle, he holds no truck with Marxist ideas that the working class should seize and conquer political power. The reason for this is quite simple. Revolutionary dictatorships are as bad as the state. In fact, for Bakunin, their differences are no more than 'superficial'. According to Bakunin,

> they both represent the same principle of minority rule over the majority in the name of the alleged 'stupidity' of the latter and the alleged 'intelligence' of the former. Therefore they are both equally reactionary since both directly and inevitably must preserve and perpetuate the political and economic privileges of the ruling minority and the political and economic subjugation of the masses of the people.[34]

Perhaps the essence of Bakunin's concerns is summarized most effectively in the document known as the Sonvillier Circular. Although not written by Bakunin, it does encapsulate the full spirit of his objections toward Marxist revolutionary strategy. In response to the General Council's abolition of the autonomy of the sections and federations that constituted the First International a document was dispatched by the new Jurassic Federation of the International to all other federations on 12 November 1871.[35] The Sonvillier Circular was, in reality, an argument from the Jura anarchists supporting Bakunin against Marx during the First International's turbulent and vitriolic decline. 'How,' it was written, 'can you expect an egalitarian and free society to emerge from an authoritarian organisation? It is impossible. The International, embryo of the future human society, must be from this moment the faithful image of our principles of liberty and federation, and reject from its midst any principle leading to authority and dictatorship.'[36] As has been so often observed, the Sonvillier formulation lay at the heart of the libertarian critique of Bolshevism–Leninism.

Bakunin's defence of the International and his belief that workers must emancipate themselves constitute something of an irony. For whilst he relished the prospect of the 'total abolition of politics', he saw the revolutionary methods of the International Working Men's Association as the 'true politics of the workers'.[37] It is these methods, Bakunin hopes, that will lead to the institution of a free society by way of three principles: a) the destruction of political power; b) a preclusion of any temporary revolutionary authority; and c) the rejection of politics. His position is clearly defined. Bakunin was expelled, along with Guillaume and others, from the First International at its Hague Congress on 5 September 1872. Another congress was convened by the same group of outcasts at St-Imier in Switzerland. A resolution outlining part of their policy was passed there. Its author was Bakunin. It reads as follows:

That no one can legitimately deprive the sections and autonomous federations of the incontestable right to determine and carry out whatever political policies they deem best, and that all such attempts must inevitably lead to the most revolting dogmatism;

That the economic aspirations of the proletariat can have no other aim than the establishment of absolutely free organisations and federations based on the labour equally of all and absolutely separate and independent from every political state government; and that these organisations and federations can be created only by the spontaneous action of the proletariat itself, [that is, by] the trade bodies and the autonomous communes;

That every political state can be nothing but organised domination for the benefit of one class, to the detriment of the masses, and that should the proletariat itself seize power, it would in its turn become a new dominating and exploiting class;

For these reasons, the Congress of St.-Imier declares:

1. That the destruction of all political power is the first task of the proletariat;

2. That the establishment of a so-called 'provisional' (temporary) revolutionary authority to achieve this destruction can be nothing but a new deception and would be just as dangerous for the proletariat as any existing government;

3. That the proletariat of all lands, absolutely rejecting all compromise in order that the Social Revolution be attained, must create the solidarity of revolutionary action; this is to be done independently of and in opposition to all forms of bourgeois politics.[38]

The real difficulty for Bakunin, though, is that the pleasantries of theory have to be rendered practicable in the real world. As a result, reality forces a tactical retreat from the high ground of theory. As Dolgoff has mused: 'For anarchists, intent upon guiding the revolution in a libertarian direction by libertarian means, the question of how to stop authoritarians from seizing power without instituting a dictatorship of their own becomes increasingly complicated.'[39] Bakunin's writings and activities constitute no exception.

Notwithstanding the difficulties, Bakunin's preference for a future society organized on the basis of free autonomous federations remains obvious. His faith in the proletariat's capacity to achieve this is markedly less evident. Indeed, it could be argued that Bakunin placed more faith in the peasantry and the lumpenproletariat than he did in the proletariat itself. This is not as strange as it might first seem, especially if one realizes that Bakunin's conception of the lumpenproletariat is larger than that of Marx.[40] More importantly, Bakunin believes that the lumpenproletariat, or the downtrodden classes, have been spared from the corrupting influences of modern capitalism. Thus Bakunin dispenses with Marx's assessment of the submerged classes. 'Marx,' he writes, 'speaks disdainfully of this *Lumpenproletariat* . . . but in them, and only in them – and not in the bourgeois-minded strata of the working class – is crystallised the whole power and intelligence of the Social Revolution.'[41] However, even this faith in the lower classes has to be questioned; for as Dolgoff points out, Bakunin was always aware that such groups as the peasantry 'were ignorant, superstitious, and conservative'.[42] Furthermore, 'Bakunin understood that the people tend to be gullible and oblivious to the early harbingers of dictatorship until the revolutionary storm subsides and they awake to find themselves in shackles.'[43] If human nature, by way of humanity's inherent inclination for rebellion, is partly responsible for the initiation of the revolution, so its failings, or humanity's gullibility, may lead to the revolution's downfall. The answer to this problem, if one can be found, lies in the principle of organization. Long before the events of the First International forced Bakunin to defend his cherished revolutionary principles, he had conceded the need for the revolution to be organized. Even with Bakunin's revolutionary zeal his naïvety had its bounds. Hence he acknowledges, in his *Appeal to the Slavs* (1848), that it 'is a sacred duty for all of us, soldiers of the revolution, democrats of all countries, to unite our forces, to come to an understanding and to organise'.[44] First impressions may lead one to assume that what Bakunin intends is some form of international revolutionary alliance. And indeed he did accept that if a revolution was to prove successful, then it would have to be international in character.[45] But there is more to it than that. Organization means more than co-operation at an international level. During the period when his anarchist ideas were beginning to assume their final shape[46] he finally recognized the need for some kind of revolutionary élite to orchestrate the masses in their endeavours to secure success amidst the revolutionary turmoil. As Dolgoff comments, it was during this period (1864–67) that

> Bakunin saw that the workers were still very far from attaining the necessary revolutionary consciousness. To imbue the masses with this consciousness and to prevent the deformation of the revolution, Bakunin felt that the only alternative was to organise the secret International Fraternity. Bakunin was convinced that this kind of vanguard movement was indispensable to the success of the Social Revolution.[47]

Thus it was that Bakunin introduced into his revolutionary methodology the notion of the secret society, which opened a Pandora's Box and plagued both Bakunin and anarchism in general ever after.

The question is, why did he reach this conclusion? His predisposition for activism before theoretical tidiness undoubtedly had some part to play. For as James Joll says, throughout his life Bakunin 'was to see himself as the great conspirator, at the centre of a web of clandestine organisations controlled by himself and organised, in theory, on the basis of a "strict hierarchy and unconditional obedience"'.[48] Even if many of these organizations were purely imaginary, as Joll suggests, it is, nevertheless, difficult to escape the conclusion that 'they were still central to his notion of anarchist strategy'.[49] There have been many attempts to explain Bakunin's incorporation of the notion of a secret society into his revolutionary strategy. One of the most vociferous has been provided by Kelly. In what is a serious and scholarly account, Kelly countenances Carr's assessment of an innate urge to dominate in Bakunin.[50] Parallel to this, she argues, rests his 'insatiable thirst for authority'.[51] Additionally, secret societies may be explained by the fact, according to Kelly, that Bakunin 'loved mystery and mystification and had a mania for codes of a simple kind which he used for his conspirational correspondence.[52] Many of these secret societies may well have been fantasies rather than real; nonetheless they offered an outlet for the personal realization or fulfilment of Bakunin's self. As Kelly comments, for Bakunin 'a mystically conceived personal wholeness remained for him the ultimate "reality", and that as before he would seek to accomplish it through the concept of a mission: a sublimation at one and the same time of his need for self-assertion and of his longing to identify with a meaningful collective entity'.[53] Seemingly, the secret society is to be the vehicle of this mission, the means by which Bakunin will become a revolutionary leader ready to identify with the masses.

The vision of Bakunin as revolutionary leader is certainly at odds with his self-declared philosophy of life discussed previously.[54] It elicited from Bakunin himself an admission that, given 'such direction to my thoughts and feelings I could not think of myself as a dictator, I could not nurture ambitious designs in my soul'.[55] Yet this did not prevent him from arguing that revolutionary movements may be directed by dictatorial powers, as his plans for a Bohemian revolution prove. The secret society directing the revolution 'was to consist of three separate societies, independent of one another and unknown to one another. . . . Each [however] was to be subordinate to a strict hierarchy and to unconditional discipline . . . according to a single plan.'[56] Moreover, Bakunin, who instructed a German student, Ottendorfer, to establish a secret society among the Bohemian Germans, was to be the 'secret leader' of this society.[57] Furthermore, Bakunin instructed the Straka brothers to set up secret societies in an endeavour to establish 'a kind of revolutionary battalion on which I could rely unconditionally and with whose aid I could gain control of all the other less organised or completely unorganised Prague elements. Having gained control of Prague, I hoped to gain control of all Bohemia as well . . . [if necessary] by force.'[58] In light of the discussion above one has to judge that Bakunin's pretence at being unable to harbour dictatorial designs is pretty thin.

Besides the hankering for a revolutionary dictatorship that seems to pervade Bakunin's personality, there is another argument to be considered. Within Bakunin's confession to the Tsar there are a number of occasions when he suggests that some form of political centralism, usually a dictatorship, is necessary if the revolution is to succeed. Commenting on the need for a dictatorship in Russia, Bakunin believed

> that in Russia more than anywhere else a strong dictatorial government that would be exclusively concerned with elevating and educating the popular masses would be necessary; a government free in the direction it takes and in its spirit, but without parliamentary forms; with the printing of books free in content but without the freedom of printing; surrounded by like minds, illuminated by their counsel, strengthened by their willing assistance, but not limited by anyone or anything.[59]

It is possible that such sentiments arise from his appreciation of the situation in Paris during the 1848 revolution. His acquaintance with events there appears to have left an indelible impression of the Parisian workers' desire for leadership and discipline. These workers, he notes, 'demanded orders, they demanded leadership, they obeyed with punctiliousness, with fervour; they would perform heavy work for twenty-four hours at a stretch without eating and never grow despondent, but were always cheerful and amiable'.[60] Whether or not there exists a direct correlation between Bakunin's personality and his advocacy of secret societies is a matter that is not susceptible to final proof. It does seem, however, that Bakunin certainly learned something about revolutionary tactics whilst engaged in his numerous revolutionary escapades throughout Europe during the 1840s. But Dolgoff insists that Bakunin's critics are missing an important point: that

> in his time all revolutionary organisations were forced to operate in secret – that the survival of such a group and the safety of its members depended on strict adherence to certain rules of conduct which the members voluntarily accepted. The elaborate style of the statutes that Bakunin worked out for the Brotherhood, in the manner of the Freemasons and the Carbonari, is largely attributable to his romantic temperament and to the generally conspirational atmosphere then prevailing in Italy.[61]

Perhaps Dolgoff's analysis contains more than a grain of truth. It seems only reasonable, given the political climate of the age, that revolutionary societies should maintain an air of secrecy. However, Dolgoff is less convincing in another respect. For whilst these societies may each have their own body of rules, that does not excuse the introduction of a 'strict hierarchy and unconditional obedience'. Moreover, to attempt to attribute this solely to some kind of personality trait is tantamount to psychological reductionism and is grossly irresponsible.

The danger is a double-edged one. On the one hand, this requirement of unconditional obedience contradicts directly Bakunin's own belief in the freedom of the individual. As Marshall has illustrated, there is an unmistakable authoritarianism exuded in Bakunin's description of the role of the individual as member of a revolutionary society. Writing in a series of articles for *L'Egalité*, Bakunin emphasized that new members of the International should be prepared 'to subordinate [their] personal and family interests as well as [their] political and religious beliefs to the supreme interests of our association'.[62] As Marshall comments himself, such writing 'sounds distinctly authoritarian, and would horrify Godwin, who thought the right to private judgment paramount: one should not join a political association which insists on loyalty and obedience contrary to one's own conscience'.[63] In arguing that one should surrender unconditionally to the obedience of the revolutionary organization, Bakunin is guilty of another contradiction. 'Freedom,' he writes in his *Revolutionary Catechism*, 'is the absolute right of every adult man and woman to seek no other sanction for their acts than their own conscience and their own reason, being responsible first to themselves and then to the society which they have *voluntarily* accepted.'[64] In addition to this, Bakunin would also be denying the conditions which human nature requires for its own fruition. A society without freedom is a society in which the growth of human nature is severely curtailed.

On the other hand, Bakunin has simply sacrificed his revolutionary principles. By incorporating the values of hierarchy and obedience into his concept of the secret society, he was, as Avrich has astutely noted, guilty of committing 'the very sin he denounced'. Thus, although 'he recognised the intimate connection between means and ends, while he saw that the methods used to make the revolution must affect the nature of society *after* the revolution, he nonetheless resorted to methods which were the precise contradiction of his own libertarian principles'.[65] The inconsistency is rendered even more bewildering in light of Bakunin's battle with Marx over the nature of the First International. Gone are the concerns of the Sonvillier Circular, whilst the principles that underpinned the St-Imier resolution are seriously undermined. In his defence of the freedom and autonomy of the federations and sections of the International, Bakunin remained faithful to the principles that were closest to his heart. In his countenancing of secret societies in his revolutionary theory, Bakunin not only sacrifices any pretension to a sustainable claim to theoretical consistency but jeopardizes his own status as an anarchist.

Bakunin may have insisted that the invisible dictatorship will never 'take any kind of public office'[66] but it is difficult to conceive that Bakunin actually believed this. It is equally difficult to reconcile it with his wider ideological narrative. Put simply, it contradicts his contextualist conception of human nature. The indisputable fact is that power is attractive to individuals. As Bakunin admits himself, every person 'carries within himself the germs of this lust for power'.[67] This innate feature of human nature becomes active when nurtured by environmental factors. Thus Bakunin counsels that humankind's 'nature is so constituted that, given the possibility of doing evil, that is, of feeding his vanity, his ambition, and his cupidity at the expense of someone else, he surely will make full use of such an opportunity'.[68] 'Take the most sincere democrat,' he argues, 'and put him on the throne; if he does not step down promptly, he will surely become a scoundrel.'[69] This lust for power is so inveterate that its basis is to be found in the struggle for survival that drives evolution forward. Power and authority corrupt all in their presence. Accordingly, Bakunin is forced to submit that 'anyone invested with authority must, through the force of an immutable social law, become an oppressor and exploiter of society'.[70] Clearly, there is an irreconcilable contradiction between Bakunin's belief in the power of moral education and an irreducible powerlust immune to it.

On the basis of the evidence above there is no point in denying that Bakunin's revolutionary theory is racked by élitism and authoritarianism. Nevertheless, Bakunin still has his defenders. In what is, arguably, the most comprehensive analysis of anarchist thought and practice to date, Peter Marshall takes up the torch, but not without some reservations. He is not prepared, for example, to defend Bakunin against what he perceives as justified criticism. And he is willing to concede that there is much that gives cause for concern. Thus Marshall acknowledges, with some degree of gravity, amidst a generally sympathetic approach, that 'there can be few fantasies for exercising absolute dictatorial power as lamentable as this in the history of political thought'.[71] Whilst accepting that Bakunin's theoretical discrepancies may be due in part to a schizoid personality, Marshall is honest enough to declare that there are other issues at stake. As he remarks, Bakunin's ambivalence over revolutionary strategy 'undermines his criticisms of Marx, and shows a profound flaw in his tactics'.[72] Yet in spite of the fact that liberty and the invisible dictatorship sit rather uneasily together, Marshall remains confident that Bakunin is an important figure in the anarchist movement. Such ambivalence, he suggests, 'does not change the validity of his public statements on freedom nor does it alter his importance in the history of anarchism. It merely shows his failure to achieve an adequate praxis.'[73] Perhaps Marshall should add that this failure is rooted in an inadequate political theory. Nonetheless, the integrity of Marshall's examination appears to be beyond reproach. Having suggested that Bakunin is a central figure in anarchist thought, Marshall proceeds to associate him with a number of thinkers who are certainly not anarchists. Thus Marshall reflects on the fact that it is difficult not to conclude that Bakunin's invisible dictatorship would be even more tyrannical than a Blanquist or Marxist one, for its policies could not be openly known or discussed. It would be a secret party; it would operate like conspirators and thieves in the night. With no check to their power what would prevent the invisible dictators from grasping for absolute power? It is impossible to imagine that Bakunin's goal of an open and democratic society could ever be achieved by distorting the truth and manipulating the people in the way he suggests.

It is not enough to excuse Bakunin's predilection for tightly organised, authoritarian, hierarchical secret organisations by appealing to his 'romantic temperament' or the oppression of existing States. His invisible dictatorship is a central part of his political theory and practice, and shows that for all his professed love of liberty and openness there is a profound authoritarian and dissimulating streak in his life and work.[74]

This is a very sober and very accurate assessment, even if it underestimates the trust Bakunin places in moral education, and it triggers what for many, including Marshall, is another telling comparison. Like Lenin, Bakunin proclaimed 'violent revolution and shared a faith in a secret vanguard controlled by himself'.[75] That such sympathetic commentators as Marshall are obliged to utter such statements indicates that there is something sadly amiss with Bakunin's position. These remarks are not gratuitous, far from it. They are born out of Bakunin's ambiguity and abandonment of principle. And when read in conjunction with Bakunin's own works they offer a telling indictment of a purported admirer of freedom and autonomy. It is impossible to say that Bakunin has been erroneously included in the school of anarchist thought on this evidence alone. To make that judgment an examination of his vision of future society will be necessary. The signs, however, are not encouraging. And if he repeats the misgivings of his revolutionary tactics, then the ground on which any reasonable defence can be offered looks increasingly small.

Bakunin's Political Theory

Before ascertaining whether Bakunin's belief in a temporary revolutionary dictatorship evolves, whether it be by some inadvertent progression or a more deliberate strategy, into support for the idea of the state, there is at least one problem that requires immediate attention. For in adumbrating the ambiguity of his position above there was one thorny issue that remained outside the debate. That is, the controversy surrounding the *Catechism of a Revolutionary* (1869), which should not be confused with the earlier *Revolutionary Catechism* (1866) that was written solely by Bakunin, and which will be the subject of examination below. To some of Bakunin's critics, the *Catechism of a Revolutionary* is conclusive proof of Bakunin's spirit of authoritarianism and his disrespect for liberty. That the document arouses such feelings is not surprising. It is, as Marshall has described it, 'one of the most repulsive documents in the history of terrorism'.[76] Furthermore, the text itself employs the argument that the ends of the revolution may be used to justify the means. Obviously, if Bakunin was to be identified as the author of this work then the substance of the criticism outlined above would receive a degree of reinforcement that his defenders would find hard to resist.

Fortunately for Bakunin, most commentators absolve him from the responsibility of authorship. Dolgoff, for example, has argued that 'research by Michael Confino has conclusively shown that Nechaev was the sole author of the *Catechism*'.[77] Continuing in a less assertive tone, Dolgoff contends that the important thing 'is that Bakunin shortly repudiated both Nechaev and his ruthless amoralism in the strongest possible terms'.[78] Others have been less willing to exonerate Bakunin completely. Avrich takes a more cautious approach within the same volume, suggesting that the 'burden of authorship seems to have been Nechaev's, but Bakunin probably did have a hand in it'.[79] In his later text, *Bakunin and Nechaev*, Avrich maintains his position, claiming that 'it is by no means certain that Bakunin had no role in [the *Catechism*'s] composition or revision'.[80] Similarly, Marshall concludes that the *Catechism of a Revolutionary* was probably written by Nechaev in the main, and that, more importantly, Bakunin sharply dismisses Nechaev's 'unprincipled use of violence and deception'. Elaborating further Bakunin's objections, he cites a letter, written in June 1870, that Bakunin addressed to his younger co-author. In it Bakunin seems to vent some anger at Nechaev by stating that his disciple seems intent on making his 'own self-sacrificing cruelty . . . a rule of life for the community'.[81] This is an understandable reaction by Bakunin, particularly as it occurs at a time when his own fight with Marx was becoming increasingly acrimonious. Nevertheless, it is only with great difficulty that one could accept Bakunin's concern for Nechaev's 'total negation of man's individual and social nature' as genuine.[82] If the preservation of the salutary conditions necessary for human nature to flourish are so important to Bakunin, then one has to question why he completely disregarded such concerns in his own revolutionary methodology.

Such inconsistencies in Bakunin's work introduce difficulties when attempting to decipher his true political standpoint. But the real challenge to Bakunin's anarchism emerges from his central and principal works, in particular those that offer the greatest access to his thoughts on how future society should be organized. Initially, this may sound problematical, if only because it is claimed that Bakunin, in common with others that are labelled anarchist, does not expound any detailed blueprint for the construction of future society.[83] A first reading of the texts might seem to corroborate this position; for in rejecting the metaphysical idealism of Hegel's philosophy Bakunin is evading what he regards as a serious and dangerous possibility. Metaphysicians, he contends, are 'those who by one means or another . . . have created for themselves an ideal social organisation into which, like new Procrustes, they want to force the life of future generations whatever the cost'.[84] This is not to say that Bakunin offers no guidance whatsoever. He plainly does; not to do so would be extremely foolhardy. Nevertheless, it is said that even when considering 'future social organisation' Bakunin's thoughts are maintained within tight parameters. Thus Marshall explains that Bakunin proffered only the 'most general principles' for future social construction.[85] Accordingly, Bakunin informs his reader that this future society should be organized 'from the bottom up, by the free association or federation of workers, starting with the associations, then going on to the communes, the regions, the nations [sic], and, finally, culminating in a great international and universal federation'.[86] Such advice, we are led to believe, is fundamental to the anarchist argument against elaborate conjecturing on the nature of future society. 'We revolutionary anarchists,' remarks Bakunin,

> have neither the intention nor the least desire to impose on our own people or on any other an ideal social organisation that we have drawn from books or thought up on our own. In the belief that the masses bear all the elements of their future organisational norms in their own more or less historically evolved instincts, in their everyday needs and their conscious and unconscious desires, we seek that ideal within the people themselves.[87]

The rationale that inspires Marshall's argument also underpins Dolgoff's interpretation of Bakunin's *Revolutionary Catechism*.

However, Dolgoff's urgency to inform his reader that the text is not designed as an 'attempt to picture the perfect anarchist society' reveals more than he is willing to admit. For in suggesting that the *Revolutionary Catechism* merely describes 'a society in transition',[88] Dolgoff tries to disguise the true nature of the document, but fails. Transitional the society *may* be, but the document's field of enquiry is truly extensive.[89] Ranging from the political structure of society, through procedures for the arbitration of disputes, to social and economic equality, the text appears to relate something more solid than a temporary state of affairs. However, the work is manifestly important for two other reasons. First, whether transitional or lasting, its depiction of future society carries considerable significance in determining the degree of commensurability that exists between means and ends, and between human nature and freedom, in Bakunin's political theory. If the document does outline a transient society, and it is difficult to provide conclusive evidence one way or another, then it has to be viewed in conjunction with his revolutionary strategy adumbrated above. If the text is, conversely, an illustration of what Bakunin believes a future anarchy should look like, then its relevance remains.[90] Comparison could then be had between means and ends. Whatever the nature of the society under examination, however, be it ephemeral or fixed, it has to be regarded as a necessary element in the final decision about Bakunin's status as an anarchist.

Judging by the opinions of commentators regarding the text's general significance in Bakunin's overall body of works, the status of his *Revolutionary Catechism* as some kind of touchstone of anarchism is beyond dispute. As the major document of the *Principles and Organisation of the International Brotherhood* (1866), the *Revolutionary Catechism* is the place where he 'elaborated his fundamental anarchist principles'.[91] Moreover, in the eyes of Kaminski the *Principles and Organisation* texts constitute nothing less than 'the spiritual foundation of the entire anarchist movement'.[92] Even with hyperbole constrained, the fact remains that Bakunin's *Revolutionary Catechism* has to be viewed as a seminally important work when engaging in an analysis of his political theory.

The *Revolutionary Catechism* is reputed to be built upon Bakunin's principal objections to the state. Within his *œuvre* it is probably the most telling critique that Bakunin directs toward the state. Certainly, the importance of the text cannot be underrated. It is in this light that Bakunin's emphasis on free association and federalism at the expense of centralized authority is to be understood, as expressed in points VII and VIII of the *Revolutionary Catechism*.

> *Absolute rejection of every authority including that which sacrifices freedom for the convenience of the state. . . .* The political and economic structure of society must now be organised on the basis of freedom. Henceforth, *order in society must result from the greatest possible realisation of individual liberty, as well as of liberty on all levels of social organisation.*

> The political and economic organisation of social life must not, as at present, be directed from the summit to the base – the centre to the circumference – imposing unity through forced centralisation. On the contrary, it must be reorganised to issue *from the base to the summit – from circumference to the centre – according to the principles* of free association and federalism.[93]

There can be little doubt then that the state, for Bakunin, is the 'supreme case of illegitimate and imposed authority'. As he subsequently argued in *Statism and Anarchy*, no state is able to meet the demands of the people. These demands include

> the free organisation of their own interests from below upward, without any interference, tutelage, or coercion from above. That is because no state, not even the most republican and democratic, not even the pseudo-popular state contemplated by Marx, in essence represents anything but government of the masses from above downward, by an educated and thereby privileged minority which supposedly understands the real interests of the people better than the people themselves . . . for the state *means* coercion, domination by means of coercion, camouflaged if possible but unceremonious and overt if need be.[94]

The state is, moreover, an organ of power that fosters centralization and negates the spontaneity of the people. Likewise, representative government is characterized as a fraud. Vindicated in terms of elected representatives and universal suffrage, which is 'nothing but a swindle and snare for the people', representative government rests solidly on its exploitation and oppression of the masses.[95] Representative democracy, claims Bakunin, is

> based on the pseudo-sovereignty of a sham popular will, supposedly expressed by pseudo-representatives of the people in sham popular assemblies, [and] combines the two main

conditions necessary for their success: state centralisation, and the actual subordination of the sovereign people to the intellectual minority that governs them, supposedly representing them but invariably exploiting them.[96]

The strength of the state lies in political power.

> Political power means domination. And where there is domination, there must be a substantial part of the population who remain subjected to the domination of their rulers; and subjects will naturally hate their rulers, who will then naturally be forced to subdue the people by even more oppressive measures, further curtailing their freedom. Such is the nature of political power ever since its origin in human society.[97]

Subtracting political power from the centralized state and investing it in the people affords neither resolution nor sense. For in shifting the location of power, power itself remains intact. The equation, as Bakunin notes, is fundamentally flawed. Rather than abolishing political power its relocation does nothing more than establish a people's state. Thus it becomes necessary to question the logic of the Marxists' proposals. As Bakunin says: 'If their state is to be truly a people's state, then why abolish it? But if its abolition is essential for the real liberation of the people, then how do they dare call it a people's state?'[98] Bakunin's thoughts reach their crescendo when he directs his attention towards Marx. There is no advantage, thinks Bakunin, to be had from investing authority in a revolutionary dictatorship as Marx does. In fact, he sees little if any difference between this and the state. Hence his argument that the

> only difference between revolutionary dictatorship and the state is in external appearances. Essentially, they both represent the same government of the majority by a minority in the name of the presumed stupidity of the one and the presumed intelligence of the other. Therefore they are equally reactionary, both having the direct and inevitable result of consolidating the political and economic privileges of the governing minority and the political and economic slavery of the masses.[99]

Bakunin takes no consolation from arguments about the dictatorship of the proletariat being only a transitional arrangement. The fault with the Marxists is that they have failed to perceive the true nature of political power. Given the argument above concerning Bakunin's countenancing of revolutionary dictatorships his points against Marx look a trifle shallow. Nevertheless, striking a heavy blow against Marxist theory, Bakunin offers what he believes is a clearer version of reality.

> [T]he only way to render any political power harmless, to pacify it and subdue it, is to destroy it. The philosophers did not understand that there can be no guarantee against political power except its complete abolition . . . any political power, as long as it remains a real power, by its very nature and under the threat of self-destruction must inexorably and at all costs strive for the realisation of its objectives, regardless of or even against the will of the authorities and princes wielding it.[100]

Even if those in command are the proletariat the same rules apply, and the same results impose themselves: government of the majority by the minority. Addressing the objections raised by the Marxists, Bakunin dismisses what he considers to be an ill-conceived strategy.

> But this minority, the Marxists say, will consist of workers. Yes, perhaps of *former* workers, who, as soon as they become rulers or representatives of the people will cease to be workers from the heights of the state. They will no longer represent the people but themselves and their own pretensions to govern the people. Anyone who doubts this is not at all familiar with human nature.[101]

The above argument has its roots in Bakunin's conception of human nature. Having sounded the alarm that all men possess a 'natural instinct for power' it naturally follows that no 'one should be entrusted with power, inasmuch as anyone invested with authority must, through the force of an immutable social law, become an oppressor and exploiter of society'.[102] One should not forget the lesson that humankind's 'nature is so constituted that, given the possibility of doing evil, that is, of feeding his vanity, his ambition, and his cupidity at the expense of someone else, he surely will make full use of such an opportunity'.[103] Parallel to this warning concerning human nature, however, is an awareness of the contextual causes that lead to the propensity for evil. Thus it is the 'evil organisation of society', and in particular the state, that is responsible for crimes and vices. Neglect of the environmental component involved would lead to an imbalance that is not reflected in Bakunin's conception of human nature itself. Human nature, then, serves a dual purpose here. On the one hand it is identified as the factor which underscores the problems associated with the exercise of political power through central state mechanisms. On the other it fulfils a justificatory role in Bakunin's arguments to overturn the state.[104]

Without the favourable circumstances of a free society to bolster it, the growth of human nature will be severely restricted. Thus Carr writes that Bakunin's 'hostility to the State flows directly from his belief in individual human nature'.[105] As Bakunin observes: 'It is in the nature of the State to disrupt human solidarity and in a sense to deny humanity.'[106] Such is the importance of freedom to human nature. Facilitation of the development of human nature demands the abrogation of all imposed authority and excessive centralization of power. Hence Bakunin's insistence that the essential conditions for freedom (and by default the flourishing of human nature) include: a) the abolition of all state religions; b) a refusal to grant political rights to churches coupled with measures to dissociate them from the education of children; c) the substitution of the commonwealth for a monarchy; d) the erasing of all classes and privileges and in their place the establishment of political equality for men and women; and e)

> *Abolition*, dissolution, and moral, political, and economic dismantling of the *all-pervasive, regimented, centralised State*, the alter ego of the Church, and as such, the permanent cause of the impoverishment, brutalisation, and enslavement of the multitude. This naturally entails the following: *Abolition of all state universities:* public education must be administered only by the communes and free associations. *Abolition of the state judiciary:* all judges must be elected by the people. *Abolition of all criminal, civil, and legal codes now administered in Europe:* because the code of liberty can be created only by *liberty itself.* *Abolition of banks and all other institutions of state credit. Abolition of all centralised administration, of the bureaucracy, of all permanent armies and state police.*[107]

It would be difficult to misjudge the tenor of Bakunin's objections, framed within the rhetoric of destruction. But such is the special characteristic of this language of disapprobation that it fortifies the desire for change. For as Bakunin enlightens his audience, one should invest trust in 'the eternal Spirit which destroys and annihilates only because it is the unfathomable and eternal source of all life. The passion for destruction is a creative passion, too!'[108]

Unleashed from their shackles these forces of destruction provide a new basis for freedom. Unlike Proudhon, for example, Bakunin is not what we in the twentieth century would call a sexist. Exhibiting an urgency for absolute equality between the sexes, Bakunin transcends some of the limitations surrounding Proudhon's doctrine. In a similar manner Bakunin encourages the abolition of the patriarchal family, the discontinuation of marriage law and the right of inheritance, together with an espousal of equal education for all. It is worth recalling, however, that these freedoms are, for Bakunin, only secured within the wider political framework of federalism. Central to Bakunin's philosophy is the belief 'that the people can be happy and free only when they create their own life, organizing themselves from below upward by means of independent and completely free associations'.[109]

Authoritarian Federalism

Bakunin's vision of future society is essentially federalist. In this he follows the precedent set by Proudhon. But whereas Proudhon was somewhat ambiguous in his consideration of the right to secession, Bakunin is quite unequivocal. For Bakunin, the right to secession is imperative, because in its absence freedom perishes. Hence his belief that *'every individual, every association, every commune, every region, every nation has the absolute right to self-determination, to associate or not to associate, to ally themselves with whomever they wish and repudiate their alliances without regard to so-called historic rights . . . or the convenience of their neighbours'*.[110] Moreover, even if a country joined a 'State of its own free will, it does not follow that it is under obligation to remain forever attached to that State. No perpetual obligation can be admitted by human justice . . . The right of free reunion, as well as the right of secession, is the first and most important of all political rights.'[111] This is not to say that Bakunin felt the right to secession would be exercised frequently. On the contrary, once the right has been 'established, secession will no longer be necessary'.[112] The reasoning behind this, as Dolgoff observes, is that Bakunin felt that people who shared many common interests would naturally co-operate. Whereas those who secede because they have little if anything in common with others in the federation will, by the act of secession, 'eliminate a source of friction'.[113]

One might suggest here that Bakunin covers the issue of secession very lightly. He makes no effort to distinguish between the different types of right that belong to individuals and groups, nor does he seem to be cognizant of the difficulties that are associated with secession. Analysis and understanding are obviously increased with hindsight, but a cursory glance at the recent problems experienced in the former Yugoslavia, and in the former USSR whose constitution embodied the right to secede, indicates that it would be naïve to assume that secession guarantees an elimination of conflict or friction. This may be merely a simple attitude of mind on Bakunin's part. Conversely, it may be a position that is influenced by his conception of human nature – humanity's sociability overcoming its egoism allowing the positive development of social relations outside a federal framework. Whatever the answer, it seems that Bakunin either has chosen to ignore or underestimates the propensity of human nature to identify with ethnic and national rivalries and differences, which can be so skilfully manipulated by nationalist movements.

If Proudhon and Bakunin share a commitment to federation, their paths part quite markedly when thinking about the economic organization of future society. Unlike Proudhon, Bakunin favours the principle of collectivism over mutualism. Accordingly, Bakunin advocates the communal ownership of land and argues for a collective basis to labour. Having recognized that it is collective labour that creates wealth, he contends that collective wealth should be owned collectively.[114] There is, however, a strict condition attached to this. That is, distribution of this wealth is to be based on work done rather than need.[115] Here enters the thin edge of an increasingly authoritarian wedge. Such coercion, and that is what it amounts to as will be shown below, signals the start of a further inconsistency between his desire for liberty and his leaning toward authoritarianism. Despite being hailed as the 'spiritual foundation of the anarchist movement', the *Revolutionary Catechism*, which purportedly depicts a free society, looks markedly less free the further one's analysis proceeds. To suggest then, like Dolgoff, that Bakunin never departed from the fundamental principles defined in these documents is vacuous. Unless it is assumed that Bakunin's authoritarianism is part and parcel of his fundamental philosophy, it makes little sense to submit that his anarchist ideas, as found in the *Principles and Organisation of the International Brotherhood*, were his constant guiding light. Marshall offers a more sober assessment, acknowledging that although the *Revolutionary Catechism* may be the storehouse of the author's 'fundamental anarchist principles' the text also reflects 'the tension between Bakunin's libertarian sympathies and his authoritarian strategy of manipulating others through secret societies'.[116] Marshall proceeds to temper his initial statement with a frank admission and obvious concern regarding the contradictory and authoritarian nature of the *Revolutionary Catechism*. Hence he documents the fact that, 'Bakunin writes that the only legitimate restraint would be the "natural salutary power of public opinion". Yet Bakunin also declares that society can deprive all "antisocial" adults of political rights and those who steal or break their agreements and violate the freedom of individuals will be "penalised according to the laws of society".'[117] This is suspiciously analogous to Proudhon. Bakunin's future society, like his predecessor's, is infused with a coercive power that is comparable to that exercised by centralized states. An examination of the *Revolutionary Catechism* confirms such misgivings.

Having surmounted some of the difficulties that surrounded Proudhon's concept of federalism, it would appear that Bakunin is unable to evade a number of proposals that bedevil his own federal society. Labour is a prime example. In the tradition of Marx and Proudhon, Bakunin deploys the concept of labour in the role of humanizer of humankind and society. So he argues that labour 'is the foundation of human dignity and morality. For it was only by free and intelligent labour that man, overcoming his own bestiality, attained his own humanity and sense of justice, changed his environment, and created the civilised world.'[118] Collective labour is preferred to mutualism as the basis of production simply because 'association marvellously multiplies the productive capacity of each worker; hence, a co-operating member of a productive association will earn much more in less time'.[119] Co-operative workers' associations are seen by Bakunin as the basis for future 'worldwide economic federalism'.[120] The rub arises, however, when it is realized that whoever wants to live in Bakunin's so-called free society has to work. For whilst Bakunin insists that everyone has the right to free association for whatever purpose except for the exploitation of minors, even the right to be lazy, he also maintains that 'whoever wants to live in society must earn his living by his own labour, or be treated as a parasite who is living on the labour of others'.[121] As Marshall has witnessed, Bakunin's labour proviso unlocks the door to a 'potential world of tyranny and oppression'.[122]

Such apprehensions are not unfounded. For example, Bakunin's concern to promote the absolute freedom of both sexes to live as they please, being accountable to no-one, in point H.3 of his *Revolutionary*

Catechism, is mercilessly overridden at H.6, just one page later. It is here that the author reveals that society cannot

> leave itself completely defenceless against vicious and parasitic individuals. Work must be the basis of all political rights. The units of society, each within its own jurisdiction, can deprive all such antisocial adults of political rights (except the old, the sick, and those dependent on private or public subsidy) and will be obliged to restore their political rights as soon as they begin to live by their own labour.[123]

As if that were not enough, those who lose 'their political rights will also lose custody of their children'.[124] Recommendations of this nature not only are frighteningly authoritarian, but also belie Bakunin's revolutionary methodology and jeopardize his credentials as an anarchist.

But why this emphasis on the necessity of labour? It is quite possible that the answer lies in that Bakunin is elaborating a teleological account of human nature.[125] Writing in his *Federalism, Socialism, and Anti-Theologism* (1867), Bakunin suggests that the

> cardinal points of the most refined human existence, as well as of the most torpid animal existence, will always remain the same: to be born, to develop and grow; to work in order to eat and drink, in order to have shelter and defend oneself, in order to maintain one's individual existence in the social equilibrium of his own species; to love, reproduce and then to die.[126]

Seemingly, Bakunin regards labour as essential in order to live and maintain oneself in society. He sustains this position in his *Philosophical Considerations* (1870).

> All animals must work in order to live. All of them, according to their needs, their understanding, and their strength, take part, without noticing or being aware of it, in this slow work of transforming the surface of the earth into a place more favourable to animal life. But this work becomes properly human only when it begins to satisfy, not merely the fixed and inevitably circumscribed needs of animal life, but also those of the thinking and speaking social being who endeavours to win and realise his freedoms to the full.[127]

Perhaps it is this understanding of the relationship between labour and human nature that leads Bakunin to suggest that work is the base of political rights in future society. If it is, then it is strikingly similar to Marx's argument about alienation. It may be that Marx was the source of Bakunin's thinking here, but that is not an important matter. A more serious consideration is the reason behind Bakunin's stress on the role of labour. One could argue that his strategy of insisting that refusal to labour results in a loss of political rights is an outcome of his design or intention to recapture those elements of human nature, and the values associated with them, that have been lost through the actions of capitalism. That is, prior to the development of capitalism individuals knew of and naturally engaged in the process of labour to fulfil themselves, together with the need to live and maintain an existence within the community. Thus Bakunin writes: 'Every animal works; it lives only by working. Man as a living being, is not exempt from this necessity, which is the supreme law of life. He must work in order to maintain his existence, in order to develop in the fulness of his being.'[128] The contextualist paradigm of this argument is obvious. As Bakunin argues,

> man does not become man, nor does he achieve awareness or realisation of his humanity, other than in society and in the collective movement of the whole society; he only shakes off the yoke of external nature through collective or social labour, the one force capable of transforming the earth's surface into an environment favourable to the growth of humanity; and without this material emancipation there can be no intellectual and moral emancipation for anyone.[129]

Humanity expresses itself through labouring; but since the onset of capitalism humanity labours only to acquire the basic prerequisites of life: food, drink and shelter. No longer is work seen as a process which secures one's own existence in the social equilibrium. That position is now given at birth, with individuals assigned their social rank according to the class they are born into. Rather than working 'in order to develop the fulness of his being', the individual works to survive in a fiercely competitive society.

Whatever the merits or demerits of Bakunin's argument about labour and alienation, one has to say that, given the insistence on labour as an obligatory contribution to society, it seems virtually impossible to agree with Bakunin's recommendations. Such measures demand a grossly interfering social power that renders present-day states havens of freedom in comparison. Not only is there a heavy-handed coercion that forces people to labour, whether they wish it or not, but there is in partnership with it an admission that some kind of punishment is to be based on a system of legislation. Immediately after his announcement on the custody of children, Bakunin warns his reader that those 'who violate voluntary agreements, steal, inflict bodily harm, or above all, violate the freedom of any individual, native or foreigner, will be penalised according to the laws of society'.[130] Parallel to the maintenance of order through law, both as moral law and as social rules, Bakunin, in common with others labelled anarchist, has recourse to the concept of public opinion to act as the guardian of freedom. It is this reliance upon public opinion that facilitates his confident prediction that idlers and parasites would not represent a problem for future society. In a society characterized by liberty, equality and justice, public opinion, he claims, 'will then reflect the new humanity and become a natural guardian of the most absolute liberty'.[131] Furthermore, 'given a rational organisation of education and upbringing and likewise the pressure of public opinion, which, being based upon respect for labour, must despise idlers – in such a society idleness and parasites will be impossible'.[132] And if parasitic individuals are to be found then they are subject to the short, sharp shock of losing their political rights.

Public opinion is expected to police people's rights and freedoms. Left at that, such expectations are not outrageously controversial. However, the remit of public opinion extends into public morality. As Bakunin outlines, to 'combat charlatans and pernicious associations is the special affair of public opinion. But society is obliged to refuse to guarantee civic rights of any association or collective body whose aims or rules violate the fundamental principles of human justice.'[133] It is at this juncture that public opinion begins to lose its effectiveness as a safeguard to the free society. The difficulties arise from the dilemma of deciding what is and what is not just. After all, who or what has the responsibility of determining whether the principles of human justice have been violated? Matters are compounded even further on consideration of the extent to which freedom apparently pervades Bakunin's free society. As he informs us, there should be boundless 'freedom of propaganda, speech, press or private assembly, with no other restraint than the natural salutary power of public opinion. Absolute freedom to organise associations even for allegedly immoral purposes including even those associations which advocate the undermining (or destruction) of individual and public freedom.'[134] Presumably, freedom has something to do with justice; for if individuals were deprived of all freedoms then society could scarcely be called just. So how is one to determine when the principles of human justice have been violated? Are associations that attempt to undermine public freedom unjust? Such issues are not always amenable to straightforward solutions; particularly when Bakunin regards justice as a matter for human conscience. Violations of human justice would have to be measured against the moral law that sanctions the actions of each individual. Consequently, as justice is a matter of conscience then there would be as many notions of justice as there are human consciences.

What this boils down to is a profound potential for dispute. Bakunin himself seems to have anticipated this. Within his federal political matrix there exists a fully incorporated legislative and judicial structure. 'The provincial tribunal (also elected by universal suffrage) will adjudicate, without appeal, all disputes between communes and individuals, communes and communes, and communes and the provincial administration or parliament.'[135] Decisions reached by the provincial tribunal are based on a framework of law, particular to a specific commune. Provision of the law is, naturally, the task of legislators. Every 'commune elects all functionaries, lawmakers, and judges. It administers the communal property and finances. Every commune should have the incontestable right to create, without superior sanction, its own constitution and legislation.'[136] In itself, public opinion is not strong enough or sufficiently embracing to cover all possible sources of dispute within society. To that effect, a body of judges, together with a framework of law and tribunals, is required to facilitate resolution of possible conflicts. Again, it has to be said that such procedures and structures have more than a passing resemblance to those that operate under states today. Even if those procedures are designed to establish a system of authority from the bottom up, rather than from the top down, Bakunin is perilously close to countenancing a democratic state or society, or both, rather than anarchy.

Detailed plans for legislative and judicial frameworks account for only one part of Bakunin's vision of future society. Accompanying this there is a very descriptive discussion of where power should lie in society. The discussion commences by way of an acknowledgement that each country should be organized on slightly differing lines, to suit the variety of traditions and circumstances prevailing in each. But Bakunin continues by insisting that there are two fundamental and indispensable principles which must be put into effect by any country seriously trying to organise a free society. *First: all organisations must proceed by way of federation from the base to the summit, from the commune to the co-ordinating association of the country or nation. Second: there must be at least one autonomous intermediate body between the commune and the country, the department, the region, or the province.*[137]

The demand for an intermediate body between commune and country is designed to obviate the danger that without it each commune 'would be too isolated and too weak to be able to resist the despotic centralistic power of the State'.[138] Bakunin is aware that, given half a chance, the old, usurped state will endeavour with all its might to regain control of the country. Each commune's autonomy has to be defended and preserved, for that is the *'basic unit of all political organisation in each country'*. But the autonomy of the commune is not infinite. Because 'in order to join and become an integral part of the provincial federation, the commune must conform its own particular charter to the fundamental principles of the provincial constitution and be accepted by the parliament of the province. The commune must also accept the judgments of the provincial tribunal and any measures ordered by the government of the province.'[139] Unsurprisingly, one soon learns that the provincial constitution is to be 'based on the principles of this catechism'.[140] Moreover, the provincial parliament enacts 'legislation defining the rights and obligations of individuals, communes, and associations in relation to the provincial federation, and the penalties for violations of its laws. It will reserve, however, the right of the communes to diverge on secondary points, though not on fundamentals.'[141]

There are two issues that need to be addressed here. The first is the demand that provincial constitutions ought to be founded on the principles inherent in the *Revolutionary Catechism*. Given Bakunin's supposed aversion to formulating detailed blueprints for future society, this is somewhat confusing. Either Bakunin believes that these societies, once consolidated and when the threat from the former centralized state has receded, should be allowed to develop in whatever manner they choose – this, of course, assumes that the society portrayed in the *Revolutionary Catechism* is a transitional society, and it seems difficult to provide convincing evidence one way or another here – or he has flatly rejected, or perhaps never sincerely held, his apparent revulsion for laying out the plans for future society. Bakunin does talk of a 'transitional period', but fails to elaborate its exact nature or the length of time he envisages it will exist.

> During the transitional period, however, society will be confronted with the problem of individuals (and unfortunately there will be many of them) who grew up under the prevailing system of organised injustice and special privileges and who were not brought up with a realisation of the need for justice and true human dignity and likewise with respect for and the habit of work. In regard to those individuals revolutionary or revolutionised society will find itself facing a distressing dilemma: it will either have to force them to work, which would be despotism, or let itself be exploited by idlers; and that would be a new slavery and the source of a new corruption of society.[142]

Without a clear definition of what a 'revolutionised society' is meant to be it is difficult to know whether Bakunin was referring to a post-revolutionary society (a transitional society) or a fully fledged anarchy. My feelings are that Bakunin is not referring to an anarchy when he talks of a 'revolutionised society', because he appears to refer to that in a different manner. The paragraph that follows immediately after the previous one (as structured in Maximoff) talks of 'a society organised upon the principles of equality and justice'. To my mind, this is Bakunin's free society, his future anarchy.[143]

The second issue concerns the degree of autonomy that remains after the functions of the provincial parliament have been subtracted from the federal equation. Despite flying in the face of Proudhon's outright repudiation of constitutions, Bakunin's emphasis on government is, according to Marshall, not as extensive as it might seem. Thus Marshall explains that 'Bakunin only wishes to retain political government in its most extenuated form'. According to Marshall, Bakunin employs the term 'government' to describe the elected parliament at the local level 'which defines the rights and obligations of the communes and the elected tribunal which deals with disputes between communes'.[144] Thus parliament is to be viewed as nothing other than a 'co-ordinating association'. There is indeed a co-ordinating role for parliament to play. Not only is parliament involved in the distribution of national income to the communes, it also embraces the task of co-ordinating and planning industrial production. This is acknowledged by Marshall himself. The problem that remains is that of defining how far the tentacles of government extend. It would seem that Marshall is slightly confused here. For whilst he wants to say that Bakunin's parliament operates only at a local level, he is compelled to admit that this government is actually absorbed into a national and international framework of decision-making. In particular, parliament is at the hub of a potentially explosive predicament: the administration of national finance. Besides directing the nation's industrial production, it also has the responsibility of distributing national income. How this is to be determined Bakunin does not say. The problem is a tricky one. Intimation of the likely procedure by which financial and other matters would be settled is given by Bakunin in his description of the nature of communes themselves. Below parliament but representing the '*basic unit of all political organisation in each country* [is] *the completely autonomous commune, constituted by the majority vote of all adults of both sexes*'.[145]

Despite the hankering for free associations within a federal structure, decisions are still to be based on the majority vote under universal suffrage. Indeed, given that the offices of functionaries, legislators and judges are all filled through popular vote, it would seem that communes are founded on a system of majority voting, and likewise the provincial parliament. How else could the representatives of the parliament ratify the actions of the provincial government? Decisions of how to allocate the national income, then, must be put to the vote. The problem that confronted Proudhon faces Bakunin in turn. Majoritarianism, whilst arguably the only feasible system on which to run social affairs, is plagued by an element of coercion. The point is, if communes are to be subjected to the outcome of a majority vote by the provincial parliament then it is extremely difficult to maintain the argument that they are fully autonomous. Even if disputes are few and far between, the ground rules have been set. Coercion is the measure to be applied in the face of opposition. Consequently, the freedom of both individuals and communes within Bakunin's federal society looks very fragile. In both the social and the political spheres, Bakunin's sketch is illuminated by an authoritarian backdrop that threatens to extirpate freedom before it has even laid down the barest of roots. From the enforcement of labour to rule by the will of the majority, freedom is hounded in a series of successive, albeit to some extent prophylactic, measures that appear to jeopardize its very existence rather than actualize it across society.

At the same time, many of Bakunin's social measures receive more than a modicum of support by way of education. It is hardly surprising that Bakunin utilizes the process of education to reinforce the presiding status quo, if only because the contextualist dynamic of his conception of human nature compels it. Bakunin was a firm believer in the idea that morality is inculcated through the processes and apparatus of socialization. Because of this Bakunin places great stress on the importance of education. Public education is one of the obligations that society has to meet for everyone, and on that basis it is to be administered by the communes. It is the 'right of every man and woman, from birth to adulthood, to complete upkeep, clothes, food, shelter, care, guidance, education (public schools, primary, secondary, higher education, artistic, industrial, and scientific), all at the expense of society'.[146] Insistence on such things as upkeep and education represents an area of Bakunin's thought that appears to be inconsistent with other proposals that are elucidated in his *Revolutionary Catechism*. Before addressing this matter, however, it is imperative that his policy on education be analysed further. Ignoring the tension or perplexity hinted at above, it may be assumed that some form of education will be delivered by society. The questions that need to be asked are, first, who or what will be responsible for this delivery? And, more importantly, what is the function of education, as Bakunin sees it?

It is difficult to elicit a straightforward answer to the first question. The most that Bakunin seems to offer is a simple commitment that the education of children will be 'assured by society'.[147] The question remains: who or what will be doing the educating, parents or teachers appointed by the commune to educate all children therein? Examination of the text reveals that there may be a division of responsibility here between parents and those acting as teachers to other children apart from their own. As Bakunin stipulates, parents are involved in this process but would appear to be monitored by the commune. 'Parents shall have the right to care for and guide the education of their children, under the ultimate control of the commune which retains the right and the obligation to take children away from parents who, by example or by cruel and inhuman treatment, demoralise or otherwise hinder the physical and mental development of their children.'[148] Apparently, then, parents do have a role to play. But as Bakunin suggests almost immediately afterwards, whilst still too young to look out for themselves 'children must be brought up under the guidance of their elders. It is true that parents are their natural tutors, but since the very future of the commune itself depends upon the intellectual and moral training it gives to children, the *commune must be the tutor.* The freedom of adults is possible only when the free society looks after the education of minors.'[149] The emphasis on public education suggests that teachers rather than parents would bear the greater responsibility, particularly as Bakunin appears to indicate that some form of schooling will exist after the abolition of state mechanisms. What consequences this has for the acquisition of a moral law within the human conscience Bakunin neglects to mention. The content of any public education system is bound to colour individual and public opinion.

Revelation of the purpose of public education is, however, clear for all to see. There is a significant absence of ambiguity here. With the secular school superseding the church, Bakunin announces that 'the sole purpose of secular public education is the gradual, progressive initiation of children into liberty by the triple development of their physical strength, their minds, and their will'. All of this, it may be argued, is quite commendable; but praise may well be suspended on familiarization with the latent agenda behind a child's educational development. 'Reason, truth, justice, respect for fellowmen, the sense of personal dignity which is inseparable from the dignity of others, love of personal freedom and the freedom of all others, the conviction that work is the base and condition for rights – these must be the fundamental principles of all public education.'[150] Public education is overtly designed to support public morality. That is the simple reason why ultimate control over education rests with the commune. Education serves a social and political function, to instil and legitimize the belief that work is the basis for rights. Without the impregnation of this public morality into children, society, as Bakunin sees it, would be at the mercy of free riders. Hence the fear of demoralization becomes literally true. Demoralization assumes a new meaning. To deprive children of the social understanding that labour secures political rights is not only a punishable offence, but is something the commune has to avoid for the sake of its own future. Recourse to a commune-controlled system of education is a vital cog in the wheel that turns Bakunin's future society.

Charges of conspirational authoritarianism gather on the horizon and seem all the more menacing because of the ambiguity inherent in Bakunin's work. It might be the case that he had in mind some form of state-like control for education; it might not. Certainty is denied by ambiguity. It may be the case that Bakunin envisaged that some kind of social welfare system would be responsible for children and others. The quotation above provides some justification for such a remark, especially when it is noted that these indispensable provisions are supplied 'at the expense of society'. Alternatively, it could be that under Bakunin's formulation society simply replaces the state. It is imperative, however, that one should avoid importing some alien meaning into the author's writings. Much effort may be invested into unravelling the intricacies of Bakunin's thought but that in itself may not produce a conclusive result. It seems that the most that one can say with any confidence is that his writings are often confused and therefore lack the clarity essential to the development of an irrepressible argument of whatever persuasion.

If an answer is to be found, then perhaps it may be located by way of human nature. The argument about to be offered parallels that which was proposed earlier concerning the possible reason why Bakunin places so much importance on the concepts of work and alienation. In suggesting that compulsory labour may be Bakunin's way (rather perverse it has to be said) of encouraging the recrudescence of those elements of human nature that were lost under capitalism, so Bakunin's portrayal of anarchist society, in his *Revolutionary Catechism*, may be the wider framework to nurture human nature back to its old self. As labour is one element in the strategy, so the transitional society is the larger enveloping environment that is designed to nourish human nature so that a fully-fledged anarchy becomes possible. To accomplish this it has first to negate or restrict the egoistical side of human nature. The development of a society organized from below upward and erected on a foundation of federated, free, autonomous communes is designed to achieve this. With no-one at the top, unlike in the Marxian concept of the dictatorship of the proletariat, the opportunities for the egoistical side of human nature to outdo its sociable side are constrained. With egoism in check, humankind's sociability will be allowed to express itself through freedom. It may be said, then, that Bakunin's *Revolutionary Catechism* represents the contextual framework under which the two key elements of his conception of human nature are worked out. First, the acquisition and control of power is curtailed, thereby restraining the likelihood of egoism coming into play through the development of the lust for power present in human nature. Second, this lack of political power creates a background for freedom and sociability. Given the importance of the contextualist account of human nature in Bakunin's ideological narrative, this may be a role the society pictured in his *Revolutionary Catechism* was designed to play.

Support for such an idea, if it does not already seem too outlandish, may be derived from a number of sources within Bakunin. Two of the most renowned and perhaps notorious are his notions of the secret society and the intellectual proletariat. Both were envisaged as facilitating the successful progress of the social revolution, supporting the lumpenproletariat in their drive to abolish the state. The emphasis, though, is on the relationship between individuals and their environment. Working out of this contextualist paradigm, Bakunin, as Shatz has highlighted,

> believed that social solidarity, a deep-rooted social and communal instinct, was an innate feature of human nature. If it failed to manifest itself consistently in contemporary society, that was only because it had been suppressed, or distorted, by the artificial structure of the state. To create a new and better society, therefore, did not require the re-education of its inhabitants or the transformation of human nature, but only the release of the masses' pent-up natural instincts and social energies by destroying the institutions thwarting them.[151]

Abolition of the state is the first step along this road. However, it appears that human nature does require some coaxing from education, despite what Shatz has to say. It is worth recalling that the element of sociability in human nature is accompanied by an equally important component, egoism. It was Bakunin's hope that, in aiding both the successful outcome of the revolution, whether it be through secret societies or the role of the intellectual proletariat, and the development of the individual after it, he could create a more salutary climate for human nature to flourish in an anarchist society.

A second endeavour to furnish a broader meaning to Bakunin's work is derived from his conception of freedom. It is a conception of freedom that is essentially egalitarian. That is, a person cannot be free unless all others are free at the same time. Hence in a society based on oppression individuals cannot be truly free. Accordingly, Bakunin's conception of freedom, as a goal which is to be achieved by the community as a whole or not at all, has some connection to his conception of human nature and how that corresponds to his ideas of work and alienation. There seems to be a parallel between the idea that the whole community has to be free if it is to be truly free, and the argument that individuals should be forced to labour or else be deprived of their political rights and children. With a twist of the imagination one might also argue that this is simply Bakunin's version of Rousseau's more famous paradox of individuals being *forced to be free*.[152] For both freedom and human nature, the community or society (the terms are employed interchangeably) appears as some kind of collective repository through which the development of each is mediated. As Bakunin writes, 'the individual, his freedom and reason, are the products of society, and not vice versa: society is not the product of individuals comprising it; and the higher, the more fully the individual is developed, the greater his freedom – and the more he is the product of society, the more does he receive from society and the greater his debt to it'.[153] Put more simply, perhaps both freedom and human nature are concepts that Bakunin utilizes to vindicate his collectivism, striving as it were to maintain a delicate balance between the individual and society.

If this is the intention of Bakunin's work then the spectre of collectivism raises grave doubts about the very viability of his arguments concerning human nature and freedom. Mechanisms of coercion or the mere suggestion that one should simply acquiesce in the face of a hostile society that has the power to dispossess you not only of rights but of your children, may well signal that Bakunin is guilty of a blatant contradiction of his own belief that freedom requires no other sanction than conscience. As he puts it in his *Revolutionary Catechism*: 'Freedom is the absolute right of every adult man and woman to seek no other sanction for their acts than their own conscience and their own reason, being responsible first to themselves and then to the society which they have *voluntarily* accepted.'[154] Additionally, Bakunin would also be denying the conditions which his conception of human nature requires for its own fruition. A society without freedom is a society in which the growth of human nature is severely restricted. Perhaps he was, as Shatz comments, 'too impatient, and too domineering, to abide strictly by his own principles'.[155] One way or another, however, Bakunin still manages to create a dilemma out of which it is difficult if not impossible to escape. If, as Shatz implies, he is merely forcing the pace of change and abandoning his principles in the process, then the conflict between means and ends remains. If, alternatively, he is earnestly attempting to provide a salubrious environment for the development of human nature, then his thoughts on the future society engender a similarly troublesome conclusion.

On the one hand, Bakunin is quite enthusiastic to impart his belief that 'no scholar can teach the people or even define for himself how they will and must live on the morrow of the social revolution'.[156] This reaction towards blueprints for post-revolutionary society is quite understandable in light of his arguments against idealism. Consciousness, for Bakunin, is determined by life, not vice versa. Society, therefore, is built upon the practical experiences of everyday life. Anarchism, in this sense, is a grass-roots movement. Thus Bakunin continues by suggesting that the nature of future society 'will be determined first by the situation of each people, and secondly by the desires that manifest themselves and operate most strongly within them – not by guidance and explanations from above and not by any theories invented on the eve of the revolution'.[157] Thought, he continues, 'follows from life', and in order to alter thought one has to change the circumstances that govern one's life. 'Give the people a broad human existence,' he claims, 'and they will amaze you with the profound rationality of their ideas.'[158] On the other hand, this notion of a society designed to elicit the best out of human nature is entirely at odds with his conviction that metaphysical idealism raises the ugly prospect of social theorists forcing people into the equivalent of a Procrustean bed. Bakunin cannot have it both ways. Either he abides by his principles concerning idealism and abandons any pretence at social planning, or else he reneges on his commitments and offers a detailed insight into what he considers the best means to achieve a harmonious society in the future. There are elements in Bakunin's work to indicate that he believes in both strategies; but the overwhelming evidence leads unerringly to the conclusion that it is the latter he opts for. His concern for freedom and its relationship with human nature forces Bakunin into the development of a political theory his anarchism was supposed to abandon. Perhaps this is because he adopts what one might label a teleological conception of human nature. Once enmeshed in politics, however, he suffers the same fate that befell Proudhon. Politics releases the food that egoism feeds on. In striving to protect and invigorate human nature through an eventual absence of politics, Bakunin's concern for human nature and freedom seems to be so strong that he is forced into reintroducing politics into his own ideological framework. Consequently, his endeavours to create a sanctuary from capitalism effectively mean that his demand for liberty is constantly eroded by an increasingly authoritarian brand of politics.

Notes

1. P. Marshall, *Demanding the Impossible: A History of Anarchism*, (HarperCollins, London, 1992) pp. 263, 265 and 295. Paul Avrich concurs with Marshall's assessment that Bakunin was not a systematic thinker. See his 'Preface', in S. Dolgoff (ed.), *Bakunin on Anarchy*, (George Allen & Unwin, London, 1973) p. xiv. Rudolf Rocker argues similarly that whilst Bakunin is not a systematic author he was an original thinker. See his 'Introduction' to G.P. Maximoff (ed.), *The Political Philosophy of Bakunin: Scientific Anarchism*, (Free Press, Glencoe, 1964) pp. 21–4. E.H. Carr, in his *Michael Bakunin*, (Macmillan, London, 1937) p. 435, judges that Bakunin's 'thought is not perfectly consistent, even in the years after 1867, when it underwent no substantial change.' Aileen Kelly concurs, suggesting that 'Bakunin's activities from 1868 onwards seem to indicate acute schizophrenia.' See her *Michael Bakunin: A Study in the Psychology and Politics of Utopianism*, (Clarendon Press, Oxford, 1982) p. 193. At the outset of her text (p. 3), Kelly argues that Bakunin's contradictions stem 'not from a contempt for theoretical consistency, but from excessive attachment to it'. Richard B. Saltman, *The Social and Political Thought of Michael Bakunin*, (Greenwood Press, Connecticut, 1983) p. xi, notes the general perception 'that Bakunin lacked a coherent political theory', but goes on to argue that the consistency of Bakunin's thought stems from his 'opposition of mutual to official forms of authority . . . [thus a] close and careful analysis of Bakunin's political writings, therefore, reveals something quite different from the fragmented, internally contradictory theory attributed to him by commentators.' (pp. 163–4.) The most recent biographer of Bakunin disagrees with Saltman's interpretation. Brian Morris, in his *Bakunin: The Philosophy of Freedom*, (Black Rose Books, Montréal, 1993) p. 1, contends that 'Bakunin was not an intellectual – if anything, he was anti-intellectual – and so never produced a systematic account of his ideas in the manner of Marx or Herbert Spencer.' Despite this judgment, Morris maintains that Bakunin's collectivist anarchism 'combined liberalism, socialism and atheism into a coherent theory.' (p. 152.)

2. For those uninitiated in the problematics of historiography a useful starting-point is Quentin Skinner, 'Meaning and Understanding in the History of Ideas', in James Tully (ed.), *Meaning and Context: Quentin Skinner and his Critics*, (Polity Press, Cambridge, 1988) pp. 29–67.

3. J. Keane, 'More Theses in the Philosophy of History', in Tully, *op. cit.*, pp. 204–17.

4. J. Guillaume, 'A Biographical Sketch', in Dolgoff, *op. cit.*, p. 51.

5. Maximoff, *op. cit.*, p. 136.

6. Ibid., p. 153.

7. Dolgoff, *op. cit.*, p. 147. Italics in original.

8. Ibid., p. 91. It is worth noting that 'depends much more on' is not as strong as 'wholly the product of' which is how Bakunin refers to the relationship between humans and their environment earlier.

9. Marshall, *op. cit.*, p. 276. James Joll, *The Anarchists*, (Methuen, London, 1979) p. 82 argues similarly to Marshall that Bakunin is a materialist. Whilst this is not in doubt, it remains a moot point to

what degree if any Bakunin remained an Hegelian in elucidating his conception of freedom. George Woodcock, *Anarchism*, (Penguin, Harmondsworth, 1975) pp. 172–3, for example, argues that 'however emphatically [Bakunin] might declare himself a materialist and try to adapt his ideas to the scientific progressivism of the Darwinian age, it was still a semi-mystical vision of salvation through destruction derived from the Hegelian 1840s that dominated his development from a revolutionary nationalist into an anarchist internationalist.' Carr, *op. cit.*, p. 434 is firm in his opinion that Bakunin 'remained a Hegelian idealist'.

10. Maximoff, *op. cit.*, p. 65.
11. For a brief commentary of the meeting see Marshall, *op. cit.*, p. 269. According to Kelly, *op. cit.*, p. 46, Bakunin began studying Hegel in 1837. And we know from Bakunin himself that in 1840, whilst at the University of Berlin, he studied German metaphysics 'in which I was exclusively immersed almost to the point of insanity, seeing nothing day and night besides Hegel's categories.' See M. Bakunin, *The Confession of Michael Bakunin*, (Cornell University Press, London, 1977) p. 34. And as Carr, *op. cit.*, p. 109 states, Bakunin was 'a full-blown Young Hegelian' by 1842. At the same time Carr believes that Proudhon held principal responsibility 'for transforming Bakunin's instinctive revolt against authority into a regular anarchistic creed.' (p. 131) Contrary to this, Kelly, *op. cit.*, p. 117, opines that it was Bakunin's dislike of Marx that was the most important shaping factor in his political ideology.
12. Bakunin, *The Confession of Michael Bakunin*, p. 92. Bakunin's

confession was written at the beginning of his incarceration in the infamous Peter and Paul fortress. He spent eight years in solitary confinement. Elicited by Count Orlov, an emissary of the Tsar, the confession is addressed to Tsar Nicholas I. The work has been described as a 'highly ambivalent document [that] appears to be both a cunning ruse as well as an outright betrayal of his beliefs.' See Marshall, *op. cit.*, p. 273.

13. M. Bakunin, *Marxism, Freedom and the State*, (Freedom Press, London, 1984) p. 17.
14. Ibid., p. 17.
15. M.S. Shatz, *The Essential Works of Anarchism*, (Bantam, New York, 1971) p. 141.
16. I. Berlin, 'Two Concepts of Liberty', in his *Four Essays on Liberty*, (Oxford University Press, Oxford, 1969) p. 136. The part of the quotation within double inverted commas refers to Rousseau's *Social Contract*, Book I, Ch. 8. Crowder's argument seems indebted to Berlin. See G. Crowder, *Classical Anarchism: The Political Thought of Godwin, Proudhon, Bakunin and Kropotkin*, (Oxford University Press, Oxford, 1991) p. 125.
17. Dolgoff, *op. cit.*, p. 76.
18. Ibid., p. 236.
19. Ibid., p. 237.
20. Ibid., p. 236.
21. Crowder, *op. cit.*, p. 129.
22. Marshall, *op. cit.*, pp. 294–5.
23. Maximoff, *op. cit.*, p. 84. Bakunin wrote this in his *Federalism, Socialism, and Anti-Theologism*, published in 1867.
24. Dolgoff, *op. cit.*, p. 6.
25. Ibid., p. 5.
26. Ibid., pp. 76–7.
27. Ibid., p. 245.
28. Ibid., p. 95.
29. Marshall, *op. cit.*, p. 293.

30. Dolgoff, *op. cit.*, p. 68.
31. M. Bakunin, *Statism and Anarchy*, (Cambridge University Press, Cambridge, 1990) p. 179.
32. Joll, *op. cit.*, p. 92.
33. Quoted in ibid., pp. 91–2.
34. Bakunin, *op. cit.*, p. 137.
35. The First International is the widely used name for the first incarnation of the International Working Men's Association. The International was founded in St Martin's Hall, London on 28 September 1864. Marx was a member of the General Council from its inception, and of the Committee that was given the task of drawing up the rules of the association. Marx also sounded the death knell of the First International when, following his dispute with Bakunin at The Hague Congress in 1872, he proposed the General Council be transferred from London to New York.
36. Quoted in Joll, *op. cit.*, p. 87.
37. Maximoff, *op. cit.*, pp. 314 and 313.
38. Quoted in Dolgoff, *op. cit.*, pp. 390–1. Parentheses in the original.
39. Ibid., p. 8.
40. Bakunin's definition covered all the depressed classes. See Dolgoff, *op. cit.*, pp. 13–14. Marx's definition of the lumpenproletariat may be found in K. Marx, 'The Eighteenth Brumaire of Louis Bonaparte', in his *Surveys from Exile: Political Writings, Volume 2*, (Penguin, Harmondsworth, 1973) p. 197.
41. Dolgoff, *op. cit.*, p. 14.
42. Ibid., p. 17.
43. Ibid., pp. 8–9.
44. Ibid., p. 65.
45. Note point 3 of the St-Imier resolution above. Alternatively, see point XI of Bakunin's 'Revolutionary Catechism', in Dolgoff, *op. cit.*, p. 95. Cf. also Bakunin, *Statism and Anarchy*, pp. 45 and 49.
46. There is disagreement between commentators as to when Bakunin became an anarchist. Adjudicating over such an issue is particularly complex, if only because an individual's acquisition of the ideological status of anarchist is seldom susceptible to specific dates. However, there is some consensus that the formative years began in 1864, with Bakunin making the final transition in 1867.
47. Dolgoff, *op. cit.*, p. 74.
48. Joll, *op. cit.*, p. 70.
49. Marshall, *op. cit.*, p. 303.
50. Kelly, *op. cit.*, p. 22. Cf. Carr, *op. cit.*, p. 5.
51. Kelly, *op. cit.*, p. 61.
52. Ibid., p. 163.
53. Ibid., p. 97.
54. Note p. 79 above.
55. Bakunin, *Confession*, p. 93.
56. Ibid., pp. 118–19.
57. Ibid., p. 119.
58. Ibid., p. 127.
59. Ibid., p. 91.
60. Ibid., p. 56.
61. Dolgoff, *op. cit.*, p. 11. Kelly, *op. cit.*, p. 241 recognizes that secret societies proliferated in Europe during the 1840s. Bakunin himself presents plenty of evidence for this. See Bakunin, *op. cit.*, pp. 54, 59, 105–6 and 136.
62. Quoted in Marshall, *op. cit.*, p. 281. Founded in 1869, *L'Egalité* was the journal of the French-speaking sections of the International in Switzerland.
63. Ibid.
64. Dolgoff, *op. cit.*, p. 76.
65. P. Avrich, 'Preface', in Dolgoff, *op. cit.*, pp. xxii-xxiii. Italics in the original.
66. Ibid., p. 10.

67. Maximoff, *op. cit.*, p. 248.
68. Ibid., p. 249.
69. Dolgoff, *op. cit.*, p. 91.
70. Maximoff, *op. cit.*, p. 249.
71. Marshall, *op. cit.*, p. 272.
72. Ibid.
73. Ibid.
74. Ibid., p. 287. The reference to temperament is directed to Dolgoff. It is only fair to say that even Dolgoff himself articulates a number of serious concerns along the lines of those expressed by Marshall. See Dolgoff, *op. cit.*, p. 9.
75. Marshall, *op. cit.*, p. 305. Cf. also Dolgoff, *op. cit.*, pp. 10–11. April Carter, in her *The Political Theory of Anarchism*, (Routledge & Kegan Paul, London, 1971) pp. 76–7, questions Nomad's thesis (with which Marshall agrees) that Bakunin foreshadowed Lenin. See M. Nomad, *Apostles of Revolution*, (Secker & Warburg, London, 1939).
76. Marshall, *op. cit.*, p. 283.
77. Dolgoff, *op. cit.*, p. 13. A. Masters in *Bakunin: The Father of Anarchism* (Sidgwick & Jackson, London, 1974) p. 203 follows Dolgoff's line.
78. Dolgoff, *op. cit.*, p. 13.
79. Ibid., pp. 381–2.
80. P. Avrich, *Bakunin and Nechaev*, (Freedom Press, London, 1987) p. 14.
81. Marshall, *op. cit.*, p. 284.
82. Quoted in ibid., p. 284. Morris, *op. cit.*, argues that the *Catechism* 'was essentially written by Sergei Nechaev' (p. 30), but confesses later that 'Bakunin may well have had a hand in the drafting of the document' (p. 45). Kelly, *op. cit.*, pp. 268–9 observes correctly that Bakunin's reference to 'your Catechism', in his letter of 2 June 1870 to Nechaev, does not constitute proof that Bakunin played no part in the document's authorship.
83. One example of this is provided by G.D.H. Cole, *History of Socialist Thought: Marxism and Anarchism 1850–1890*, (Macmillan, London, 1964) p. 227.
84. Bakunin, *Statism and Anarchy*, p. 133.
85. Marshall, *op. cit.*, p. 298.
86. Dolgoff, *op. cit.*, p. 270.
87. Bakunin, *op. cit.*, p. 135.
88. Dolgoff, *op. cit.*, p. 74.
89. I emphasize *may* because there is little evidence other than Dolgoff's own assertion, which in itself cannot count as evidence, to indicate what Bakunin himself actually intended the document to be.
90. Marshall, *op. cit.*, p. 276 argues that the three related works, *The International Family, Revolutionary Catechism* and *National Catechism*, known collectively as *Principles and Organisation of the International Brotherhood* (1866), 'not only offers the most detailed glimpse of Bakunin's version of a free society but also sketches the prototype of all his subsequent secret societies.' According to Morris, *op. cit.*, p. 31, Bakunin's *Revolutionary Catechism* is 'the first outline of his anarchist creed.' Kelly, *op. cit.*, p. 177, argues that Bakunin's *Principles and Organisation of the International Brotherhood* 'contains the most detailed outline of his ideal of human society to be found anywhere in his work.'
91. Marshall, *op. cit.*, p. 277.
92. Quoted in Dolgoff, *op. cit.*, p. 73.
93. Ibid., pp. 76–7. Emphasis in original. Bakunin makes a similar point about federalism obviating centralization in his *Statism and Anarchy*, p. 44.
94. Bakunin, *Statism and Anarchy*, p. 24. Emphasis in original.

95. Dolgoff, *op. cit.*, pp. 224 and 221.
96. Bakunin, *op. cit.*, p. 13.
97. Dolgoff, *op. cit.*, p. 221.
98. Bakunin, *op. cit.*, p. 179.
99. Ibid., p. 137.
100. Ibid., p. 150.
101. Ibid., p. 178. Emphasis in original.
102. Maximoff, *op. cit.*, p. 249. It has to be said, though, that in light of Bakunin's own position on revolutionary dictatorships he appears oblivious to his own conception of human nature.
103. Ibid.
104. Obviously, the two are not entirely unrelated. In effect it is seen as a malleable concept capable of both good and evil, the predominance of which is largely due to environmental circumstances.
105. Carr, *op. cit.*, p. 436.
106. A. Lehning (ed.), *Michael Bakunin: Selected Writings*, (Cape, London, 1973) p. 264.
107. Dolgoff, *op. cit.*, p. 78. Emphasis in original. The list of conditions drawn up by Bakunin constitutes the vast bulk of the *Revolutionary Catechism* itself.
108. Ibid., p. 57. It ought to be noted that this quotation is drawn from *The Reaction in Germany*, published in 1842. This is the period during which commentators suggest Bakunin is indebted to idealism. Hence the reference to eternal Spirit, which might sit somewhat uneasily with his later materialism.
109. Bakunin, *op. cit.*, p. 136. Bakunin had called for a Universal Federation of European Republics as early as 1848 in his *Appeal to the Slavs*. See Dolgoff, *op. cit.*, pp. 67–8.
110. Dolgoff, *op. cit.*, p. 78. Italics in original.
111. Maximoff, *op. cit.*, p. 275.
112. Dolgoff, *op. cit.*, pp. 78–9.
113. Ibid., p. 8.
114. Bakunin, *Statism and Anarchy*, p. 198.
115. See, for example, Marshall, *op. cit.*, p. 282.
116. Ibid., p. 277.
117. Ibid., p. 278.
118. Dolgoff, *op. cit.*, p. 89.
119. Ibid., pp. 92–3. Perhaps one could also argue that given the humanizing aspect of labour, collective labour would further increase the humanization of both humankind and society.
120. Ibid., p. 93.
121. Ibid., p. 89. See also ibid., pp. 82 and 79.
122. Marshall, *op. cit.*, p. 299. Whilst Marshall shares my reservations concerning the possible development of tyranny and oppression in Bakunin's future society, he does not seem to allow his doubts to question Bakunin's standing as an anarchist.
123. Dolgoff, *op. cit.*, pp. 80–1. The comments within parentheses belong to Bakunin. The insistence on labour is rather ironic since Bakunin himself would have failed miserably to meet this criterion.
124. Ibid., p. 81.
125. By this is meant that Bakunin is operating a conception of human nature in which he ascribes a purpose or end to human existence. In depicting labour as essential to human well-being, Bakunin may be constructing a social vision that encourages or promotes this end or purpose, authoritarian strategies notwithstanding.
126. Maximoff, *op. cit.*, pp. 85–6.
127. Ibid., p. 87.
128. Ibid.
129. Lehning, *op. cit.*, pp. 146–7. Cf. Maximoff, *op. cit.*, pp. 244–5.
130. Dolgoff, *op. cit.*, p. 81.
131. Ibid., p. 80.
132. Maximoff, *op. cit.*, p. 345.

133. Dolgoff, *op. cit.*, p. 82.
134. Ibid., p. 79. The comments within parentheses are Bakunin's own.
135. Ibid., p. 84. The comments within parentheses belong to Bakunin. It has to be said that a denial of some mechanism of appeal is an aspect of Bakunin's society that does not lend itself towards an expansion of justice.
136. Ibid., p. 83.
137. Ibid., pp. 82–3. Emphasis in the original.
138. Ibid., p. 83.
139. Ibid.
140. The catechism he refers to is obviously the text itself, his own *Revolutionary Catechism*. See ibid., p. 84.
141. Ibid.
142. Maximoff, *op. cit.*, p. 345. The comments within parentheses are those of Bakunin.
143. See ibid. One should also imagine that on the basis of Bakunin's contextualist assumptions concerning human nature, it may take some time before the residual traces of capitalism have finally been eliminated from human nature, thereby making anarchy possible.
144. Marshall, *op. cit.*, p. 278.
145. Dolgoff, *op. cit.*, p. 83. Italics in original.
146. Ibid., p. 79. Parentheses in the original.
147. Ibid., p. 93.
148. Ibid., p. 94.
149. Ibid. Emphasis in the original.
150. This and the previous quotation are drawn from ibid., pp. 94–5.
151. Quoted in Bakunin, *op. cit.*, p. xxxiii.
152. See J-J. Rousseau, *The Social Contract*, (Penguin, Harmondsworth, 1968) p. 64 [Book I, Ch. 7].
153. Maximoff, *op. cit.*, p. 158.
154. Dolgoff, *op. cit.*, p. 76. Italics in original.
155. Bakunin, *op. cit.*, p. xxxiv.
156. Ibid., pp. 198–9.
157. Ibid., p. 199.
158. Ibid., p. 207.

5

Kropotkin: Mutal Aid and Anarchy

Of all the classical anarchists it is perhaps Kropotkin who corresponds most closely to informed perceptions of anarchism. Martin Miller, for example, has described him 'as the world's leading anarchist theoretician'.[1] Certainly, when compared to Proudhon and Bakunin, there are fewer doubts associated with the standing or status of Kropotkin as an anarchist. Nevertheless, doubts persist and there are strong grounds for contesting the consistency of Kropotkin's anarchist ideology. Although all three social anarchists under review endorse a conception of human nature that is comprised of both sociability and egoism, the emphasis on egoism in Proudhon and Bakunin, and its associated difficulties, renders it on occasion truly problematical to conceive of either as truly anarchist. Seemingly, Kropotkin's writings constitute a watershed in the development of anarchist ideology. Upon initial inspection, Kropotkin does not seem to suffer from the problems that arise from the emphasis on egoism that permeates the works of Proudhon and Bakunin. And whereas both Proudhon and Bakunin have evinced very telling critiques against the state, Kropotkin develops a significantly more positive and constructive aspect of social and political thought. Kropotkin is unlike Bakunin in that there is no accent upon the urge to destruction nor on violence. Although Kropotkin may see violence as necessary, it is to be employed very sparingly. The significant fact is that it was, as Woodcock argues, 'the positive, constructive aspect of anarchism' that appealed to him.[2] It is here that Kropotkin begins to forge a new identity for anarchism; and the hallmark of this anarchism is the synthesis which it undergoes with communism. It is this which, purportedly, distinguishes Kropotkin from his predecessors. Distribution of goods and services according to need, rather than according to labour performed, separates Kropotkin from both Proudhon's mutualism and Bakunin's collectivism. At least, that is how it is usually seen. It is my contention that Kropotkin is closer to his predecessors, and their failings, than is traditionally thought.

The Methodology of Mutual Aid

Kropotkin does differ from his anarchist ancestors in at least one respect: he is much more consistent and coherent than either Proudhon or Bakunin. In the works of these earlier writers, consistency in particular is often buried under a mountain of paradox and contradiction. This is not to say that Kropotkin's essays are unblemished by apparent contradictions. Indeed, given the multifarious nature of Kropotkin's life and studies, it is hardly surprising that the unity of his thought occasionally wanes. Rather, it is simply to suggest that the works of Kropotkin bear a degree of cohesion that other anarchists find difficult to equal. The unity of Kropotkin's work derives largely from his endeavours to establish anarchism on a sound philosophical and scientific basis. Much of this stems from his investigations into the concept of evolution, which were a major factor in the development of his understanding of the world and the creatures that inhabit it. In attempting to place anarchism on this philosophical footing, Kropotkin's thoughts on human nature are clearly dependent on his observations on the process of evolution; an unsurprising occupation given the scientific revelations of his age.

As with many other theories encountered in the natural sciences, evolution is subject to competing interpretations. Aside from Kropotkin's own observations on the matter, his chief mentor in this debate was undoubtedly Darwin. His most notable opponent is T.H. Huxley. The objective which Kropotkin is trying to secure in this debate is simple: the discrediting of the one-eyed interpretations of Darwin's work dispensed by his antagonists – and Kropotkin chastises Darwin for his failure to rebuke such exegeses – in order to provide a fuller and more valid account of evolutionary theory. It was a target that Kropotkin had to aim for if his belief in anarchism was to be maintained. Without some effort to refute the notion of perpetual struggle for existence, Kropotkin's vision of a co-operative, communist future society would perish before leaving the womb of his imagination.

Chronology dictates that it would be wrong to assume that Kropotkin's initial collation of biological facts in Siberia was coloured by a belief in anarchism.[3] At this stage in his career Kropotkin was not yet an anarchist. Siberia may have prepared him to become an anarchist,[4] but the development of his anarchism did not begin to occur until his first visit to Western Europe, during which Kropotkin came into contact with members of the International in 1872. During his sojourn in the Jura mountains, Kropotkin's political persuasion was irrevocably moulded. Hence he recalls that the

> theoretical aspects of anarchism, as they were beginning to be expressed in the Jura Federation, especially by Bakunin; the criticisms of state socialism – the fear of an economic despotism, far more dangerous than the merely political despotism – which I heard formulated there; and the revolutionary character of the agitation, appealed strongly to my mind. But the equalitarian relations which I found in the Jura Mountains, the independence of thought and expression which I saw developing in the workers, and their unlimited devotion to the cause appealed far more strongly to my feelings; and when I came away from the mountains, after a week's stay with the watchmakers, my views upon socialism were settled. I was an anarchist.[5]

His observations of nature and animal life in Siberia may have predisposed his mind to a favourable reception of anarchist ideas, but once he accepted these ideals it was imperative that he defend his original interpretation of the 'facts' of evolution; otherwise the foundation upon which the edifice of his anarchist beliefs was constructed would begin to crumble before his own eyes.

Although Kropotkin's scientific endeavours were not conducted under the aegis of an anarchist outlook, there are some very real doubts as to whether his research was undertaken with an entirely open mind. As both scientist and ideologist Kropotkin is susceptible to bias. Just as ideologists may be inclined to tender their preferred political doctrine as the most conclusive account of reality, so scientists may be willing to ignore relevant facts if they contradict the evidence that supports their theory. One of the first to question Kropotkin's scientific objectivity was the Italian anarchist, Malatesta. Recalling the nature of Kropotkin's investigative practices, he writes that his

> normal procedure was to start with a hypothesis and then look for the facts that would confirm it – which may be a good method for discovering something new; but what happened, and quite unintentionally, was that he did not see the ones which invalidated his hypothesis.
>
> He could not bring himself to admit a fact, and often not even to consider it, if he had not managed to explain it, that is to fit it into his system.[6]

Some years later Roger Baldwin alerts a possibly unsuspecting audience to the same problem.[7] When concentrating on his geographical works, however, Kropotkin reversed the methodology, eliciting facts before developing theories. According to Baldwin it was the importance Kropotkin attached to social issues that led him 'to ignore or brush aside the facts that contradicted his interpretations'.[8] Hence Baldwin's contention that whilst some parts of Kropotkin's social scientific writings are indebted to a scientific methodology other elements are tinged by preconceptions.[9] Such circumstances may be unavoidable, for as Chalmers elaborates, the sin of selective interpretation of evidence is difficult to avoid when engrossed in an inductivist endeavour to locate the facts. In this sense, science is little different from ideology. The theoretical framework which serves as the departure point for observation is so composed that it directs, latently or otherwise, the perception of what are determined as central facts or mere epiphenomena. Thus Chalmers argues that, for 'the most naïve of inductivists, the basis of scientific knowledge is provided by observations made by an unprejudiced and unbiased observer. If interpreted anything like literally, this position is absurd and untenable.'[10] Observations and experiments are performed under the auspices of some theoretical matrix, and the operational guidelines imposed by this intellectual scaffold delimit the parameters of relevancy within any experimental situation. Given the interrelationship of theory and practice, the inductivist position is, as Chalmers remarks, 'undermined by the fact that the sharp distinction between observation and theory cannot be maintained because observation, or rather the statements resulting from observation, are permeated by theory'.[11]

As a scientist engaged in the observation of nature one would like to think that an objective and disinterested approach was adopted by Kropotkin. As has been indicated, however, this may be impossible to achieve. Possibly, Kropotkin's own observations were conditioned by his own knowledge and experience of the climate and physical environment of the region in which he conducted his investigations. More significantly, as Daniel P. Todes has elaborated, Kropotkin was undoubtedly influenced by the general reaction to the Darwinian metaphor and its Malthusian overtones amongst Russian intellectuals, a reaction that reflected two factors of particular importance to Russian evolutionists. First, unlike Darwin and Wallace, who had collected much of their data from the tropical forests of the equator, Russian biologists were more accustomed to researching upon a vast continental plain that was subject to violent fluctuations in climatic conditions. Additionally, in associating his concept of the struggle with Malthus, 'Darwin almost assured the skepticism of his Russian audience.'[12] The cultural applicability of Darwin's metaphor and Malthus' argument seemed rather inappropriate to a Russian population that was comparatively small and occupied a huge territory.

Resolution of the debate is compounded by the very nature of the research. Given the obvious implications of the Darwinian thesis for humankind, which soon attracted the social Darwinists, it is hard to imagine how the arguments would not stray from the descriptive to the prescriptive. Concepts of human nature are normative constructs and are, therefore, outside the realms of pure description. This is not to say that Kropotkin completely disregarded all facts contrary to his own conception of human nature. In enunciating his own account of mutual aid, Kropotkin accepts that the struggle for existence may be found but insists that mutual aid is as important in nature as struggle. Thus Kropotkin regards his own text as an exposition of *one* of the factors of evolution. This is a reasonable point. Kropotkin's conception of mutual aid, first elaborated properly in the late 1880s after his reading of Kessler whilst interned at Clairvaux in 1883, represents only one particular gloss on the theory of evolution. Nothing more or less could be expected. Kropotkin was engaged in an ideological battle, in which he was determined to correct the imbalance created by the neo-Malthusians. To do this he was obliged to defend the conception of mutual aid that was crucial to his accepted political beliefs. From start to finish it would seem that his observations and arguments were coloured in one way or another. That *may* jeopardize his standing as an objective scientist, if such a thing exists, but it can hardly be used to discredit his ideological inclinations.

Mutual Aid and the Struggle for Existence

Kropotkin himself was keen to justify his own argument by appealing to Darwin's texts. If victory was to be attained over the neo-Malthusians it had to be sought by way of the corroboration of Darwin. Indeed, it seems likely that this was the only viable method to convince his contemporaries that notions such as Spencer's 'survival of the fittest' were at best misleading and at worst mistaken. Vindication, then, could only materialize by way of a correct interpretation of the texts. With that in mind, Kropotkin set out to explore the Vitim regions of Siberia with his friend and companion Poliakóv, an eminent Russian zoologist. Despite travelling for three months in this area, their fieldwork yielded little substantial evidence to support Darwin's thesis. Kropotkin recalls how they 'vainly looked for the keen competition between animals of the same species which the reading of Darwin's work had prepared us to expect'.[13] Lack of empirical evidence led Kropotkin, as it would have led any scientist, to question Darwin's emphasis on competition. These doubts were expressed most forcibly in his *Mutual Aid* (1902).

> No one will deny that there is, within each species, a certain amount of real competition for food – at least at certain periods. But the question is, whether competition is carried on to the extent admitted by Darwin, or even by Wallace; and whether this competition has played, in the evolution of the animal kingdom, the part assigned to it.
>
> The idea which permeates Darwin's work is certainly one of real competition going on within each animal group for food, safety, and possibility of leaving an offspring. . . . But when we look for real proofs of that competition, we must confess that we do not find them sufficiently convincing.[14]

Knowledge of the hostility of winter storms, frosts and inundations in northern Eurasia and experience of the inclemency of nature in general led Kropotkin to a recognition of 'the overwhelming importance in Nature of what Darwin described as "the natural checks to over-multiplication", in comparison to the struggle between individuals of the same species for the means of subsistence, which may go on here and there, to some limited extent, but never attains the importance of the former'.[15]

The challenge to Darwin and his followers, such as Huxley, is that they are wide of the mark when identifying competition as that factor which plays *the* leading role in evolution. There is, Kropotkin believes, more than one important or significant element in the theory of evolution; and he considers it his task to correct the imbalance. Bearing in mind the intellectual climate of the age, it is easy to understand the importance Kropotkin attaches to the repudiation of his opponents' views. Besides, the nature of the argument and the flavour of the language employed in this debate were nothing short of contentious, and as such were bound to elicit considerable criticism. Huxley's view, for instance, is presented in an article entitled 'The Struggle for Existence: A Programme', published in the periodical *The Nineteenth Century* in February 1888. 'From the point of view of the moralist,' Huxley comments, 'the animal is on about the same level as a gladiator's show. The creatures are fairly well treated, and set to fight; whereby the strongest, the swiftest, and the cunningest live to fight another day. The spectator has no need to turn his thumb down, as no quarter is given.' His discussion of humankind is similarly grim: 'the weakest and stupidest went to the wall, while the toughest and shrewdest, those who were best fitted to cope with their circumstances, but not the best in another way, survived. Life was a continuous free fight, and beyond the limited and temporary relations of the family, the Hobbesian war of each against all was the normal state of existence.'[16]

Kropotkin is exasperated by the hyperbole of Huxley, whom he denounces as being as inadequate as Rousseau. For where Rousseau saw nothing bad in nature, Huxley sees nothing but blood and gore. Kropotkin's ire is further inflamed by the Rousseauean implications of Huxley's anthropology. Kropotkin simply cannot accept that the 'first men who substituted the state of mutual peace for that of mutual war, whatever the motive which impelled them to take that step, created society'.[17] For Kropotkin, humans were never engaged in some battle for survival, largely isolated from other human beings. Humans are and always have been social creatures. Humans and society are commensurate and inseparable. Humans could not have created society because 'society existed before Man'.[18] After dismissing Rousseau's philosophical anthropology, Kropotkin insists further that the Hobbesian dimensions of Huxley's analysis are also at fault. It would be extremely odd if he did not, as the notion of mutual aid ordains the repudiation. The connotations of mutual aid invite an open rebuff of the inferred conception of human nature in Hobbes' state of nature. In developing the Rousseauean and Hobbesian dimensions of Darwin's concept of the struggle for existence, Kropotkin asserts that Huxley has deliberately compressed the wider meaning of Darwin's idea. Permeating Huxley's analysis is a conception of the individual as the focal point for competition. But Kropotkin argues that Darwin does not restrict the concept of the struggle for existence to a competition between individuals. Rather, he broadens the notion to include groups or species. Kropotkin defends his thesis by suggesting that Darwin, in his original work, neglected to outline with sufficient strength the metaphorical basis of the image of the struggle for existence. Unfortunately, Darwin died before he was able to set the record straight. Events, inescapably, dictated Kropotkin's response. Accordingly, he seeks to redress the imbalance fostered by those he believed distorted Darwin's message. He attempts this by locating alternative evidence. In place of the struggle for existence, for which there was a dearth of supporting evidence to be found during his forays in Siberia, Kropotkin discovers an abundance of mutual aid. As a factor of evolution it is manifested in a myriad species, but nowhere is this more so than among ants. Whilst there may be wars between different species, mutual aid, self-devotion and self-sacrifice are the rule within the ant's community. 'The ants and termites,' writes Kropotkin, 'have renounced the "Hobbesian war", and they are the better for it.'[19]

Kropotkin's idea of mutual aid was derived from the Russian biologist, Karl Kessler. It was whilst in prison at Clairvaux that Kropotkin came across a lecture delivered by Kessler in 1880. Kessler's work provided the key that was to unlock the door of the evolutionary debate in which Kropotkin was soon to become deeply entangled. As Kropotkin relates through his *Memoirs* (1899),

> I found in a lecture by a Russian zoölogist, Professor Kessler, a true expression of the law of struggle for life. 'Mutual aid,' he said in that lecture, 'is as much a law of nature as mutual struggle; but for the *progressive* evolution of the species the former is far more important than the latter.' These few words -- contained for me the key of the whole problem.[20]

As Kropotkin realized, however, rectification of the imbalance imposed through neo-Malthusian interpretations was only available through reference to Darwin. Whilst acknowledging his debt to Kessler, Kropotkin is keen to inform his reader that he also draws substantiation for his conception of mutual aid from Darwin. In *The Descent of Man* (1871), argues Kropotkin, Darwin indicated that another factor was at work alongside mutual struggle, that of mutual support within species. Having found the material he was searching for, Kropotkin was now in a position to employ the authority of Darwin in his critique of Huxley. 'Darwin,' he declares, 'was quite right when he saw in man's social qualities the chief factor for his further evolution, and Darwin's vulgarisers are entirely wrong when they maintain the contrary.'[21]

It is at this juncture that the time has arrived to take stock of this debate. It seems important to do so for a number of reasons. First, one should note the manner in which Kropotkin's argument unfolds. Appeal is made extensively to *The Descent of Man* rather than *The Origin of Species* (1859). It is from the former rather than the latter that Kropotkin builds his case against the 'vulgarisers' of Darwin.

Subsequently, one is forced to ask whether this is simply another instance of Kropotkin's selective interpretation of evidence to suit his own designs? On reflection it is an accusation that is hard to resist, if only because Kropotkin himself has admitted that there is little headway to be made from Darwin's earlier work. The first edition of The Origin of Species confirms Kropotkin's fears that Darwin relies very heavily on a tight interpretation of the struggle for existence. Whilst it is true that Darwin wishes to impress upon his reader that he intends to 'use the term Struggle for Existence in a large and metaphorical sense', it soon becomes obvious that his actual employment of the phrase is rather more conservative.[22] So, although the author acknowledges that there are three mediums within which the struggle occurs, (within and between species, and with the environment), it is the former which becomes foremost in Darwin's narration of the tale. As he puts it himself, 'the struggle almost invariably will be most severe between the individuals of the same species, for they frequent the same districts, require the same food, and are exposed to the same dangers'.[23]

Confronted by a scarcity of desirable material Kropotkin is forced to locate it elsewhere; hence his reliance on the later exposition of evolution. Even if he is guilty of a proclivity to select only that which favours his own case, it may be too easy to overemphasize the significance of this. The observation and procurement of evidence may have an innate bias that one cannot ignore, as Darwin himself seems to recognize.[24] Whether or not one accepts this poor apology for Kropotkin's lack of disinterest, there is one thing that emerges from this that appears to be undeniably true. It constitutes another principal reason for the résumé of this debate, and may be characterized in the following fashion. The development of Kropotkin's mutual aid thesis is essential to the success of his wider political theory. For without the foundation of mutual aid his anarchist-communist philosophy is deprived of the prerequisite that ensures its survival. The conception of mutual aid, as explained in the text Mutual Aid underpins the anarchist-communist framework of The Conquest of Bread (1892).[25] Without the standing of the former the latter would collapse. Were he to allow the victory of the struggle for existence, The Conquest of Bread would represent little other than the muted cry of the vanquished. The integrity of Kropotkin's anarchist ideology is dependent upon the successful execution of the mutual aid thesis. Kropotkin himself was aware of this fact, as his 'Introduction' to Mutual Aid illustrates.

It was necessary to indicate the overwhelming importance which sociable habits play in Nature and in the progressive evolution of both the animal species and human beings: to prove that they secure to animals a better protection from their enemies, very often facilities for getting food (winter provisions, migrations, etc.), longevity, and therefore a greater facility for the development of intellectual faculties; and that they have given to men, in addition to the same advantages, the possibility of working out those institutions which have enabled mankind to survive in its hard struggle against Nature, and to progress, notwithstanding all the vicissitudes of its history.[26]

Mutual Aid and Sociability

Despite the rather unpleasant aftertaste that the notion of a struggle for existence must have left in Kropotkin's mouth (if only because it jeopardized the feasibility of his anarchist doctrine), he was not in a position to ignore it completely. As mutual aid is a factor in evolution, then so is the struggle for existence. 'Sociability,' he remarks, 'is as much a law of nature as mutual struggle.'[27] His confidence in this argument is derived from the knowledge he accumulated through his own observations, as well as from other sources, which leads him to conclude that although mutual aid must be prepared to accept the presence of another player in this evolutionary process 'it most probably has a far greater importance, inasmuch as it favours the development of such habits and characters as insure the maintenance and further development of the species, together with the greatest amount of welfare and enjoyment of life for the individual, with the least waste of energy'.[28] Provision for the possibility of mutual aid was furnished by Darwin himself. Although not elaborated as directly as Kropotkin would have liked, it seems that socialization provides the integrating factor between the origin and nature of humankind and the process of sexual selection. The construction of social relations, particularly if they lead to beneficial adaptations to the environment, by their very nature supply the bedrock of that which is known as mutual aid. As Anthony Flew has highlighted, Darwin's 'account of the struggle for existence in the natural world leaves abundant room for *mutual aid* between members both of the same species and of different species'.[29] The one does not preclude the other, it is simply a matter of emphasis.

For Kropotkin, the evidence for mutual aid is incontestable and irresistible. It is evident among birds, being displayed in their mass migrations in which thousands will congregate at a specific location, waiting until their number is sufficient before embarking upon their airborne journey. It is present also in mammals, especially in the social species which overwhelmingly outweigh the carnivores that do not associate.[30] Apes and monkeys also exhibit mutual support and mutual protection within their societies. Nothing is further from the truth, for Kropotkin, than the imagined animal kingdom dominated by vicious predators sinking their teeth into the warm flesh of their victims. Life in societies is taken to represent the supreme defence against the struggle for existence. Sociability is that eminent social faculty which constitutes the primary factor of evolution; an agent of evolution that facilitates the most parsimonious securement of the well-being of the species. Put quite simply, life in societies ensures survival. According to Kropotkin, it

> enables the feeblest insects, the feeblest birds, and the feeblest mammals to resist, or to protect themselves from, the most terrible birds and beasts of prey; it permits longevity; it enables the species to rear its progeny with the least waste of energy and to maintain its numbers albeit a very slow birth rate; it enables the gregarious animals to migrate in search of new abodes. Therefore, while fully admitting that force, swiftness, protective colours, cunningness, and endurance to hunger and cold, which are mentioned by Darwin and Wallace, are so many qualities making the individual, or the species, the fittest under certain circumstances, we maintain that under *any* circumstances sociability is the greatest advantage in the struggle for life.[31]

But what is mutual aid? What Kropotkin terms mutual aid is what Darwin would regard as a 'permanent instinct'; and these instincts, such as 'maternal love' or 'mutual sympathy', are, according to Kropotkin's interpretation of Darwin, more permanently at work in social animals than even self-preservation. It is mutual aid that will insure that humanity progresses 'in the direction of putting the wants of the individual *above* the valuation of the services he has rendered, or might render, to society; in considering society as a whole, so intimately connected together that a service rendered to any individual is a service rendered to the whole society'.[32] Humankind may be the product of both its congenital instincts and its education, but its actions are directed by the benevolent hand of mutual aid. Inherited through the process of evolution, mutual aid has acquired a psychological dimension. It is almost as if mutual aid is a psychological drive that compels us to act for the good of our neighbour and therefore the good of society. Human actions are piloted by a consciousness of the individual's shared identity with his or her fellow human beings. In Marxist terminology it would probably be explained through the recognition that individuals' actions correspond to the consciousness of their species-being. And as Kropotkin accentuates, these 'actions in which men are guided by their mutual-aid inclinations constitute so great a part of our daily intercourse that if a stop to such actions could be put all further ethical progress would be stopped at once. Human society itself could not be maintained for even so much as the lifetime of one single generation.'[33] Mutual aid, acting through sociability, is responsible for delimiting the boundaries of the physical struggle whilst simultaneously expanding the potentiality 'for the development of better moral feelings'.[34] But if mutual aid is the basis for morality, which will be discussed more fully below, then it has to extend the parameters of that morality beyond the concerns of love and sympathy. For human society, constructed around the practices of mutual aid, is grounded in the consciousness of human solidarity. 'It is the unconscious recognition of the force that is borrowed by each man from the practice of mutual aid; of the close dependency of every one's happiness upon the happiness of all; and of the sense of justice, or equity, which brings the individual to consider the rights of every other individual as equal to his own.'[35]

There is some mixing of the differing philosophies of materialism and idealism here. Evolution may well have endowed humans with some permanent instinct, but that is only properly brought to bear through a consciousness of one's own position in society vis-à-vis the position of others. Contemplating such matters in his *Ethics* (1924), Kropotkin maintains that modern science has demonstrated that humankind does not constitute the centre of the universe. Conversely, it 'has taught him that without the whole the "ego" is nothing; that our "I" cannot even come to a self-definition without the "thou"'.[36] An analogous reference to Hegelian philosophy establishes what may seem to be a symbiotic relationship in Kropotkin's theory. That is, the elaboration of the idealist dimension of mutual aid is an outgrowth of and is therefore dependent upon shared social instincts. Likewise, these instincts can only surface through the medium of consciousness. Without the one the other would be severely debilitated. In this sense, evolution has equipped us with the ability and propensity to engage in mutual aid. Of this Kropotkin was convinced. Mutual aid, he argues, is all around us. One only has to recognize the numerous institutions which are founded upon mutual aid to appreciate the extent of its actions. Kropotkin's favourite example was the Royal National Lifeboat Institution, but many others could be cited even today. For instance, mountain rescue teams, the St John's Ambulance Brigade, trade unions, and the almost innumerable clubs, societies, organizations, alliances and associations that satisfy some of the needs of human beings. So widespread are such institutions, so extensive the practice of mutual aid, Kropotkin avers, that, 'in short, there is not a single direction in which men exercise their faculties without combining together for the prosecution of some common aim'.[37] In practice, mutual aid is most obvious within the activities and remit of the voluntary rescue services. Evidence of their often heroic endeavours to save lives is sufficient proof, for Kropotkin, that mutual aid is inherent in human nature. For Kropotkin, such acts exhibit 'the gist of human psychology'. And it is this psychology which dictates that humans cannot bear 'to hear appeals for help, and not respond to them. . . . The sophisms of the brain cannot resist the mutual-aid feeling, because this feeling has been nurtured by thousands of years of human social life and hundreds of thousands of years of pre-human life in societies.'[38]

Having formerly repudiated the notion of a Rousseauean emergence of society elaborated within Huxley's argument for the struggle for existence, it would appear that Kropotkin is not averse to accepting the analysis of human nature offered in Rousseau's second *Discourse*. There is no reference to Rousseau at this stage in Kropotkin's text, but given the resemblance of the two renditions it is difficult to believe that Kropotkin was not influenced by Rousseau. Even if Rousseau offers an account of a pre-social human nature, which Kropotkin obviously could not accept, the affinity of the analysis denotes correspondence rather than coincidence.[39] Utilizing a language that is echoed by Kropotkin, Rousseau suggests, in his *Discourse on the Origins of Inequality* (1754), that humankind's one natural virtue is compassion, a disposition that 'serves to moderate the ardour he has for his own wellbeing by giving him an innate repugnance against seeing a fellow creature suffer'. In fact it is so much a part of nature that no animal ever 'passes the corpse of a creature of its own species without distress'.[40] This sympathy that is shown for the suffering of others leads beyond the good of the individual to the good of the species. As Rousseau's anthropology reveals, it is 'very certain that pity is a natural sentiment which, by moderating in each individual the activity of self-love, contributes to the mutual preservation of the whole species'.[41] However, the initial disagreement between the two thinkers still holds good. Kropotkin's rejection of the Rousseauean notion of a pre-social primitive existence leads to a further difference on the success of mutual aid in the state. In Rousseau's illustration of events, pre-social human nature is severely corrupted upon individuals' entrance into civil society and their subsequent familiarization with the mechanisms of the state. Kropotkin, on the other hand, maintains that the excesses of the state have done nothing to diminish the efficacy of mutual aid in human nature. The powers of the state have failed to 'weed out the feeling of human solidarity, deeply lodged in men's understanding and heart, because it has been nurtured by all our preceding evolution'.[42] Thus, whereas both Rousseau and Kropotkin agree that mutual aid or sympathy is a pre-human phenomenon, it is only the latter who believes that it constitutes the basis of social institutions.

Mutual Aid and Morality

To some the above may be a trifle confusing, if only because it seems difficult to resolve the apparent puzzle of the coterminous existence of a repressive state with Kropotkin's conception of mutual aid. To understand the nature of this seemingly paradoxical predicament it is necessary to know something about the relationship between mutual aid and morality. After identifying the presence and role of mutual aid in evolution, with regard in particular to the survival of the species and adaptation to the environment, Kropotkin proceeds to explain why social instincts lead to the development of morality in society. Contrary to Hobbes and Rousseau, it is indubitable, for Kropotkin, that humans are a social animal, and that this is the origin of morality. Society, for Kropotkin, is not an artificial creation but existed long before humankind staked its claim on the planet. Morality is a consequence of combination in societies. And as one might expect, this process commences ahead of humanity's entry into the evolutionary network. 'No animal society is possible without resulting in a growth of certain moral habits of mutual support and even self-sacrifice for the common well-being.'[43] Consequently, when living in the tribe or clan, the primitive individual is already beginning to work out what Kropotkin designates as 'the primary foundations of morality'. Humankind is becoming conscious of its morality. The so-called savage is not, as Rousseau depicts, a noble, virtuous creature; nor, as Hobbes announces, the paradigm of barbarity. Rather the primitive individual is the proprietor of one fundamental quality, according to Kropotkin. The individual 'identifies his own existence with that of his tribe; and without that quality mankind never would have attained the level it has attained now'.[44] Repulsing the Rousseauean notion of moral autonomy, Kropotkin stresses that humankind does not become moral by acting in accordance with the command of law, regardless of whether the law be prescribed by the state or oneself. Rather, human morality has its genesis in the fact that the individual identifies his or her own existence with that of the tribe or wider collective. Morality flows from the consciousness of the individual's shared identity with his or her fellows. Sociality, for Kropotkin, is inherent in human nature. There was no need, as Hobbes signals, to create a 'social covenant' or a 'Leviathan-state' to promote the growth of sociality.

Having ascertained the significance of the social context of morality there remains one question to address: if humans are naturally moral, why does the state exist? The argument has been invoked most recently by Peter Marshall. As he sees it, Kropotkin is facing a dilemma. If humans are naturally social, co-operative and moral, then how does one account for the existence of inequalities, which in many instances may be sanctioned by the state?[45] One way to respond to this is by examining the notion of potential. According to Kinna, the spirit of mutual aid becomes habit in the right environment. 'As it does so the biological impulse gives rise to particular ethical sentiments.'[46] And it is these ethical sentiments that culminate in morality. Seemingly, the environment can serve as a trigger or potential that can spark into life a natural sense of morality. But given the wrong social context, namely the state, mutual aid and morality become increasingly moribund. Attainment of the correct environment then becomes a matter of will. However, this strikes a discordant note with Marshall. In light of Kropotkin's endeavours to establish anarchism on a scientific footing, in which his evolutionary theory contributes substantially to that effort, the anarchist has, according to Marshall, become too fatalistic. Whilst agreeing that Kropotkin was essentially right in viewing anarchy as natural order, Marshall contends that 'he erred by talking of nature as if it were a kind of providence. By insisting that anarchy is a tendency within a mechanical universe which must inevitably triumph, he underestimated the role of creative will.'[47]

Certainly, Kropotkin should not be regarded as naïvely optimistic, but the reason why he plays down the capacity of the human will may have more to do with his recognition of the power of circumstance or environment. Besides, there are other elements at play that may counteract the forces of morality in human nature. Just as there are two opposed feelings in humans, namely, struggle and mutual sympathy, so there are two conflicting tendencies that dominate the progression of human history: 'the striving for justice, i.e., equity, and the striving for individual domination over others, or over the many'.[48] Kropotkin was quite willing to accept that sometimes people do not always act out of the best of intentions. In other words, people are not necessarily 'those free-minded, independent, provident, loving, and compassionate fellows which we should like to see them.' But it is precisely because humans are not as good as we would like them to be that 'they must not continue living under the present system which permits them to oppress and exploit one another'.[49] By contrast, conservatives, whilst keen to draw attention to the moral and intellectual imperfections of humankind, are unwilling to apply their argument universally to all people. Burke, for instance, is quick to register humankind's unsuitability to live a life according to reason, 'because we suspect that this stock in each man is small', but proceeds, rather hypocritically, to make an exception for the rulers and aristocracy of society.[50] Anarchists, on the other hand, make no distinction. As Kropotkin writes in his *Anarchism: Its Philosophy and Ideal* (1897), there are 'not two measures for the virtues of the governed and those of the governors; we know that we ourselves are not without faults and that the best of us would soon be corrupted by the existence of power'.[51] The imperfections of human nature affect not some but all. This kind of selective, subjective immunity to the vicious aspects of human nature is that which Kropotkin finds most irksome. Not only is it wrong, but it patently ignores the responsibility for changing humankind's social, political and economic environment. To adopt the conservative attitude that humans are simply bad, and that the capitalist system is required to maintain order, is to absolve oneself from the necessary task of social reconstruction. Kropotkin might not believe like Rousseau that humankind was originally innocent, but he certainly shares his opinion that the social context is partly responsible for the adverse aspects of human nature. Anyone with half an eye can see the ill consequences of things as they now stand: 'that the present capitalist, authoritarian system is absolutely inappropriate to a society of men so improvident, so rapacious, so egoistic, and so slavish as they are now'.[52] Kropotkin was a realist, standing firm against the brute facts of a harsh world. In common with most if not all anarchists there is something of the nihilist within him. But Kropotkin never let his pessimism overtake his grasp of reality. In this sense, Kropotkin cannot be characterized as a blithe admirer of human nature. As he admits himself, whilst feelings of sociality may prove to be the source of morality, other less attractive facets of human nature may intervene. 'Unfortunately,' he notes, 'the rapacious instincts that still survive in men from the time of the primitive stages of their development interfere with the recognition of the feeling of sociality and the consciousness of equity as the fundamental principle of the moral judgments.'[53]

Kropotkin's Philosophy of History

Just as human nature is intricately woven into an evolutionary matrix, society too is subject to a process of development. The historical pattern of civilization may be represented in a number of stages: the tribe; the village community; the free city and the state.[54] Underpinning this process there are two politico-historical trends. According to Kropotkin, and one may note the influence of Proudhon here, two opposed recurrent traditions have vied with each other, throughout the history of civilization, for supremacy: 'the Roman and the Popular; the imperial and the federalist; the authoritarian and the libertarian'.[55] Three years later the development of this struggle was rendered even more explicit. Writing in his *Modern Science and Anarchism* (1901), Kropotkin argues that since time immemorial

> two currents of thought and action have been in conflict in the midst of human societies. On the one hand, the masses, the people, worked out, by their way of life, a number of necessary institutions in order to make social existence possible, to maintain peace, to settle quarrels, and to practice mutual aid in all circumstances that required combined effort. . . . On the other hand, there have always flourished among men, magi, shamans, wizards, rain-makers, oracles, and priests, who were the founders and the keepers of a rudimentary knowledge of Nature, and of the first elements of worship (worship of the sun, the moon, the forces of Nature, ancestor worship).[56]

That the balance of forces now lies with the state does not mean that the contest has always been one-sided. It is only recently that the might of authoritarianism has consolidated its hold over humankind. Until about the sixteenth century, mutual aid was the champion of the libertarian trend sitting on the throne of the medieval city. Enlivened by a spirit of 'free agreement and individual initiative' and organized on the basis 'of the free federation of the interested parties', mutual aid predominated in these bastions of liberty.[57] Constructed upon a federation of village communities and medieval guilds, the city was perhaps a state in itself. Its ultimate objective was to guarantee peace, liberty and self-administration. It achieved this through 'a close union for mutual aid and support, for consumption and production, and for social life altogether, without imposing upon men the fetters of the State, but giving full liberty of expression to the creative genius of each separate group of individuals in art, craft, science, commerce, and political organisation'.[58]

The question that needs to be addressed now, is how the state managed to usurp the power of the medieval city. There are two dimensions to the answer: history and human nature. The latter facilitates the development of the former. In historical terms the capitulation of the medieval city was brought about by an association of rising interest groups. Thus Kropotkin notes that it was only upon reaching 'the sixteenth century that a mortal blow was dealt to the ideas of local independence, to free union and organisation, to federation of all degrees among sovereign groups, possessing all functions now seized upon by the State'.[59] Rising in anger with every sentence, Kropotkin continues his analysis by outlining what he believes is the common understanding of how

> this association of lord, priest, merchant, judge, soldier, and king founded its domination. It was by the annihilation of all free unions: of village communities, guilds, trade unions, fraternities, and medieval cities. It was by confiscating the land of the communes and the riches of the guilds. It was by the absolute and ferocious prohibition of all kinds of free agreement between men. It was by massacre, the wheel, the gibbet, the sword, and the fire that church and State established their domination, and that they succeeded henceforth to reign over an incoherent agglomeration of "subjects" who had no more direct union among themselves.[60]

The historical development of the state, however, has its origin in human nature. Commentators are unanimous in their assessment that Kropotkin has to establish something analogous to a lust for power to explain the appearance of institutions like the state. As Marshall remarks, Kropotkin 'had to posit in human nature a will to power which leads to the domination and exploitation of one's fellows'.[61] In a more explicit tone, David Miller contends that, for Kropotkin, both private property and political authority arose from humankind's instinct of self-assertion.[62] There is then, an implicit relationship between human nature and historical progress, with the rise of the state corresponding to the rise of self-assertion or egoism. Like Proudhon and Bakunin before him, Kropotkin posits a Janus-faced conception of human nature. The struggle of historical forces, the battle between libertarianism and authoritarianism, is occasioned by a comparable contest within human nature. As Kropotkin remarks, sociability has been developed by nature 'in opposition to the egotism of the self-preservation instinct'.[63]

As a parallel to the evolutionary debate and the admission by Kropotkin that mutual aid is simply one factor of evolution, with the struggle for existence another, the conception of human nature adopted by Kropotkin could be said to represent a simple reflection of that argument. But it is not as straightforward as that. The problem is engendered by the kind of conception of human nature proffered by Kropotkin. And it has obvious consequences for his philosophy of history. Emphasizing that human nature envelops both sociability and egoism presents the question of their origins. Are these features permanently inherent in humankind, or are they a result of the context within which human beings find themselves? On the one hand, Kropotkin gives the impression that he is offering a contextualist conception of human nature. Commenting on human nature in his first political essay, Kropotkin says that 'every individual is a product of the views surrounding him'.[64] But in the same essay, just one page later, Kropotkin gives a clear indication that egoism will remain in some people regardless of their environmental context.[65]

Academic analysis compounds the confusion. David Miller, for instance, argues that Kropotkin sees egoism 'as a perversion engendered by a competitive society, and one which will be replaced by an altruism which is "natural" to man'.[66] Martin Miller provides a similar interpretation. In his opinion, Kropotkin believed that the worst effects of egoism manifested themselves 'only insofar as inequality existed'.[67] Given the evolutionary matrix which supports Kropotkin's ideology this would appear to be a compelling argument. Egoism is a consequence of capitalism. The story differs, however, when viewed from the perspective of Marshall. It is not that Marshall furnishes an implacably opposed argument, far from it. Focusing on Kropotkin's statement in *The State: Its Historic Role* (1898) that humans prefer peace and quiet to soldiering, which illustrates the lack of natural aggression in humankind, Marshall proceeds to enunciate a contextualist position that apparently concurs with the two Millers. In his interpretation of Kropotkin it is by way of the media of 'higher education' and 'equality of conditions' that humans will 'be able to free themselves from their slavish instincts'.[68] But Marshall's account raises a possibility that is precluded in both David and Martin Miller and is possibly unseen by Marshall himself. The difficulty surrounds the notion of instincts, referred to by Marshall, which implies that Kropotkin incorporated a universal or given element into his conception of human nature. An understanding and possible resolution of the difficulty may be facilitated through an analysis of two factors that are embedded in Kropotkin's conception of human nature: habit and human motivation. The impact or seriousness of this omission, however, can only be gleaned through an appreciation of the support that the contextualist principle receives from Kropotkin himself.

Considering the degree of commitment Kropotkin attaches to the contextualist dimension of his conception of human nature, it is understandable that this tension has gone unnoticed in the past. As the aforementioned imply, Kropotkin does make effective use of the environmental territory. As will be illustrated below, it is an integral part of his critique of the Marxist–Leninist conception of revolutionary strategy. It is not my intention to deny that Kropotkin operated a contextualist conception of human nature, because it is quite plain that he did. However, as was demonstrated in the chapter on ideology and human nature, ideologists are often the proprietors of a concept of human nature that draws on both contextualist and given elements and Kropotkin is no exception. The contextualist parameters of Kropotkin's conception of human nature are presented in a fashion that resembles a Rousseauean argument. It was noted above that whilst Rousseau believes that human nature is corrupted by civil society, Kropotkin considers, in *Mutual Aid*, that the state has had a negligible impact on the efficacy of mutual aid in human nature. Nevertheless, the power of mutual aid is obviously affected by the predominance of the state, if only because capitalism brings out the worst in human nature. Kropotkin's reflections on prison life confirm that people 'live now in too much isolation. Everybody cares only for himself, or his nearest relatives. Egotistic – that is, unintelligent– individualism in material life has necessarily brought about an individualism as egotistic and as harmful in the mutual relations of human beings.'[69] If individuals are a product of the environment in which they are raised, it is not surprising that Kropotkin believes, after the manner of Rousseau, 'that society at large is responsible for the vices that grow in it'.[70] In light of this assessment it is not difficult to imagine Kropotkin locating the source of egoism in the environment. Capitalism, a society marked by 'servitude and exploitation', is a principal factor in the degeneration of human nature.[71]

But what of these instincts that Marshall refers to? Although they may be a product of humanity's evolutionary inheritance, are they not impervious to environmental changes? Viewed from Marshall's standpoint it would appear not. The power of education will release individuals from these 'slavish instincts'. As intimated above, though, it is not certain that Marshall has fully recognized the implications of his own statement. The difficulty that Marshall either is unconscious of or chooses to ignore is how to explain the presence of a concept that would appear to be an indelible aspect of humankind's evolutionary baggage. There appear to be two ways of explaining this. First, what Marshall terms instincts are what Kropotkin refers to as habits. Indeed slightly earlier in his text Marshall hints at this. Focusing on the development of Kropotkin's moral theory in *Anarchism and Anarchist Communism* (1887), he points to the author's argument that moral actions are 'a mere necessity of the individual to enjoy the joys of his brethren, to suffer when some of his brethren are suffering; a habit and a second nature, slowly elaborated and perfected by life in society'.[72] As Kropotkin informs us in *Words of a Rebel* (1885), because humans are not solitary creatures they develop within themselves 'the feelings and habits that tend to sustain society and propagate the race'. These feelings of sociability do not emanate from human institutions; rather they 'develop spontaneously, through the nature of things like those habits among animals which men call instinct; they emerge from a useful and even necessary process of evolution that sustains society in the struggle for existence in which it is involved'.[73] This may help to clarify what look like rather off-the-cuff remarks by Kropotkin. If moral actions become second nature and are to be thought of as habits, then that would help explain why Kropotkin believes that virtually all our moral actions arise from habit.[74] Morality may be pre-human in origin, but it is refined throughout the course of human evolution. Whether or not it also assists in clarifying what Kropotkin meant by the unconscious is another matter. Kropotkin was of the opinion that our unconscious life occupied three-quarters of our relations with others. Above and beyond this, however, little is said. It may be construed that our unconscious is an element of our mind that corresponds to something like the innate sense of justice or morality that Kropotkin describes in humankind.[75] That is, that an individual's unconscious is somehow locked together with, or is perhaps a deeper depository of, the sympathy that resides in humankind. But as there is no direct evidence for this linkage, one has, in assessing Kropotkin's works, to be cautious in attributing a union of ideas that may not actually exist.

It might be objected that whilst the preceding elucidation of the relationship between instinct and morality, in terms of an innate sense of justice, may possess some accuracy, it hardly accounts for the 'slavish' in Marshall's narrative. Prima facie this may be true, but such reasoning ignores the fact that the rationale of the argument advanced by Kropotkin in respect of sociability and habits also serves to explain the existence of other social customs. Continuing his chronicle of social evolution in *Words of a Rebel*, Kropotkin remarks that

> alongside these customs, necessary for the life of societies and conservation of the race, other passions and desires appear and other habits and customs emerge from them. The desire to dominate others and impose one's will on them; the desire to lay hold the products of a neighbouring tribe's work; the desire to subjugate other men . . . such personal and egoistic desires create another current of habits and customs.[76]

Here, then, is the most probable meaning of Marshall's 'slavish instincts'. Society has fostered the development of higher and lower instincts in human nature. Nonetheless, the initial objection still persists. For as Marshall was aware, considered as social habits these egoistic desires may be subdued by the process of education. They are not, as Kropotkin admits, intrinsic to human nature. 'Without being inherent in man (as the priests and metaphysicians say) these qualities are the result of life in common.'[77] As such these social habits are not ineradicable features of human nature. They are susceptible, as Marshall indicates, to amelioration through education. They are the result of social evolution, the development of human societies rather than an innate element of humanity's evolutionary inheritance. Accordingly, the first explanation, that of habits, does not in itself present an insuperable problem either to Marshall or to the wider perspective of Kropotkin's contextualist conception of human nature. The desire to dominate is cultivated by capitalism. A change in environment would induce a change in morality. This is the essence of the contextualist paradigm. Such thinking allows anarchists to argue that a social revolution would bring about a new morality, thereby obviating many of the difficulties and objections that might be raised about humanity's supposed suitability to live in an anarchist society. However, if the second explanation, that of human motivation, were to be acknowledged as representing a given or fixed dimension of human nature, then Kropotkin's argument concerning the plausibility of anarchism might suffer a serious setback. For if his philosophy of history is predicated upon a corresponding conception of human nature, the introduction of a given or universal element could jeopardize his hopes for anarchism, especially if that fixed constituent of human nature threatened the triumph of mutual aid and sociability.

Kropotkin's theory of human motivation is outlined in his *Anarchist Morality* (1892). Here one finds Kropotkin in agreement with the Epicurean notion 'that all the acts of man, good or bad, useful or baneful, arise from a single motive: the lust for pleasure'.[78] Whether people steal a child's food or share their last morsel with a stranger, the motivation for such action springs from the same source, the impulse of egoism. Of course, hedonistic psychology was not original to Kropotkin; and even if it was the basis of the political theory of some of his rivals (n.b. Hobbes), that did not detract from the truth of its conclusion that humans seek pleasure and attempt to avoid pain. Indeed, Kropotkin considered egoism so powerful a factor in human motivation that it can override the compulsion of pity and compassion. 'Take for example the worst of scoundrels: a Thiers, who massacres thirty-five thousand Parisians, or an assassin who butchers a whole family in order that he may wallow in debauchery. They do it because for the moment the desire of glory or of money gains in their minds the upper hand of every other desire. Even pity and compassion are extinguished for the moment by this other desire, this other thirst. They act almost automatically to satisfy a craving or their nature.'[79] It is extremely unlikely, then, that such passions can be forever contained. Even a change in environment may be insufficient against the inherent egoism in human nature. Love may live in and appeal to every mind, but Kropotkin's realism forces him to concede that there will forever 'be men whose passions may occasionally lead them to commit acts of an anti-social character'.[80] Even in *The Conquest of Bread*, Kropotkin's realism persists. Once in an anarchist society 'some inequalities, some inevitable injustices, undoubtedly will remain. There are individuals in our societies whom no great crisis can lift out of the deep mire of egoism in which they are sunk.'[81] Obviously, social habits and human actions have a deeper, more fundamental, cause than mere environmental stimuli. Egoism is rooted in human psychology. It is, therefore, an ineradicable trait of human nature. Marshall's assessment of the 'slavish instincts' does not hold good here. Whether or not Marshall's phrase actually embodies the concept of egoism is not that important. It is the inference of his account that is of particular consequence. For the meaning of Marshall's arguments suggests that the worst aspects of human nature can be mitigated by education. This may be partly true, even with reference to egoism. But it is not entirely true. As Kropotkin has revealed, his conception of human nature incorporates a factor of egoism that has the capacity to rear its ugly head regardless of context or occasion. Morality may be improved by creating the circumstances in which individuals will be discouraged from deceiving and exploiting others, but as Kropotkin recognizes, the anti-social habits of humankind can only be weakened not eliminated.[82]

There are, then, two distinct components in Kropotkin's conception of human nature. The first is sociability that, in conjunction with sympathy, nurtures the advance of mutual aid. The second is egoism that gives rise to anti-social behaviour. And both aspects of human nature correspond to the two trends that Kropotkin identifies shaping the passage of human history. Whether or not one could say that these features of Kropotkin's conception of human nature determine the outcome of history is a moot point. Perhaps the best way to describe the relationship between Kropotkin's philosophy of history and conception of human nature is to say that these trends stand in a symbiotic relationship to human nature. By that is meant that whilst human nature provides the food upon which history feeds, furnishing the sustenance for the development of history in one particular direction, history itself releases the possibility of its own fulfilment. This relationship is alluded to in *The Great French Revolution* (1909). It is here that Kropotkin attempts to portray 'the mighty currents of thought and action that came into conflict during the French Revolution – currents so intimately blended with the very essence of human nature that they must inevitably reappear in the historic events of the future'.[83] In other words, social circumstances may inaugurate the consummation of an historical trend. Human nature acts as a catalyst establishing a basis for the victory of one trend over another. In this sense a political movement or other event or phenomenon acts as an environmental trigger liberating both the forces of history and the potential of human nature. The one feeds off the other as they chart their progress through the course of social evolution. If this analysis is accurate then Kropotkin is relieved of the charge of historical determinism. Given the relationship between history, human nature and circumstance, Kropotkin is unlikely to concede that history proceeds according to some pre-defined plan. The dual dimension of human nature prohibits it. In this respect, Kropotkin had more in common with Bakunin than with Marx. Revolution, as Crowder has noted, is regarded 'as a means of positively determining the course of history in accordance with human will'.[84] Progression from one environment to another, by way of a revolution, demands the exercise of human will.

Kropotkin's Revolutionary Methodology

One could be forgiven for attributing a charge of historical determinism to Kropotkin, if only because of the frequency of his enunciations on the imminence of revolution. This is not to say that speculations of revolutionary activity vindicate the conclusion of determinism; rather that they create an ambience in which the erroneous deduction of determinism is, at least, understandable. Kropotkin was often convinced that a social revolution was casting its shadow over bourgeois society. During his trial at Lyon in 1883, for example, Kropotkin's defence speech was marked by an insistence that the social revolution was looming on the horizon.[85] At times such emphatic prophesizing assumes the appearance of historical determinism. His message in *The Conquest of Bread*, 'that Communism is not only desirable, but that existing societies, founded on Individualism, *are inevitably impelled in the direction of Communism*' is somewhat reflective of a determinist position. Yet more often than not this is little more than the language of expectant revolutionaries. Kropotkin's rhetoric simply encapsulates the prevalent revolutionary fervour; an ardour that finds material expression in his radical journalism. Writing in an article entitled 'The Breakdown of the State', Kropotkin requests his reader to contemplate all state forms, 'from the police autocracy of Russia to the bourgeois oligarchy of Switzerland, and you will not find a single example today . . . of a State that is not set on an accelerating course towards disintegration and eventually, revolution'.[86]

Besides the rhetoric of revolutionary anticipation, Kropotkin's speculation has its origins in yet another source, the faith he invested in the masses. In conjunction with his outspoken belief in the portentous revolutionary cataclysm, Kropotkin, as Martin Miller recognizes, clung steadfastly to an 'unquestioned faith in the revolutionary instinct of the masses'.[87] Kropotkin's confidence in the revolutionary potential of the people reflects more than a mere contemporary intoxication. To understand Kropotkin's reasoning three other factors need to be taken into account. The first concerns the epistemology of Kropotkin's position. As Marshall has highlighted, Kropotkin's faith matured out of his experiences in Siberia. Consequently, the basis of his faith was provided during his stay in Siberia, when 'his contact with the peasants and their communities gave him a lasting faith in the solidarity and the creative spontaneity of the people'.[88] A second consideration invokes the concept of spontaneity. Seemingly, the influence of Bakunin has had some effect on Kropotkin. Although the two never met, Kropotkin appears to be have been inspired by his predecessor's idea of an instinct of rebellion in humankind. Never exhibited with Bakunin's vigour, Kropotkin's notion of a 'spirit of independence that is in man' does rest firmly within the tradition of Bakunin's argument.[89] Furthermore, Kropotkin's faith in the masses is more than a high regard for their ability to implement the principles of equity in a revolution. Given the results of Kropotkin's observations in Siberia, and bearing in mind the spirit of independence that he posits in human nature, it is only to be expected that he accommodates the philosophy of the anarchist sections of the First International in their expression that the task of the revolution is the task of the people themselves. In other words, his faith in the revolutionary potential of the masses serves to underscore his belief that the revolution must be carried out by the people themselves, a lesson brought firmly home by Kropotkin's reading of the history of the French Revolution.

The significance of this revolutionary philosophy extends beyond the fact that it complements his observations on spontaneity and independence. It is, more importantly, a necessary and coherent outcome of his conception of human nature, precisely because his conception of human nature infers a will to power. The rationale of the assessment of an innate egoism in human nature recommends that revolutions should at no cost be directed by revolutionary minorities. His notion of human nature warns 'that any group of people entrusted with deciding a certain set of activities often of an organisational quality *always* strives to broaden the range of these activities and its own power in these activities'.[90] Humans cannot be trusted with power. Again his own personal experience helped to cement his theoretical inclinations. Recalling the relationship of prisoners to warders in Clairvaux, Kropotkin remarks: 'Men are men; and you cannot give so immense an authority to men over men without corrupting those to whom you give the authority. They will abuse it; and their abuses of it will be the more unscrupulous, and the more felt by the abused, the more limited and narrow is the world they live in.'[91] Situated within the province of power, humans are compelled to acquire it. The context of power teases out and reinforces that lust for power that resides within humankind. Just as individuals are made worse by the state, so *ipso facto* they will be corrupted by the power of revolutionary cabals, parties or committees. Revolutionary dictatorships contravene Kropotkin's anarchist formula. 'Nothing good and lasting,' he comments, 'is made except by the free initiative of the people, and all power tends to kill it.'[92] Indeed, there is nothing like a small clique of officials, whether in a revolutionary situation or not, to encourage the instinct of egoism. As he remarks in *The Conquest of Bread*, 'there are plenty of egoistic instincts in isolated individuals. We are quite aware of it. But we contend that the very way to revive and nourish these instincts would be to confine such questions as the housing of people to any board or committee, in fact, to the tender mercies of officialism in any shape or form.'[93]

However, the disquiet that Kropotkin voices about revolutionary dictatorships and small groups of officials does not prevent him from countenancing, albeit briefly, something analogous to Bakunin's secret societies. Caroline Cahm cites an open letter from Kropotkin to Malatesta, Cafiero and Schwitzguébel, probably written in June 1881, in which the author reveals his thoughts about two levels of revolutionary organization. For Kropotkin, it was clear 'that the secret organisation must be *national* and that the international bond must be as *secret* as the organisation itself. I do not see any other way than to return to the international brothers.'[94] Shortly afterward Kropotkin seems to have frowned upon the efficacy of conspiratorial struggle, progressing to the viewpoint that the overthrow of the state could only be facilitated by a popular struggle.[95] Certainly, it is this kind of outlook that Marshall notes in Kropotkin. According to Marshall, Kropotkin had 'rejected the kind of deceit and manipulation practised by Bakunin, preferring open and sincere propaganda'.[96]

An abandonment of the methodology of secret societies squares with Kropotkin's thinking on the nature of revolutions. For as he puts it in *The Conquest of Bread*, revolution encompasses more than an amendment to existing social institutions. 'It implies the awakening of human intelligence, the increasing of the inventive spirit tenfold, a hundredfold; it is the dawn of a new science – the science of men like Laplace, Lamarck, Lavoisier. It is a revolution in the minds of men, as deep, and deeper still, than in their institutions.'[97] Seen from this angle, secret societies facilitate the development of a revolutionary consciousness. They are not the organs that anarchists should depend on to usher in the forthcoming revolution. If they have any role to play at all it is in disseminating information and generally preparing people for the event itself. They are certainly not, as Kropotkin observes, the instruments of revolution 'that give the fatal blow to governments. Their function, their historic mission, is to prepare people's minds for the revolution. And when the people's minds are prepared – with the help of external circumstances, the last push comes, not from the initiating group but from the masses that have remained outside the society.'[98]

Similarly, Kropotkin is somewhat sceptical of the value of industrial action. In general, he thought strikes too limited in their aims, often detracting from the real objective of workers' struggle. Although the strike may have some educational effect, it 'serves as a good method for arousing the consciousness of one's power only when it ends in victory'.[99] Correspondingly, trade unions are unable, and indeed unsuitable organs, to provide the foundations for a free society. Hence Kropotkin gave only 'qualified support to syndicalism', expressing doubts about possible authoritarian elements, shying away from 'the establishment of centres of new economic power' and casting a suspicious glance at the favour bestowed on the proletariat at the expense of the peasantry.[100] Kropotkin was in broad agreement with Malatesta's concern that anarchists increasingly envisaged syndicalism as an end rather than a means.

The issue of means and ends should not be underestimated. Although not so directly involved in the dispute that split the International as Bakunin was – the debate about revolutionary methodology – Kropotkin did admit much of Bakunin's argument. The conscious involvement of the people themselves in the revolutionary process is consistent with Kropotkin's desire to nurture a new morality. This methodology obviates the difficulties associated with reliance on revolutionary parties or minorities and increases the opportunities for a successful conclusion to the social revolution. It also has consequences for the issues of terrorism and 'propaganda by the deed', which became associated with anarchism at the end of the nineteenth century. Apart from the contradictions raised in the approach to means and ends, Kropotkin disliked the notion of 'propaganda by the deed' for other reasons. First, Kropotkin was always in favour of collective action rather than individual acts of terrorism, even if he displayed public sympathy for those who took it upon themselves to engage in acts of revolt. Additionally, Kropotkin suspected that the rationale behind 'propaganda by the deed' lent itself too easily to the attractions of publicity rather than the authentic desire to rid the masses of exploitation and subjugation. More importantly, concessions to violence threaten the integrity of Kropotkin's ideology. The contextualist dynamic of his conception of human nature indicates that if individuals become accustomed to violence and oppression of others in the revolution, then these features could well constitute the hallmark of any resultant society.

Kropotkin's Anarchist Vision

But what was the new society to look like? What did Kropotkin's vision of a new social order entail? The first thing worth noting is that Kropotkin's anarchist future is closely associated to his conception of human nature. In common with his predecessors, Kropotkin builds the possibility of anarchism on a specific conception of human nature. Like all ideologies, anarchism carries an outline of how it would like to see society develop – whether it cares to admit this or not. In Kropotkin's works this vision is presented in two distinct stages. The first conveys his thinking as to why it is necessary to discuss such images in the first instance. Once this is concluded, Kropotkin embarks on the second step of the process, revealing the details of that vision. This section of the chapter is concerned to adumbrate the arguments presented by Kropotkin as he proceeds to develop his vision of an anarchist future, whilst the following section examines his specific vision in greater detail.

To begin with Kropotkin was not only convinced that anarchism would be the next stage in the evolutionary process, he was also persuaded that contemplations of future society are an integral part of the revolutionary process itself. He writes in Emile Pouget's and Emile Pataud's *Syndicalism and the Co-operative Commonwealth* (1913):

> It is often said that plans ought not to be drawn up for a future society. . . . On the other hand, it is necessary to have a clear idea of the actual concrete results that our communist, collectivist

or other aspirations might have on society. For this purpose we must picture to ourselves these various institutions at work. Where do we want to get to by means of the Revolution? We need to know this. There must, therefore, be books which will enable the mass of the people to form for themselves a more or less exact idea of what it is they desire to see realised in a new future.[101]

Given the requirements of ideological argument, Kropotkin is obliged to portray a vision of how society ought to be, regardless of the detail elaborated. Kropotkin appears to be cognizant of this prerequisite himself. Writing in his *Modern Science and Anarchism*, he proclaims that no revolutionary

struggle can be successful if it is unconscious, if it has no definite and concrete aim. No destruction of existing things is possible if men have not already settled for themselves, during the struggles leading to the destruction, and during the period of destruction itself, what is going to take the place of that which is destroyed. Even a theoretical criticism of what exists is not possible without one picturing to oneself a more or less exact image of that which he desires to see in its place. Consciously or unconsciously, the *ideal*, the conception of something better, always grows in the mind of whoever criticises existing institutions.[102]

An image of a better society is an inherent part of any ideology. Ideologies are proprietary bodies of thought that each contain a vision of a better future that derives from a critique of contemporary society. They are both descriptive and prescriptive. Both present and future tenses exist in parallel in ideological argument.

Almost inevitably then, Kropotkin engages in a form of speculative sociology, constructing a vista of anarchy that encourages the development of the revolutionary process itself. The question that has to be resolved is to what extent does Kropotkin's examination of the possible uncover the fine detail of the future? Some, such as Woodcock, argue that Kropotkin offers little more than a general framework for overcoming the problems of contemporary society.[103] Others, such as Miller, contend that 'Kropotkin was not afraid to be specific about the kind of society he would like to see after a revolution'.[104] I side with the latter interpretation. There are three texts in particular which support it: Kropotkin's first major essay in politics, *Must We Occupy*

Ourselves with an Examination of the Ideal of a Future System? (1873); *Fields, Factories and Workshops* (1899); and *The Conquest of Bread* (1892). From the outset of his first political tract, Kropotkin is keen to answer the question of his essay title in the affirmative. He believes that one should think about the ideal of a future system; for if one is afraid to contemplate that ideal it is most unlikely that it will be established in practice. Nevertheless, he does not consider himself to be furnishing a detailed scheme that will correspond to the society of the future; rather he is simply producing 'an outline of this future system in the most general terms'.[105] He considers himself unable to do more than this for epistemological reasons. In an argument that shares more with Herbert Read than Malatesta, Kropotkin asserts that 'there does not even exist now that mind which comprehends all the future moral ideas of mankind. Consequently, any contemporary idea will be a manifestation of present-day conceptions of morality, a manifestation which will be impossible, because before it is realised, in its totality, new conceptions of justice will be created and *begin to be realised.*'[106]

To my mind Kropotkin underplays the specificity of his argument here, for the text reflects a concentration on detail that is possibly only surpassed in *The Conquest of Bread* and *Fields, Factories and Workshops*. In many respects Kropotkin's wider ideological concerns are prefaced in his 1873 essay. It is not long, for example, before Kropotkin warns his audience that assigning functions and power to a government or state will lead nowhere. No matter how responsive and dynamic that body proves to be, the danger is that 'the group of individuals to whom society cedes its rights would always be the power, separate from society, trying to broaden its influence, its interference in the business of each separate individual. And the wider the circle of activity of this government, the greater the danger of enslavement of society, the greater the likelihood that the government would stop being the expression of the interests and desires of the majority.'[107] The consistency of such statements with his conception of human nature is plainly visible. Moreover, these dangers cannot be prevented by way of checks and balances. Liberalism holds little attraction for Kropotkin. The state cannot be rendered acceptable by tinkering and fine tuning; it has to be abolished. Radical action is a prerequisite for remedying social injustices because the inconveniences of the state 'lie in the most basic conception of the institution, in its very essence, and so cannot be eliminated by any measures such as limitations, control, and so on as long as the very essence of the institution continues to exist'.[108]

One of the first measures to be taken in reaching the objective of an anarchist society is the expropriation of capital. This is designed to promote equality in rights to work. Additionally, expropriation occurs within a federal framework, which was favoured by Kropotkin as a means of organizing society. Kropotkin is seemingly under the influence of Proudhon here, especially as he goes on to say that products will be exchanged between artels on the basis of labour receipts.[109] But Kropotkin suffers from the same types of problems that beset the earlier anarchist. For instance, there is no mention here of who or what is to attempt to broker an agreement concerning 'necessary measures'. This is a little surprising in light of Kropotkin's own admission that there are likely to be problems of exchange in that society. Anticipating the possible causes of such disputes, Kropotkin reasons that the farmers of one commune might value their ten hours of labour at ten measures of wheat, whereas the farmers of another commune believe that their ten hours of work is equal to eleven measures of wheat. Obviously, other communes would prefer to exchange their products with the first set of farmers, and this in itself will probably lead to problems and 'even quarrels'.[110]

One possible solution ventured by Kropotkin is that of the committee, which is responsible for issuing labour notes. Committees are an important tool in Kropotkin's assessment of how to realize the goals elaborated in this document. They are involved in many organizational tasks, including the division of land, the allocation of housing and the economy. Their economic remit is quite broad, covering the appraisal of cargo transportation and the responsibility for purchasing provisions at the market.[111] Apparently, economic or trade disputes would be settled by committees, comprised of elected representatives. As with Proudhon, the resolution of difficulties is accomplished by means of majoritarianism. The writing was on the wall, so to speak, when Kropotkin referred to 'the interests and desires of the majority' when considering how government constantly strives to extend the tentacles of its power and influence.[112] And when situated within the context of the committee Kropotkin's apparent solution sounds increasingly like the foundations for authoritarian centralism, operating through a planned economy, rather than the free production he talks of in other places. Suspicions of the imposition of a majoritarian culture are corroborated upon recognition that the condition of equality in labour dictates 'that everyone should be compelled to earn his livelihood through his own labour'.[113] A better, or perhaps this should be worse, example of Kropotkin's indebtedness to Bakunin could not be found. If individuals wish to live in and partake of the benefits offered by life in community then they have to labour. Although free to choose an occupation, everyone must comply with the assignment received from the artel. Whilst individuals may wish to prosecute their own private ends, they are free to do so only after they perform what is deemed to be socially useful as decreed by the majority of society.[114] In the tradition of Bakuninian collectivism, Kropotkin constructs a labour proviso that is at odds with the declared aims of a free society.

Perhaps this residue of collectivism is necessary to counteract the free-rider problem, a not infrequent objection levelled at utopias. Consider, Kropotkin asks, a person who does no work and is compelled to steal in order to live. Once apprehended 'an autonomous communal court will deal with him – by itself or through elected representatives'. There is no need of government, for 'in all its own internal affairs the *obshchina* [a Russian peasant commune], just as now, is and will be able to be in command without creating a government'.[115] If, Kropotkin continues, one commune were to seize the land of another commune on which to feed its own cattle then there are mechanisms for settling the dispute. Both communes are likely to belong to the same agricultural union or federation; hence it is obvious to Kropotkin 'that the *offended obshchina* has to appeal with the complaint to its own union of agricultural *obshchiny*'.[116] The elected representatives of the *obshchiny* would resolve the altercation. Once again the spirit of Proudhon radiates through Kropotkin's vision of future society, and just as equally through his rather vague description of the remit of the representatives. Reticence compels a conclusion in favour of majority voting, a judgment not out of line with the remainder of the work. The question that has to be asked now, is whether such a judgment casts a mould into which his later political writings were confined? On the specific subject of majoritarianism an unequivocal answer cannot be tendered. David Miller, for instance, accepts that Kropotkin depends on majority decisions to determine socially useful work, but remarks that 'this is not mentioned later, and one must take it that he is relying on a universal consensus'.[117] But why assume that? There is no hard evidence, to my mind, that can be cited in favour of that conclusion, and what intimations Kropotkin does make in later works suggest the opposite. The problem is real and relevant. For whilst it might present itself as little more than speculative semantics, anarchists, as Woodcock and Avakumovic hold, do not accept majority decisions.[118]

There are potentially more serious objections to be levelled at Kropotkin's work, one of which emanates from the adoption of committees into his revolutionary society. Seen as part of his whole ideology, the introduction of committees would constitute a major difficulty for Kropotkin, creating a fundamental inconsistency between his conception of human nature and his programme of revolutionary action. The committee cannot be regarded in any way as a solution to the problems of social organization, it can act only as an irritant. In this respect, the position Kropotkin held in 1873 was abandoned in his later works, notably *The Conquest of Bread*, in which his conception of human nature served as a warning that committees and other organs of officialism breed egoism in individuals.[119] Evolution of Kropotkin's economic argument resulted in the development of his theory of anarchist-communism, a brand of anarchist theory distinct from both Proudhon and Bakunin. The employment of labour notes in his 1873 essay bears a striking resemblance to Proudhon's economic theory. But in formulating a mechanism of distribution according to deed rather than need Kropotkin placed himself quite squarely in the collectivist camp of Bakunin. This was to change, or so it is told, as Kropotkin worked out a new basis for the economic organization of anarchist society.

Cahm, for example, relates how Kropotkin began to explore anarchist theory in depth in the late 1870s. The re-examination, she holds, was stimulated principally by Elisée Reclus and Paul Brousse in a debate at the Congress of the Jura Federation at Fribourg in 1878, during which Brousse edged toward communism as opposed to collectivism.[120] By 1879 Kropotkin appears to have been partially persuaded. At the Congress of the Jura Federation at La Chaux-de-Fonds in 1879 Kropotkin made a speech entitled *The Anarchist Idea from the Viewpoint of Its Practical Realisation*. In it he seemingly adopted a compromise position, adhering to a collectivist standpoint on property, but expressing that anarchist-communism was to be the final aim of the revolution.[121] By the time of the 1880 congress, held in the same location, Kropotkin had jettisoned collectivism in favour of communism. In a speech given at the congress and published in *Le Révolté* on 17 October 1880, Kropotkin remarks how the collectivist stance on property can be nothing more than a transitory stage in the revolution rather than the pinnacle of the revolution itself. This shift in position was to be the launching-pad from which Kropotkin was to expand his theory of anarchist-communism that was expressed fully in *The Conquest of Bread*.

The principal objection against collectivism is that it inferred the existence of collective property, which as a result might give rise to the prospect of competition. 'Collectivists,' argues Kropotkin, 'begin by proclaiming a revolutionary principle – the abolition of private property – and then they deny it, no sooner than proclaimed, by upholding an organisation of production and consumption which originated in private property.'[122] Fundamentally, this criticism contained two separate but related points: the remuneration of labour and distribution according to work done rather than need. Neither Proudhon nor Bakunin foresaw the problems associated with collectivism, whereas Kropotkin purports to surmount both of these obstacles. The introduction of labour cheques will, for Kropotkin, result in the peasants withholding their produce. 'We must offer to the peasant in exchange for his toil not worthless paper-money, but the manufactured articles of which he stands in immediate need.'[123] An integral part of the problem is that the labour theory of value subscribed to by the collectivists glosses over a number of potential pitfalls. Principal among these are three areas of obvious concern to any anarchist society. First, it is exceedingly difficult to rationalize individual contributions in what is effectively a collective enterprise. Thus Kropotkin attacks Proudhon for asserting that the value and quantity of work necessary to produce an object are proportional. Rejecting the labour theory of value, Kropotkin denies that the exchange value of commodities necessarily corresponds to the labour required to produce them.[124] Secondly, maintenance of the wages system and differential rewards corresponding to different types of work will inevitably create social stratification. Thirdly, social division will furnish the kind of environment in which egoism thrives.[125]

All three objections listed here reside under the broader umbrella of Kropotkin's belief that society's wealth is a common inheritance. 'There is not even a thought, or an invention,' Kropotkin states, 'which is not common property, born of the past and the present.'[126] All inventions of mind and labour depend on the discoveries of the past and the assistance of others in the present. Accordingly, it is unjust of anyone to appropriate part of the whole and claim it for themselves. Thus, 'the means of production being the collective work of humanity, the product should be the collective property of the race. Individual appropriation is neither just nor serviceable. All belongs to all. All things are for all men, since all men have need of them, since all men have worked in the measure of their strength to produce them, and since it is not possible to evaluate every one's part in the production of the world's wealth.'[127] In recognition of the interdependency of industry and manufacturing one should, Kropotkin claims, abandon the collectivist position 'that payment proportionate to the hours of labour rendered by each would be an ideal arrangement, or even a step in the right direction'. As far as Kropotkin is concerned, 'the Collectivist ideal appears to us untenable in a society which considers the instruments of labour as a common inheritance'.[128] The formula for the distribution of social goods has undoubtedly been altered to that which is commensurate with human need rather than deed. Or has it? One would expect that it had, but a closer examination of the texts reveals that Kropotkin may have retained a remnant of collectivism in his theory of anarchist-communism that was present in his 1873 essay. That residue is the labour proviso.

If Kropotkin had entirely discarded any notion of compulsory labour, then he would have stood apart from both Proudhon and Bakunin. Initially, one is led to believe that the transformation of the collectivist formula is complete. Kropotkin himself attempts to buttress the revision by declaring without hesitation that an anarchist-communist society is 'a society that recognises the absolute liberty of the individual, that does not admit of any authority, and makes use of no compulsion to drive men to work'.[129] If by this Kropotkin means that people will not be compelled to engage in wage-labour then there is really nothing to worry about. But this does not seem to be Kropotkin's meaning. Whilst he makes clear, in both *The Conquest for Bread* and *The Place of Anarchism in Socialistic Evolution*, that anarchist-communism entails the free consumption of goods, so long as they are abundant, because everyone has the right to live, access to these goods is conditional upon performing socially useful labour.[130] In the very same two texts Kropotkin transgresses the essential barrier between his putative anarchist-communism and the collectivism of previous writers. 'All is for all!' he declares in the chapter entitled 'Our Riches' in *The Conquest of Bread*, immediately before delivering a collectivist left hook. 'If the man and woman bear their fair share of work, they have a right to their fair share of all that is produced by all, and that share is enough to secure them well-being.'[131] And in 'Expropriation', in the same text, Kropotkin confirms that the resident of an anarchist society 'knows that after a few hours of productive toil he will have a right to all the pleasures that civilisation procures'.[132] *The Place of Anarchism in Socialistic Evolution* contains an identical message. 'All belongs to everyone! And provided each man and woman contributes his and her fair share of labour for the production of necessary objects, they have a right to share in all that is produced by everybody.'[133]

These are not documents only relevant to the contemporary Russian populist struggle, as might be said about Kropotkin's first political essay of 1873. *The Conquest of Bread* was first published in 1892, although it originated as a series of articles that first appeared in 1886 when Kropotkin was at the apogee of his revolutionary journalism. And *The Place of Anarchism in Socialistic Evolution*, first published in 1886, was originally delivered as a lecture in Paris on 28 February 1886, shortly after Kropotkin's release from Clairvaux prison.[134] The gap between these works and Kropotkin's original essay is at the very least thirteen years, but arguably more, given the publication date of *The Conquest of Bread*. Sufficient time, one would think, to allow for the expression of an evolution of thought, and a clear three or four years since Kropotkin last defended the vestiges of his collectivism at the Jura Federation congresses in the early 1880s.

Any difference that existed between Kropotkin and the collectivists was quashed by the restatement of the fundamental collectivist demand, that the enjoyment of social privileges requires work. Kropotkin may not be requesting remuneration proportionate to labour, as the collectivists enjoin under a wages system, but it is undoubtedly remuneration of social privileges for the contribution of labour. The charge of collectivism is given further credence by Kropotkin's treatment of the land question. The subject was of immense significance to the Russian populists, simply because of the demographic imbalance between peasants and proletarians in favour of the former. In light of that, Kropotkin drew up a series of measures to be implemented after the revolution in Russia. The following steps he thought it imperative to undertake:

The land should be declared the property of all, of the whole Russian people.

Every village and countryside settlement should receive the use of those lands which they now control.

All the lands taken by the whole countryside or by separate peasants of the village or countryside should become the possession of this village or countryside.

All the landowner's lands which are lying fallow should become the possession of the former peasants of this landowner.

All the lands bought by separate peasants for themselves should become the possession of the whole community of the village where such peasants are registered.[135]

It seems that whilst the land is to be the common property of all it is to be held in collective possession of local villages or communes. In essence this is a position not too far removed from Proudhon, and one that Kropotkin generally adheres to in his later writings. In *Modern Science and Anarchism*, Kropotkin again talks of the people regaining 'possession of the land and of all that is required for producing all sorts of necessaries of life' in a future society.[136] Elaboration of detail is rather thin in the aforesaid text, in what amounts to a rather vague antecedent of a more concrete argument in *Words of a Rebel*. To be sure, Kropotkin's standpoint is not unambiguous. In the essay 'Expropriation', for example, Kropotkin consolidates the position he initially took up in his first political essay of 1873, referring to the 'collective possession' of the land. A few pages later he enunciates that whilst the individual holding of the land would remain, the social revolution 'would expropriate all land that was not cultivated by the hands of those who at present possess the land'. Seemingly, there would exist a 'communist cultivation' alongside peasant proprietors.[137]

The above reflects a similar argument advanced in a previous essay, 'Representative Government', but contrasts somewhat with what Kropotkin has to say in 'The Paris Commune'.[138] Here Kropotkin appears to return to the argument of Proudhon. The people, he argues, will take possession 'of the whole of social wealth', whilst simultaneously establishing 'their rights of usufruct immediately'.[139] Bafflement arises because of the nature of the usufructuary relationship to the land. As Proudhon makes clear, rights of usufruct establish only rights of use and possession, not of proprietorship. Kropotkin, then, conflates notions of possession with ideas of proprietorship. Hence it is not entirely clear what he intends to happen to the land. Individual ownership by peasants stands firmly at odds with the idea of collective possession and use. Either one assumes that Kropotkin has retreated from his earlier outlook and permits the existence of individual ownership, or that peasants retain individual possession of their holdings whilst becoming subject to collective ownership by the village or commune. The only other alternative available is that individual proprietors enjoy the privilege of proprietorship on condition that they pool their resources and produce under the aegis of the free organization, production and consumption that is the hallmark of anarchist-communism. Either way, individual ownership seems a peculiar concession to grant. Not only does it undermine the process and standing of common or collective ownership, it is also bound to lead, like differential rewards for workers, to the recrudescence of egoism.

The Politics of Anarchy

It is at this juncture that an investigation of the finer details of Kropotkin's conception of anarchy is called for. It is important to do this for two reasons. First, it allows an assessment of the extent to which his vision of anarchist society corresponds to his conception of human nature. And, secondly, it will provide a basis from which to analyse the consistency of Kropotkin's anarchist ideology. Much of Kropotkin's earlier and some of his later writings bear witness to the vacillating influence of both Proudhon and Bakunin. However, it is Rousseau who seems closest to equipping Kropotkin with a foundation for his conception of anarchist society. Before illustrating the margins of Rousseau's influence, it is worth noting that Kropotkin accepts the Marxist idea that the political regime 'is always an expression of the *economic* regime which exists at the heart of society'.[140] Absorption of this mode of analysis has obvious consequences for Kropotkin's own theories; for if his own economic arguments exude mechanisms of compulsion or coercion then that might well be reflected in the political territory of his anarchist ideology. As means influence ends so the economic base of Kropotkin's ideology will influence his anarchist politics.

To determine whether that is true it is first necessary to sketch out the details of the society Kropotkin upholds as his ideal. That society is reached through a revolution, and the task of the revolution, as Kropotkin sees it, is to establish an environment in which everyone 'may live by working freely, without being forced to sell his work and his liberty to others who accumulate wealth by the labour of their serfs'.[141] Communism, then, embodies 'the conquest of perfect liberty by the individual, by free agreement, association, and absolute free federation'.[142] Put differently, anarchist-communism is built upon a commitment to abolish authority. At times Kropotkin approaches this subject rather blithely, insisting on one occasion that anarchism 'works to destroy authority in all its aspects'.[143] At other times Kropotkin's attitude is more conservative. Thus in *Modern Science and Anarchism* authority is only partially rejected. Here it is only centralized authority that Kropotkin objects to, not authority *per se*.[144]

Authority bears a moral capacity, in that authority is a reflection of accepted moral norms within anarchy, that is fundamental in most of what Kropotkin says about revolutionary society. Kropotkin outlines how anarchism is impregnated with moral feeling in his *Anarchist Morality*. In 'proclaiming ourselves anarchists we proclaim beforehand that we disavow any way of treating others in which we should not like them to treat us; that we will no longer tolerate the inequality that has allowed some among us to use their strength, their cunning or their ability after a fashion in which it would annoy us to have such qualities used against ourselves. Equality in all things, the synonym of equity, this is anarchism in very deed.'[145] Morality plays a multi-faceted role in Kropotkin's anarchism. First, it underpins the prescriptive element of his ideology. By fabricating an argument that links morality to human nature, Kropotkin establishes the necessity of revolution if individuals are to enjoy freedom. Morals improve or decline as the social environment improves or declines. The resurgence of mutual aid, for Kropotkin, will lead to a betterment of human morality. Severing the sinews of authority, by ushering in a social revolution, engenders a climate in which mutual aid and sociability can flourish. Because morality is essential to the well-being of society and to freedom, anarchist society enshrines certain moral rules. Absence of moral rules and obligations would, for Kropotkin, render the functioning of society impossible.[146] Morality, then, fulfils an important role in prescribing how individuals ought to behave toward one another, as well as providing a basis for the more formal agreements that individuals might enter into. Kropotkin's vision of anarchy, as expounded in *Modern Science and Anarchism*, embraces 'a society in which all the mutual relations of its members are regulated, not by laws, not by authorities, whether self-imposed or elected, but by mutual agreements between the members of that society, and by a sum of social customs and habits'.[147] No actions are to be imposed upon individuals as in bourgeois society. Individuals are free to enter into contracts that are fair and self-imposed.

Outside personal agreements and contracts, the freedom of the commune is best maintained through a federal structure. Local communities and villages need to marry themselves together under a federation in order to sustain relations with their neighbouring urban centres and organize themselves around these centres. The partnership between urban and rural is not balanced in favour of the former. As Kropotkin notes in his essay 'The Commune', the

> centre will not be able to establish an intrusive preponderance of its own over the communes in its environment. Thanks to the infinite variety of the needs of industry and commerce, all inhabited places have already several centres [to] which they are attached, and as their needs develop, they will enter into relations with further places that can satisfy new needs. Our needs are in fact so various, and they emerge with such rapidity, that soon a single federation will not be sufficient to satisfy them all. The Commune will then feel the need to contract other alliances, to enter into other federations.[148]

Relations between and within communes are consistent and commensurate with the principle of federalism. For if, as Kropotkin ponders in 'The Paris Commune', 'we concede to the free initiative of the communes the task of coming to an understanding between themselves on enterprises that concern several cities at once, how can we refuse this same initiative to the groups of which a Commune is composed? A government within the Commune has no more right to exist than a government over the Commune.'[149]

After countenancing the desirability of revolution and having served as the framework for personal and collective behaviour and action, it would be surprising if morality did not permeate Kropotkin's critique of contemporary society. In this third role of morality in Kropotkin's anarchism, the influence of Rousseau is visibly obvious. This is not to say that Kropotkin considers Rousseau to have been an anarchist; it is simply to suggest that Kropotkin shares some of the concerns of Rousseau and seems to invoke the spirit of Rousseau when formulating his vision of anarchy. Rousseau's *First Discourse*, for example, underscores Kropotkin's critique of the excesses of greed and luxury in his *An Appeal to the Young* (1885).[150] But the resemblance to Rousseau does not end there. In attempting to mitigate the passions resident in humankind, Kropotkin insists, like Rousseau, that anarchists 'take men as they are'.[151] And in an analogy of Rousseau's fusion of liberty and law in the general will, Kropotkin proceeds to argue that society should be arranged 'so that each man may see his interest bound up with the interests of the others';[152] only then will evil passions be subjugated. Like Rousseau, Kropotkin wants to create a community of self-governing individuals whose morality is fully developed and given practical expression in mutual agreements and free contracts. To Kropotkin's mind anarchism represents 'the ideal of a society where each governs himself according to his own will (which is evidently a result of the social influences borne by each)'.[153] Human morality, as expressed through mutual aid and sociability, manifests itself in its most developed form in anarchist-communism. Anarchism's strength is that it understands human nature. Hence anarchist-communism, as explained by Kropotkin in *Anarchism: Its Philosophy and Ideal*, transpires to be 'the best basis for individual development and freedom . . . that which represents the full expansion of man's faculties, the superior development of what is original in him, the greatest fruitfulness of intelligence, feeling and will'.[154] Anarchy is not a utopian ideology. Rather it is the tendency of modern social development and the realization of human nature.[155]

An Assessment of Kropotkin's Anarchism

Without doubt Kropotkin is a compassionate and persuasive writer, who is often held to be both systematic and clear. That may be a rather charitable assessment, but it should be said that in comparison to Proudhon and Bakunin, Kropotkin stands proud as a paragon of clarity and coherence. He was, moreover, fully cognizant of the charge that anarchists are little more than romantic dreamers, a charge levelled recently by George Woodcock among others.[156] Kropotkin responded to the criticism that anarchists are romantic dreamers by exhibiting a measure of realism that not only contradicts Woodcock's concomitant allegation that the anarchist was the proprietor of an especially benign account of human nature, but is seldom found in other anarchist writings.[157] Thus Kropotkin's reflection that people 'will not turn into anarchists by a sudden transformation; yet we know that on the one hand the insanity of governments, their ambitions, their bankruptcies, and on the other hand the incessant propaganda of ideas will result in great disturbances of equilibrium. At such a time we must act.'[158] Even amidst his realism, then, Kropotkin exercises a cautious optimism that the revolutionary opportunity will present itself.

But on what grounds does he base his optimism? Why will people revolt? And why, as David Miller has questioned, should we accept that it is anarchism that will evolve out of capitalism rather than some other form of social organization?[159] According to Miller there are two possible answers within Kropotkin's writings. The first is that

Kropotkin has a theory of moral progress; and the second, that he has also a theory of technological progress. For Miller, Kropotkin's moral ideas flow from human characteristics, like sympathy, that are 'unchanging' but become refined with the passage of history. And as 'anarchist principles are the fullest development of these moral ideas, anarchy is the final outcome of history'.[160] Likewise, technological progress has steadily created a situation in which individuals are increasingly dependent upon one another, rendering obsolete the view that individuals can succeed on their own. Anarchist-communism is the society best suited to enhance these technological developments.

Ultimately, Miller's responses have to be discarded. Before doing so, however, a few comments should be made. The first thing of note is that what Miller says here about Kropotkin's supposed theory of moral progress elicits a tension with what he says later about egoism. At one point Miller argues that Kropotkin regarded egotism as a perversion of capitalist society to be corrected by altruism in the long run.[161] The problem, for Miller, is that such a view invokes the contextualist account of human nature inherent in Kropotkin's writings. As such, human nature may respond to the environment in which it is situated, for humans are adaptable, but in itself human nature is incapable of determining the course of historical events. There is no assumption of an 'unchanging' human nature in Kropotkin's conception of human nature. Nor does he afford a notion of human nature that is capable of self-improvement. Human nature may recover from a prolonged bout of egoism, but the context within which human nature finds itself is integral to the process of convalescence. Altruism and sociability may resume their predominance at the expense of egoism, but human nature cannot accomplish this through some mystical self-ameliorating dynamic. If altruism and mutual aid are to be the benchmarks of future society that can only come about by way of a conscious, deliberate effort on the part of the people themselves to change history. The progression of human morality and human history is a matter of human will, ably assisted by education.

Miller's identification of a theory of technological progress is more defensible, but again encounters the difficulty discharged by the argument of non-determinism. Kropotkin's enthusiastic predictions of imminent revolution were, as noted above, inspired partly by the revolutionary climate and partly, as Miller has indicated, by a favourable assessment of technological progress. Whether this was displayed in agriculture or science matters little; what is important is that Kropotkin, as Marshall observes, shared in the nineteenth century's positivistic faith in science to bring about progress.[162] In that sense, Miller's notion of a theory of technological progress rings true. Kropotkin did place great stock in the idea that the evidence of history illustrated the coming of anarchism. The vehicle of this progress, though, is not so much the technological advancement that Kropotkin sees around him, but the tendencies present in historical development. Improvements in science and agriculture, and an optimism animated by the potential ability to change through education, amount to little more than fuel in the tank of the vehicle of history in which anarchy is a passenger. Kropotkin's objective, as Marshall informs us, was 'to demonstrate that anarchism represents existing tendencies in society towards political liberty and economic equality.' Furthermore, he endeavoured to show that 'the conclusions of anarchism could be scientifically verified'.[163]

None of the above, however, detracts from the fundamental difficulty that envelops Kropotkin's ideological narrative. In denying that anarchism is nothing but a utopian dream Kropotkin is forced to rely on an argument that placed anarchy as the outcome of existing social and historical tendencies. The state, he believed, had reached its apogee; its future progress was downhill towards disintegration. The social revolution loomed large on the horizon. History was not acting alone, however. Human nature was supporting its progress in the direction of a brighter future. But none of this can be guaranteed. History is not amenable to scientific laws of inevitability, it is a matter of human will. Thus, if Kropotkin's analysis is wrong (and history to date vindicates such a judgment), if it is simply an expression of faith rather than fact, then perhaps Kropotkin's anarchism should be considered utopian rather than scientific.

To complement his conception of human nature, as encapsulated in the concept of mutual aid, Kropotkin enunciates a vision of the good life characterized by voluntary agreements and free access, so long as one labours, to the produce of society. His brand of federal politics and free communism, set out in *The Conquest of Bread*, is consistent with his conception of human nature as expounded in his work *Mutual Aid*. The relationship between his conception of human nature and the philosophical basis of his conception of history is somewhat less satisfactory. The twin pillars of his conception of human nature, sociability and egoism, are mirrored in the dominating trends that he identifies in history: liberty and authority. But when viewed in conjunction with his philosophy of history, the contextualist element of his notion of human nature precludes any guarantee that history will evolve in a given direction. As there is no certainty that a social revolution will occur, so there is no certainty that the forces of liberty will triumph over the forces of authority. The contextualist dimension of his conception of human nature is a hurdle that history cannot cross without the assistance of human will. Capitalism, 'that bane of present society' is a 'stumbling-block in the path of intellectual and moral progress'.[164] History cannot be conceived as a unilinear development for the better, for Kropotkin.[165] Neither human morality nor human nature are bound to develop in a given direction. Which way they travel is a matter of human will. If history were perceived to be on a unilinear path of progression, then Kropotkin would have tremendous difficulty in explaining the rise of the modern state. It is because of the collapse of the medieval guilds, because history may proceed in a retrograde manner, that egoism vanquished sociability and the capitalist state secured its predominance at the expense of the medieval city-state. Kropotkin is no Hegelian idealist, but there is an admixture of ideas and material circumstances that combine to explain his philosophy of history. But, given the lack of historical determinism in Kropotkin, it is surprising that one does not discover a heavier emphasis on the role of the revolutionary in disseminating ideas. Undoubtedly, Kropotkin did support such activity, but his vocal backing of such measures is rather quiet at times. It would seem as if Kropotkin is actually caught in two minds about this, a reflection perhaps of his dualistic approach to the driving forces of history.

Traditionally, those who have relied on human will as the initiator of social revolutions, such as Bakunin, have placed great stock in the necessity of revolutionary groups and organizations in the promotion of a revolutionary consciousness. Hence the importance, to Bakunin, of secret societies and the International Brotherhood. One may argue that such thinkers have to emphasize the importance of revolutionary groups and organizations because they do not rest easy in the arms of historical destiny. Kropotkin is in a similar position. His philosophy of history disqualifies the leisurely inevitability of historical determinism. Yet he offers only qualified support for revolutionary minorities and revolutionary actions like 'propaganda by the deed'. It is not that he deliberately underestimates the prominence of ideas in the making of revolutions; the acquisition of a revolutionary consciousness in the masses reflects the fact that, for Kropotkin, a social revolution is a revolution in the minds of men as much as anything else. Rather it is that his conception of human nature warns him against investing too much authority in such organizations. Just as the perpetuity of egoism dictates caution in trusting individuals with power, so the contextualist dimension of his conception of human nature reinforces the necessity of prudence. The everlastingness of egoism, combined with a milieu that might unleash that capacity for self-assertion, shepherds Kropotkin away from the dangers of revolutionary minorities and their organizations as much as it forewarns him of the potential pitfalls of the dictatorship of the proletariat. Both the permanent and contextualist components of his understanding of human nature counsel against unqualified support for such institutions. Consequently, Kropotkin hovers in a state of limbo. Precluded from the comforts of historical determinism by his philosophy of history, his assumptions concerning human nature prevent him from bestowing too much optimism in revolutionary organizations and activity. Even if a successful revolution were to materialize, Kropotkin's problems do not disappear. To be sure, the new environment would favour the development of human morality and the consolidation of mutual aid. However, together with the contextualist conception of human nature there stands that which is permanent or given. Egoism and self-assertion survive in anarchy as sociability and mutual aid endures in capitalism. Neither can be truly eradicated. Just as Kropotkin has to assume a will to revolution so he infers a will to power. It is because of this that the dangers of the Marxist 'dictatorship of the proletariat' are of constant concern to the anarchist.

In light of the fact that altruism or mutual aid is the glue that holds Kropotkin's anarchist society together, one has to ask whether it is up to the job? On its own it is patently not capable of this task. Support is required by way of social rules and moral coercion. Acknowledging that conflict will arise both within and between communes, because of the presence of egoism, Kropotkin was forced to concede that measures of social disapproval, ostracism and public opinion would have to be employed to curtail anti-social behaviour.[166] And that in itself raises the spectre of authoritarianism. As Marshall remarks, 'Kropotkin thinks that it is right for public opinion to oblige all people to do manual work and he believes it justifiable to use force against inveterate monopolisers. There are authoritarian elements here which cannot be dismissed.'[167] The evidence is not hard to find. In discussing the problems of free riders in *The Conquest of Bread*, Kropotkin suggests that besides ostracism other workers could threaten to withdraw contracts, and if the recipient of these threats finds this to his dislike then he may leave. 'This is,' writes Kropotkin, 'what would be done in a communal society in order to turn away sluggards if they become too numerous.'[168] Evidently, as the collectivist prerequisite of labour entails compulsion so too do the excesses of egoism and self-assertion. Increasingly, the distinction between Kropotkin's two competing historical trends is beginning to look a bit thin.

Of course it could be asked why any form of compulsion or coercion is necessary in the first place? Is it not that Kropotkin has latently acknowledged that his concept of mutual aid may not be as strong as he paints it? This at any rate is the line of reasoning prosecuted by Avrich. In his *Anarchist Portraits*, Avrich accepts that Kropotkin's theory of mutual aid was 'a valuable corrective' to the arguments of the neo-Malthusians and social Darwinists. 'But,' he continues, 'Kropotkin erred in the opposite direction. He took insufficient account of the naked violence that dominates the life of most animals, from insects and fish to reptiles and mammals. He underestimated the widespread brutality in nature, the persecution of the weak by the strong, among humans as well as among animals.'[169] Although Avrich may have a point, it seems that his argument would be fairer if construed in a slightly different manner. It is not correct to say that Kropotkin underestimated the extent of the evolutionary struggle, nor that 'he underrated the urge to power in many and the willingness of the mass of people to follow charismatic leaders'. Rather it is that the concept of the struggle was considered less relevant in the formulation of his ideological narrative. This is not to say that Kropotkin completely disaccommodates the notions of struggle and egoism. Indeed, a refusal to recognize the importance of these concepts would have left his ideological programme of action open to the gate-crashing tendencies of the revolutionary avant-garde party and the centralized communist state. It is simply that mutual aid and sociability were given preference over egoism and self-assertion, for mutual aid and sociability are the bedrock of his anarchist society.

To understand why compulsion and coercion are a necessary feature of Kropotkin's anarchist society, a more subtle analysis of his concept of mutual aid is called for. As part of an ideological armoury employed by Kropotkin to defend his vision of how things are now and how they could be in the future, mutual aid, as representative of his conception of human nature, does a reasonably good job. But it may not do all that Kropotkin would like it to do. For instance, citing mutual aid as a relevant factor in the struggle for existence between a species and its environment does much to justify the weight that

Kropotkin attaches to the concept. However, that does not preclude a rival interpretation in which egoism or self-assertion is the chief motivating factor in the existence of struggle within a species. Essentially, Kropotkin's mutual-aid thesis is a concerted defence against the neo-Hobbesian view of competitive egoism. And that really is about the limit of its explanatory powers. As Cahm has noted, Kropotkin knew that his theory of mutual aid, considered as only one factor in the process of evolution, could not in itself account for the development of evolution.[170] Moreover, as David Miller has remarked, the evidence that Kropotkin cites in support of it 'does nothing to prove that species and groups are more likely to survive the more they practise it; it would be equally compatible with the view that there is an optimum level of mutual aid, above which a species' or group's chances of survival are lessened'.[171] Even in the example of mutual aid that has the most bearing on the possibility of anarchist-communism, that of mutual aid in social institutions, Kropotkin's argument may not be as comprehensive as first appears. Mutual aid, as represented in the medieval guild and city-state, is an important element in Kropotkin's ideological tale about how such institutions established precedents that predict the feasibility of an anarchist society. As such Kropotkin is full of praise for what was achieved in these institutions at this time. Nevertheless he was honest enough to admit that they were not without their own problems. Thus, there are 'conflicts' and 'internal struggles', 'bloodshed' and 'reprisals'.[172] Precious little is said, however, about their inherent inegalitarianism, and no mention is made of the fact that the medieval guilds were at the same time religious brotherhoods. Their camaraderie and practices of mutual aid, then, could have been inspired by religion as much as human nature. The upshot of this is that Kropotkin is requesting that mutual aid play a role that it cannot fulfil. The obligations imposed on Kropotkin's account of human nature by the remainder of his ideological narrative are too heavy for it to bear. Mutual aid, and therefore human nature, cannot determine the course of historical development because Kropotkin's philosophy of history forbids it. Furthermore, mutual aid is unable, in the final analysis, to guarantee the smooth functioning and well-being of any future anarchist society, because there is a parallel feature of Kropotkin's conception of human nature, namely egoism, that constantly undermines its good intentions.

Notes

1. M.A. Miller, *Kropotkin*, (University of Chicago Press, Chicago, 1976) p. vi.
2. G. Woodcock, *Anarchism: A History of Libertarian Ideas and Movements*, (Penguin, Harmondsworth, 1975) pp. 171–2.
3. Kropotkin spent five years in Siberia, exploring the Vitim region in 1865.
4. P. Kropotkin, *Memoirs of a Revolutionist*, (The Cresset Library, London, 1988) p. 148, referred to hereafter as *Memoirs*. One has to assume that this new attitude was triggered, at least in part, by his reading of Proudhon's *Système des Contradictions Economiques*, recommended by the dissident poet Mikhailov, sentenced to hard labour in 1861. Although Kropotkin neglects to mention this in his *Memoirs*, it appears to be common knowledge. See, for example, G. Woodcock and I. Avakumovic, *From Prince to Rebel: Peter Kropotkin*, (Black Rose Books, Montréal, 1990) p. 57. They argue that Kropotkin obtained the poet's annotated copy of this text after his death in 1865. Miller, however, seems to suggest that Mikhailov gave Kropotkin the book. See M.A. Miller, *Selected Writings on Anarchism and Revolution: P.A. Kropotkin*, (MIT Press, Boston, 1970) p. 9. C. Harper, *Anarchy: A Graphic Guide*, (Camden Press, London, 1987) pp. 52–3, agrees; suggesting that 'before his death from tuberculosis, Mikhailov introduced Kropotkin to Proudhon's ideas.'
5. Kropotkin, *Memoirs*, p. 188. As Caroline Cahm notes, 'Kropotkin's use of the term "anarchist" is actually anachronistic here for the Jurassians had not adopted it at this stage.' See her *Kropotkin and the Rise of Revolutionary Anarchism 1872–1886*, (Cambridge University Press, Cambridge, 1989) p. 27.
6. E. Malatesta, 'Peter Kropotkin – Recollections and Criticisms of an Old Friend', *The Raven*, 5, 4, (1992) p. 399. Malatesta's article on Kropotkin is a reprint of an essay originally published in 1931.
7. R.N. Baldwin (ed.), *Kropotkin's Revolutionary Pamphlets*, (Dover Publications, New York, 1970) p. 6.
8. Ibid.
9. Baldwin's concerns are essentially a reflection of Malatesta's suspicions of Kropotkin. In subsequent years Baldwin's doubts have been supported by Walter and Kinna. See, in the first instance, N. Walter, 'The Great French Revolution' (book review), *Freedom*, 50, 9, (1989) p. 14. Kinna too notes an implicit bias that exudes from the very selective interpretation of evidence that permeates Kropotkin's theory of mutual aid. See R. Kinna, 'Kropotkin and Huxley', *Politics*, 12, 2, (1992) p. 43. Paul Avrich, in his work *Anarchist Portraits*, (Princeton University Press, Princeton, 1988) refers to the concerns of Kropotkin's contemporaries, Cherkezov and Stepniak, who recognized Kropotkin's efforts to 'make certain ideas prevail at all costs' (p. 75).
10. A.F. Chalmers, *What is this Thing Called Science?* (Open University Press, Milton Keynes, 1980) p. 30.
11. Ibid., p. 33.
12. Daniel P. Todes, 'The Scientific Background of Kropotkin's Mutual Aid', *The Raven*, 6, 4, (1993) p. 361.
13. P. Kropotkin, *Mutual Aid: A Factor of Evolution*, (Freedom Press, London, 1987) p. 26, referred to hereafter as *Mutual Aid*.
14. Ibid., p. 63.

15. Ibid., p. 12.
16. T.H. Huxley, 'The Struggle for Existence: A Programme', *The Nineteenth Century*, (1888) pp. 163 and 165.
17. Ibid., p. 165.
18. P. Kropotkin, *The State: Its Historic Role*, (Freedom Press, London, 1987) p. 12, referred to hereafter as *The State*.
19. Kropotkin, *Mutual Aid*, p. 30.
20. Kropotkin, *Memoirs*, p. 299.
21. Kropotkin, *Mutual Aid*, p. 98.
22. C. Darwin, *The Origin of Species*, (Penguin, Harmondsworth, 1968) p. 116.
23. Ibid., p. 126.
24. J. Howard, *Darwin*, (Oxford University Press, Oxford, 1982) p. 91.
25. First published in Paris in 1892, Kropotkin's *The Conquest of Bread* preceded publication of *Mutual Aid* (1902) by ten years. Reliance on publication dates alone, however, would present a misleading picture of events. Bearing in mind that Kropotkin's first essays on the subject of mutual aid were published in *The Nineteenth Century* in 1890, it seems safe to assume that he must have been working on both texts, or was at least juggling with both theses, simultaneously. And it seems likely that Kropotkin must have begun to think seriously about the mutual aid thesis after reading Kessler's lecture whilst imprisoned at Clairvaux between 1883 and 1886. Moreover, it is known that articles constituting the basis of *The Conquest of Bread* were published in *Le Révolté* during 1886. See Cahm, *op. cit.*, p. 205. *Le Révolté*, edited by P. Kropotkin, F. Dumartheray and G. Herzig, was published from 1879 to 1887. *Le Révolte*, edited by J. Grave with some assistance from Kropotkin, was published in Paris from 1887 to 1894.
26. Kropotkin, *Mutual Aid*, p. 18.
27. Ibid., p. 24.
28. Ibid.
29. A.G.N. Flew, *Darwinian Evolution*, (Paladin, London, 1984) p. 16.
30. Of course some carnivores do associate. Kropotkin tends to ignore the fact that lions, for example, reside in family groups. Moreover, canine carnivores, such as wolves, not only associate but hunt together in a highly disciplined and co-operative manner.
31. Kropotkin, *op. cit.*, pp. 60–1. Emphasis in the original.
32. P. Kropotkin, *Anarchism and Anarchist Communism*, (Freedom Press, London, 1987) p. 44, referred to hereafter as *A&AC*. Italics in the original. Kropotkin differs from Godwin in this respect. Whereas Kropotkin believes that mutual aid outweighs any desire for self-preservation he is reluctant to follow Godwin's lead and declare that there can be no such instinct for self-preservation stamped on the minds of men. See W. Godwin, *Enquiry Concerning Political Justice*, (Penguin, Harmondsworth, 1985) pp. 97, 98 and 103.
33. Kropotkin, *Mutual Aid*, p. 184.
34. Ibid., p. 62.
35. Ibid., p. 16.
36. P. Kropotkin, *Ethics: Origin and Development*, (Benjamin Blom, New York, 1968) p. 4.
37. Kropotkin, *A&AC*, p. 49.
38. Kropotkin, *Mutual Aid*, p. 218.
39. One recent analysis of anarchism suggests that there is no positive proof that Kropotkin ever read Rousseau. See G. Crowder, *Classical Anarchism: The Political Thought of Godwin, Proudhon, Bakunin and Kropotkin*, (Oxford University Press, Oxford, 1991) pp. 119–20.

An earlier biography indicates otherwise. According to Miller, Kropotkin had come across some of Rousseau's works in the library of Nikolai Pavlovich Kravchenko, who had married Peter's older sister Yelena. Kropotkin used to visit their house on Sundays whilst studying at the Corps de Pages. It seems highly improbable that Kropotkin would not have read Rousseau. See M.A. Miller, *Kropotkin*, p. 29. Indeed, Kropotkin himself gives a distinct impression that he had read Rousseau when comparing him to Tolstoy and the moral pathos that the writings of both invoke. See P. Kropotkin, *Russian Literature: Ideals and Realities*, (Black Rose Books, Montréal, 1991) p. 161.

40. J-J. Rousseau, *A Discourse on Inequality*, (Penguin, Harmondsworth, 1968) p. 99.

41. Ibid., p. 101.

42. Kropotkin, *Mutual Aid*, p. 229.

43. Kropotkin, *A&AC*, p. 57.

44. Kropotkin, *Mutual Aid*, p. 99.

45. P. Marshall, 'Human Nature and Anarchism', in D. Goodway (ed.), *For Anarchism: History, Theory, and Practice*, (Routledge, London, 1989) p. 137.

46. Kinna, *op. cit.*, p. 46.

47. P. Marshall, *Demanding the Impossible: A History of Anarchism*, (HarperCollins, London, 1992) p. 337.

48. Kropotkin, *Ethics*, p. 263. Elsewhere Kropotkin argues that the two most prominent tendencies in history have been 'a tendency towards integrating labour for the production of all riches in common' and 'a tendency towards the fullest freedom of the individual in the prosecution of all aims, beneficial both for himself and for society at large.' See Kropotkin, *A&AC*, p. 24.

49. P. Kropotkin, *Act For Yourselves: Articles from 'Freedom' 1886–1907*, (Freedom Press, London, 1988) p. 82.

50. E. Burke, *Reflections on the Revolution in France*, (Penguin, Harmondsworth, 1982) p. 183.

51. P. Kropotkin, 'Anarchism: Its Philosophy and Ideal', in *Fugitive Writings*, (Black Rose Books, Montréal, 1993) p. 115.

52. Kropotkin, *A&AC*, p. 83.

53. Kropotkin, *Ethics*, p. 312.

54. Ibid., p. 137, n. 2.

55. Kropotkin, *The State*, p. 59. Cf. n. 48, p. 140 above.

56. P. Kropotkin, *Modern Science and Anarchism*, (Freedom Press, London, 1923) pp. 1–2, referred to hereafter as *MSA*.

57. Kropotkin, *The State*, p. 59. The rather rosy view presented by Kropotkin is challenged by David Miller, who ventures to suggest that Kropotkin conveniently neglects the less savoury elements present in medieval life. See D. Miller, 'The Neglected (II): Kropotkin', *Government and Opposition*, 18, (1983) p. 332.

58. Kropotkin, *Mutual Aid*, pp. 152–3.

59. Kropotkin, 'Anarchism: Its Philosophy and Ideal', in *Fugitive Writings*, p. 111.

60. Ibid., p. 112.

61. Marshall, *Demanding the Impossible*, p. 324.

62. D. Miller, *op. cit.*, p. 333.

63. Kropotkin, *MSA*, p. 47.

64. P. Kropotkin, 'Must We Occupy Ourselves with an Examination of the Ideal of a Future System?' in *Fugitive Writings*, p. 54.

65. Ibid., p. 55.

66. D. Miller, *Social Justice*, (Clarendon Press, Oxford, 1976) p. 246.

67. M.A. Miller, *Selected Writings*, p. 30.
68. Marshall, *op. cit.*, p. 322.
69. P. Kropotkin, *In Russian and French Prisons*, (Black Rose Books, Montréal, 1991) p. 367.
70. Ibid., p. 24.
71. P. Kropotkin, 'Anarchist Morality', in *Fugitive Writings*, p. 146.
72. Kropotkin, *A&AC*, p. 58. Kropotkin's moral theory is reviewed in Marshall, *op. cit.*, pp. 321–2.
73. P. Kropotkin, *Words of a Rebel*, (Black Rose Books, Montréal, 1992) pp. 150–1.
74. P. Kropotkin, 'Anarchist Morality', in *Fugitive Writings*, p. 144.
75. Ibid., pp. 143 and 141.
76. Kropotkin, *Words of a Rebel*, p. 151.
77. Ibid. Parentheses in the original.
78. Kropotkin, 'Anarchist Morality', in *Fugitive Writings*, p. 130.
79. Ibid., p. 131.
80. Kropotkin, *In Russian and French Prisons*, p. 367.
81. P. Kropotkin, *The Conquest of Bread*, (Elephant Editions, London, 1985) p. 94. Cf. ibid., p. 99.
82. P. Kropotkin, *The Place of Anarchism in Socialistic Revolution*, (Practical Parasite Publications, Cymru, 1990) p. 14.
83. P. Kropotkin, *The Great French Revolution. Volume 1*, (Elephant Editions, London, 1986) pp. 16–17.
84. Crowder, *op. cit.*, p. 167.
85. Details of Kropotkin's arrest and trial at Lyon may be found in M.A. Miller, *Kropotkin*, pp. 162–3.
86. Kropotkin, *Words of a Rebel*, p. 24. The following essay in this text is called 'The Inevitability of Revolution'. *Words of a Rebel* is a collection of articles written by Kropotkin for *Le Révolté* during 1879–82. A further example of Kropotkin's opinion that revolution was imminent can be found in *The Conquest of Bread*, pp. 39 and 80.
87. M.A. Miller, *Selected Writings*, p. 16.
88. Marshall, *Demanding the Impossible*, p. 310.
89. Kropotkin addresses this aspect of human nature when considering the French Revolution in his *The Conquest of Bread*, p. 83.
90. Kropotkin, 'Must We Occupy Ourselves with an Examination of the Ideal of a Future System?' in *Fugitive Writings*, p. 25. My emphasis.
91. Kropotkin, *In Russian and French Prisons*, p. 333.
92. Kropotkin, *Words of a Rebel*, p. 171.
93. Kropotkin, *The Conquest of Bread*, p. 93.
94. Quoted from Cahm, *op. cit.*, p. 145.
95. Ibid., p. 154.
96. Marshall, *op. cit.*, p. 336.
97. Kropotkin, *The Conquest of Bread*, p. 192.
98. Kropotkin, *Words of a Rebel*, p. 174.
99. Kropotkin, 'Must We Occupy Ourselves with an Examination of the Ideal of a Future System?' in *Fugitive Writings*, p. 65.
100. A useful but short summary of Kropotkin's position is provided by M.A. Miller, *Selected Writings*, p. 28.
101. Quoted in Cahm, *op. cit.*, p. 65.
102. Kropotkin, *MSA*, pp. 43–4. Emphasis in original. However, Kropotkin tempers this argument further into the text. 'It is impossible', he writes, 'to legislate for *the future*. All we can do is to vaguely guess its essential tendencies and clear the road for it.' (Ibid., pp. 87–8.)
103. Woodcock, *Anarchism*, p. 190. It should be noted that in the

biography of Kropotkin that Woodcock wrote with Avakumovic, he does acknowledge that whilst Kropotkin's *The Conquest of Bread* does not outline 'an exhaustive plan of the future' it does offer 'a somewhat elaborate sketch of the free society of the future and the anarchist answer to various social problems.' See Woodcock and Avakumovic, *op. cit.*, p. 314.

104. D. Miller, *Social Justice*, p. 236. Miller's judgment is echoed in his later work *Anarchism*, (Dent, London, 1984), p. 8, in which he argues that anarchists are not averse to elaborating 'models of the kind of society that they want to see'.

105. Kropotkin, *Fugitive Writings*, p. 32.

106. Ibid.

107. Kropotkin, 'Must We Occupy Ourselves with an Examination of the Ideal of a Future System?' in *Fugitive Writings*, p. 16.

108. Ibid., p. 25.

109. Ibid., p. 29. As Ward acknowledges, Kropotkin's theory of federalism is similar to those espoused by Proudhon and Bakunin. See C. Ward, 'Kropotkin's Federalism', *The Raven*, 5, 4, (1992) p. 328.

110. Kropotkin, 'Must We Occupy Ourselves with an Examination of the Ideal of a Future System?' in *Fugitive Writings*, p. 31.

111. See ibid., pp. 29, 34 and 35.

112. See p. 155 above.

113. Ibid., p. 16.

114. Ibid., pp. 19 and 16.

115. Ibid., p. 26.

116. Ibid.

117. D. Miller, *Social Justice*, p. 237.

118. Woodcock and Avakumovic, *op. cit.*, p. 362. It should be noted that this is a contentious point. Some anarchists find democratic decision-making the only realistic solution. See, for example, M.

Bookchin, *Social Anarchism or Lifestyle Anarchism: An Unbridgeable Chasm*, (AK Press, Edinburgh, 1995) pp. 17–18.

119. See Kropotkin, *The Conquest of Bread*, p. 93.

120. The congress took place on 3–5 August 1878. For a description of the events and debate see Cahm *op. cit.*, pp. 44–9. According to Cahm the first exposé of anarchist-communism was delivered by Reclus at Lausanne in March 1876.

121. Two slightly differing versions of this speech are provided by Cahm, *op. cit.*, p. 49 and M. Miller, *Kropotkin* pp. 141–2. The congress at La Chaux-de-Fonds was held on 12 October 1879.

122. Kropotkin, *The Conquest of Bread*, pp. 162–3.

123. Ibid., p. 84.

124. Kropotkin's argument is to be found in *MSA*, p. 76.

125. These problems have been outlined by David Miller in 'The Negelected (II): Kropotkin', p. 325. All three, however, are subsumed within Kropotkin's general position, in *The Conquest of Bread* and elsewhere, that social wealth is a common inheritance. Whilst Miller recognizes the overarching importance of Kropotkin's argument on social wealth, he fails to address in any detail the contextualist perspective of Kropotkin's conception of human nature.

126. Kropotkin, *The Conquest of Bread*, pp. 28–9.

127. Ibid., p. 33.

128. Both citations are drawn from ibid., p. 46.

129. Ibid., p. 143.

130. For details of the right to life as the basis for the free distribution of goods, see ibid., pp. 42–3. When goods are scarce preference is given to children and the aged. See

Kropotkin, *The Place of Anarchism in Socialistic Evolution*, pp. 7–8.

131. Kropotkin, *The Conquest of Bread*, p. 34.

132. Ibid., p. 61.

133. Kropotkin, *The Place of Anarchism in Socialistic Evolution*, p. 6.

134. Confirmation of the date of the Paris address can be had from M. Miller, *Kropotkin*, p. 165. The lecture was first published in *Le Révolté* between 28 March and 9 May 1886. Again Miller provides the source of information at p. 298, n. 24.

135. Kropotkin, 'Must We Occupy Ourselves with an Examination of the Ideal of a Future System?' in *Fugitive Writings*, p. 33.

136. Kropotkin, *MSA*, p. 64.

137. The details of these arguments may be found in Kropotkin, *Words of a Rebel*, pp. 211, 214, 215 and 220. Kropotkin also emphasizes that industrial plant will be returned to the community. See ibid., p. 219.

138. See P. Kropotkin, 'Representative Government', in *Words of a Rebel*, p. 143.

139. P. Kropotkin, 'The Paris Commune', in *Words of a Rebel*, p. 99. Cf. also ibid., p. 101. For details of Proudhon's argument on usufructuary, see P-J. Proudhon, *What is Property? An Inquiry into the Principle of Right and of Government*, (William Reeves, London, n.d.) pp. 98–9.

140. Acceptance of the base–superstructure paradigm is to be found in Kropotkin, *Words of a Rebel*, p. 118. Assimilation of the same model is evident in *The Conquest of Bread*, p. 54.

141. Kropotkin, *Words of a Rebel*, p. 208.

142. Kropotkin, 'Anarchism: Its Philosophy and Ideal', in *Fugitive Writings*, p. 111.

143. Ibid., p. 115.

144. Kropotkin, *MSA*, p. 5.

145. Kropotkin, 'Anarchist Morality', in *Fugitive Writings*, p. 142.

146. Kropotkin, *Words of a Rebel*, p. 30; *The Place of Anarchism in Socialistic Evolution*, p. 12.

147. Kropotkin, *MSA*, p. 45. Somewhat akin to Proudhon, Kropotkin talks of free contracts between individuals and groups in his *The Conquest of Bread*, p. 50.

148. Kropotkin, *Words of a Rebel*, p. 87.

149. Ibid., p. 97.

150. P. Kropotkin, 'An Appeal to the Young', in Baldwin, *op. cit.*, *passim*.

151. Kropotkin, *The Place of Anarchism in Socialistic Evolution*, p. 16.

152. Ibid. Cf. Kropotkin, *Fugitive Writings*, p. 114.

153. Kropotkin, 'Anarchism: Its Philosophy and Ideal', in *Fugitive Writings*, p. 106. Parentheses in the original. Such thoughts are obviously inconsistent with what he has to say in *Ethics*. See the discussion at pp. 138–9 above.

154. Kropotkin, 'Anarchism: Its Philosophy and Ideal', in *Fugitive Writings*, p. 119.

155. Kropotkin, *MSA*, p. 46.

156. Woodcock, in particular, indicts Kropotkin's *Words of a Rebel*. See his 'Introduction' to that text, p. 13. For Kropotkin's appreciation of the accusation of romanticism, see *Fugitive Writings*, p. 114.

157. For details of Woodcock's opinion of Kropotkin's supposedly kind appraisal of human nature, see Woodcock, *Anarchism*, p. 206.

158. Kropotkin, *Words of a Rebel*, p. 219.

159. D. Miller, *Social Justice*, p. 211.

160. Ibid.

161. Ibid., p. 246.

162. Marshall, *Demanding the Impossible*, p. 318.

163. Ibid., p. 336. There are numerous examples of Kropotkin's belief that anarchism would be the outcome of existing historical tendencies, two of which are to be found in *The Conquest of Bread*, p. 45, and in P. Kropotkin, *Fields, Factories and Workshops Tomorrow*, (Freedom Press, London, 1985) p. 26.

164. Kropotkin, *The Conquest of Bread*, p. 117.

165. See his comments in *The State*, p. 59. The closing pages of this text provide good reasons for thinking that Kropotkin believed that the two competing trends of historical development are forever in opposition.

166. For an extensive and informed survey of the degree to which anarchism is dependent upon notions of public censure, see A. Ritter, *Anarchism: A Theoretical Analysis*, (Cambridge University Press, Cambridge, 1980).

167. Marshall, *op. cit.*, p. 338.

168. Kropotkin, *The Conquest of Bread*, p. 154.

169. Avrich, *Anarchist Portraits*, p. 75.

170. Cahm, *op. cit.*, p. 5.

171. D. Miller, 'The Negelected (II): Kropotkin', p. 337.

172. For an appraisal of Kropotkin's treatment of the medieval guilds and city-state, see Avrich, *op. cit.*, pp. 76–7 from whom these citations are drawn.

6

Conclusion

Grappling with Ideology

All political ideologies are protean by nature, but anarchism more so than its competitors. The range and diversity of anarchist thinkers seems at times perplexing. Classification occurs at so many different levels: from the American individualist Rothbard to the communism of Malatesta; and from the violence of Bakunin to the pacifism of Tolstoy. It comes as no surprise, then, to discover some commentators proclaiming that anarchism lacks doctrinal continuity.[1] Criticism flows freely when faced with a bewildering multiplicity of ideological identities. But the endeavour to uncover the true nature or real core of an ideology is a valuable exercise, even if it is a task both difficult and fraught with dangers. Indeed, searching for the essential identity of a political ideology may at times be analogous to the quest for the Holy Grail. This is not to assert that, when it comes to investigating political ideologies, a fundamental and unmistakable identity is some form of exegetical mirage. On the contrary, some such association of core values or beliefs is a necessary element of any ideology.[2] However, the demands exacted in the process of identification vary from one ideology to another.

One complicating factor, for instance, is that ideologies are not static, moribund, monolithic monuments to a bygone golden age. They are, conversely, living, dynamic and evolving bodies of political ideas that are capable of changing both their fundamental principles and, in consequence, their political outlook to a considerable degree. Take, for example, the transformation of liberalism. Under the aegis of the likes of John Locke and Adam Smith, classical liberalism extolled the virtues of economic individualism and provided a convincing justification for the free market. By the close of the nineteenth century, liberalism, under the influence of such thinkers as John Stuart Mill and Thomas Hill Green, had acquired a social conscience. Recognizing that some people were unable to help themselves in the savage arena of capitalist market forces, liberals began to argue that the forces of capitalism be tempered and a safety net secured for the poorest in society. At the heart of this progression in political ideas is a division over the concept of human nature. Whereas the old school had seen humans as selfish, acquisitive, competitive and pleasure-seeking, the modern liberals viewed individuals as essentially social, co-operative and community-oriented.

In a more contemporary setting, conservatism has undergone a similar shift in character with the rise of the New Right or neo-conservatism. Both in America and, more recognizably, in the United Kingdom, conservatism has changed direction quite sharply. In the United Kingdom, in particular, the old familiar tradition-based, pragmatic, organic conservatism, with a distinctly limited style of politics, has surrendered to a new breed of thinker and activist. In place of the old ways of thinking enshrined in the likes of Benjamin Disraeli's 'one-nation conservatism', a radical, principled and conviction-based style of conservatism has emerged that has been more radical than anything offered by democratic socialists for the last two decades. Once again a shift in the ideology's understanding of human nature has accompanied the amended philosophy. A conception of human nature that owed much to the classical liberals underpinned the neo-conservative perspective, with a subsequent abandonment of the scepticism and belief in intellectual imperfection that supported the more moderate benevolent paternalism of organic conservatives.

Despite the differences occasioned by each ideology's evolution, both liberalism and conservatism have preserved some of their most important principles. Appreciation of liberty above all else remains central to liberalism, even if the conception of liberty may have changed from a negative to a positive interpretation. Freedom is also cherished by conservatives, but perhaps more so under the auspices of neo-conservatism and its classical liberal inheritance. However, the touchstone of both brands of conservative thinking is the maintenance of order in society.

The question that has to be addressed now is whether the same can be said of anarchism? In other words, does anarchism possess central principles too? Anarchism is a particularly slippery ideology. Even when reduced to a simple category of social anarchism, differences persist and contrasts remain strong. From Proudhon's mutualism, through Bakunin's collectivism to Kropotkin's supposed communism, the business of locating the ideology's essential unity should not be understated. As Graeme Duncan has counselled, the investigation of ideology can prove to be a frustrating experience. The difficulties arise, he warns, because ideologies 'may be incoherent in some respects, or contain contradictory elements. . . . In addition, significant internal divisions may be sheltered beneath a large ideological umbrella. . . . To pursue an ideology, even if we call it a political philosophy, may be to pursue a mysterious, ever-retreating thing, which dissolves as we clutch at it.'[3]

This seems especially true of anarchism. As expounded by Proudhon, Bakunin and Kropotkin, anarchism is often incoherent and sometimes contradictory. Yet whilst these writers are often separated from one another on the basis of economics, they do share a common prescriptive outlook. They all desire a society without the state. In this sense the ideology of anarchism is tangible. Its vision of the good life, commonly dependent upon a decentralized and federated structure of autonomous communes in all three social anarchists under review here, maintains its unity at this prescriptive level.

More importantly, the consistency of this vision of the good life is paralleled by a uniformity in its conception of human nature. All three thinkers rely on the twin dimensions of egoism and sociability when elucidating their respective conceptions of human nature. But the consensus over declared goals and the common perception of human nature belies the disparity of theories of economic organization exhibited by social anarchists. Whilst all three subscribe to some form of federal administrative structure, they differ in their observations on how the future society should be constructed on an economic basis. This should come as no surprise, since the role played by any concept of human nature in an ideology is limited to marking out the boundaries of what is possible. One particular set of assumptions about human nature does not necessarily lead to a specific conclusion on matters of politics or economics. As Robert McShea has remarked, a theory of human nature

> makes political philosophy possible, but so far as we can see, it does not determine its content. Those who accept it do not commit themselves thereby to specific political conclusions or norms. All existing programmes, from anarchism to communism, can be stated and argued for in these terms. What the theory does is to provide a common terminology within which opposing views and ideologies can find a way of coming to grips both with their opponents and with themselves.[4]

The manifestation of conflicting theories of economic organization does not necessarily reveal fundamental variations in conceptions of human nature. There may be shades of disagreement over minor matters, but the central foundation of a conception of human nature can be one and the same in different thinkers and therefore support miscellaneous political and economic arrangements. One useful way of explaining this ideological tolerance is, as Duncan has suggested, by the idea of fit. 'Accounts of human nature,' Duncan argues, 'are critical and normative instruments, used to support one kind of regime or series of developmental stages, and to dismiss others as violating or being incompatible with that nature. However, the fit may not be immaculate: on opening up a conception of human nature we may discover that it has hidden possibilities or implications, which enable it to support different recommendations from those of the author.'[5] In a technical analogy the degree of tolerance between a conception of human nature and its surrounding ideological prescriptions may be wider than one first imagined.

The question that remains unanswered is, how far does the analogy of fit hold good? For it is one thing to say that a conception of human nature may yield numerous political prescriptions, and quite another to say that a conception of human nature need bear no resemblance to the conclusions it is supposedly responsible for. As Andrew Vincent has argued, an

> ordinary expectation of the term 'ideology' implies the existence of a cluster of concepts, ideas and values which can be rationally articulated and which evince some moderate coherence. An ideology in this sense can be defined formally as a mesh of interconnected concepts, values and principles providing a set of relatively coherent beliefs about human nature, human agency, action and social, political, moral and economic interaction.[6]

A measure of coherence is obligatory in political ideologies. And in so far as a concept of human nature helps to bind the various ideas and values of an ideology together, so it has to exhibit a degree of commensurability with an ideology's political proscriptions.

Anarchism's Fundamental Inconsistency

The problem for the social anarchists is that the mandatory measure of commensurability evaporates upon close inspection of the ideology of anarchism. Whilst all three social anarchists subscribe to approximately the same description of human nature, and derive different economic conclusions from that, there is a major breakdown in the coherence between their conception of human nature and their recommendations for restructuring society. The social anarchists' conception of human nature fails to mesh or knit tightly with their vision of the good life. Indeed, it is more accurate to say that social anarchism embodies a fundamental inconsistency between its conception of human nature and the social and political prescriptions that it writes.

The nature of the disparity may be revealed through a brief comparison of anarchism with traditionalist conservatism.[7] At first sight it may seem that two ideologies so implacably opposed to one another could not possibly have anything in common. Nevertheless, there are certain parallels that exist between the anarchist and the conservative conceptions of human nature. For example, both ideologies recognize that humans have a potential for wrongdoing or even wickedness, and as such an air of realism pervades each. Both acknowledge that egoism has a role to play in human behaviour. This may manifest itself as something like a lust for power which concerns the social anarchists, or it may be a consequence of the Christian doctrine of original sin in conservative thought.

Although the two ideologies diverge in their respective ideas of how to contain the potential evil or wickedness that may afflict human action, the question to be asked is whether the disparity of prescriptive recommendations arises solely and simply from considerations of human nature? To contain outbreaks of disorder and to ensure that individuals refrain from committing wrongful acts, conservatives have long been noted for their emphasis on law and order. As such they work to reinforce social morality (n.b. the 'Back to Basics' campaign of John Major's government launched in the autumn of 1993), and thereby the status quo, by accentuating the value of traditional social institutions like the family and the church. In the event that these measures fail, conservatism relies on law enforcement agencies to clear up the mess.[8]

Beyond the prominence given to law and order, traditionalist conservatives depict themselves as reluctant to engage in the kind of detailed political conversation that, they consider, characterizes other ideologies. Indeed, conservatives deny that they are ideologists simply because they claim not to have an elaborate political theory.[9] Politics, for the conservative, is a limited activity. It is an element in one's life that is forced to compete for attention with other activities. Music, theatre, drama, literature, sports and many other pastimes are only some of the ways in which the conservative perceives individuals enjoying life. Politics, conservatives say, is not an activity that precludes almost every other activity, as it may, and often does in their eyes, for the Marxist and other ideologues.

Belying this denial of ideological attachment is the critical importance conservatives place on the moral and intellectual imperfection of humankind. As Anthony Quinton has termed it, conservatism is, in many respects, a philosophy of imperfection. Not only is humankind's moral standing challenged, its intellectual capacity is also questioned.[10] Citing the doctrine of original sin as an indelible mark of humankind's depravity, conservatives place great store in the belief that humans are inherently wicked. Religion, however, is not the only source of this line of reasoning. There are, as conservatives joyfully point out, tributaries to be found in Freud and Hobbes. For the former, the individual is subject to an ever eager id; the lascivious level of the tripartite mind. Thus, conservatives may warm to the image presented by Freud of the ego as an individual on horseback endeavouring to keep the animal under control by substituting 'the reality principle for the pleasure principle which reigns unrestrictedly in the id'.[11] Whereas in Hobbes, conservatives find appeal in his belief that human nature is the key to understanding why life was 'solitary, poore, nasty, brutish and short' in the state of nature.[12]

To the cynic, however, it would seem that moral and intellectual imperfection is not a universal malady. In particular, the ruling élite appear immune from its effects; for it is exactly this class that consider themselves naturally fit to govern.[13] In rejecting the partiality of the conservative argument, anarchists contend that it is precisely because all human beings are susceptible to the inclinations of egoism that no one should be placed into positions of power or authority. Anarchists, as Miller has observed, are cognizant 'of the imperfections of human nature'.[14] As Bakunin remarked, with the best will in the world one simply has to recognize the corrupting effects of power on all human beings. 'Take,' Bakunin suggests, 'the most sincere democrat and put him on the throne; if he does not step down promptly, he will surely become a scoundrel.'[15] Likewise, Proudhon contends: 'give power to a Saint Vincent de Paul and he will be a Guizot or a Talleyrand'.[16] Once incumbent, the occupier of power will simply abuse the privilege bestowed by that position.

To insure against the vulnerability of individuals in the face of power and privilege, anarchists suggest that the political environment be recast. The best way of avoiding an abuse of power or authority is to bar the availability of such positions. If the state is abolished and all remnants of political authority and power are thereby extirpated anarchists believe, individuals will no longer abuse, oppress or exploit one another, because the very mechanisms that encourage and facilitate such behaviour will have been dismantled in the process of social reconstruction. If the state and its mechanisms of exploitation are dissolved, power and political authority will evaporate, because their medium of existence will cease to exist.

Here, then, is to be found the crucial difference between traditionalist conservatism and anarchism. On the one hand, traditionalist conservatives have a firm perspective of human nature as a concept that embodies fixed or given elements, such as the moral and intellectual imperfection of humankind. Accordingly, they possess a vision of society and social organization that reflects their conception of human nature. One may dislike or disagree with their assumptions concerning human nature, but one cannot criticize them on the grounds that their vision of how society ought to be is out of step with the features they ascribe to human nature. The pessimism or scepticism that accompanies conservative thought is directly related to their conception of human nature. The philosophy of imperfection leads unerringly to a moderate, pragmatic and limited style of politics, which is a conscious and palpable observation on their understanding of human nature.

Anarchists, on the other hand, are plainly guilty of ignoring the implications that arise from their own conception of human nature. In suggesting that human nature comprises both egoism and sociability, and in confessing that neither of these two components can be completely eradicated, regardless of external circumstances, anarchists subscribe to the view that human nature is both something that is given and something that may vary depending on the context in which it is situated. Thus the essential optimism of anarchism, that future society will be free of the exploitation, violence and abuses of power that characterize capitalism, cannot be borne entirely by its conception of human nature.

Whilst the anarchists may argue quite legitimately that human nature is malleable, they cannot use that argument to justify their vision of the good life. That contention would only hold good if the conception of human nature they employed was one in which there were no fixed or given elements present. By importing egoism into their conception of human nature, the social anarchists are compelled to account for that fixed constituent in their vision of the good life.

As Andrew Heywood has remarked, to argue that human nature represents something fixed is to argue that society should mirror that which is considered as given.[17] Because there is something permanent in human nature anarchists have to account for how society will embrace that. The fact that they seek to radically alter society is therefore irrelevant. Even after radical surgery, society will still have to deal with that which is enduring in human nature.

Consequently, the optimism that is inherent in the expression of a society without state cannot be based on the social anarchists' conception of human nature. Or, to put it more accurately, the anarchist vision of a future stateless society is an unwarranted optimism that finds little by way of vindication in its conception of human nature. If social anarchists held that human nature was something that could be bent at will by a change in environment, then they would be justified in stressing the consistency of their ideological prescriptions by appealing to their conception of human nature. But the social anarchists do not regard human nature as wholly malleable. Their conception of human nature assumes that even in a post-revolutionary or post-capitalist society egoism will remain a thorn in the side of their endeavours for peace and harmony.

This, then, is the central tension, the fundamental contradiction of social anarchism. Anarchists share with liberals a concern for the susceptibility of human nature to a lust for power, and both liberals and anarchists believe that the actions of human beings may be directed by egoism as much as by sociability or an interest in the well-being of others. Thus both ideologies recoil from the prospect of an unrestrained power or political authority established through centralized social or political institutions. However, whereas liberals proceed to circumscribe the power of egoism inherent in human nature by instituting a series of checks and balances on government power, anarchists blithely jettison their worries in favour of the socialist-based vision of human beings as co-operative creatures perfectly capable of living harmoniously without the interference of laws or government.

Sociability, it would seem, usurps the reign of caution that was exercised in light of the dangers of egoism. Jumping from one assumption about human nature to another, anarchists may give the impression that they are working with a conception of human nature that assumes human nature to be entirely malleable. But this is simply untrue. Within social anarchism egoism is recognized as a given or innate feature of human nature, and as such it will not dissolve into non-existence upon the transition from capitalist society to anarchist society. Here is to be found the anarchists' utopian optimism. It is an optimism inspired by the inheritance of the socialist vision of human nature. And it is utopian in that the goal of a stateless, non-coercive, non-hierarchical society must forever elude the grasp of anarchists because they either fail to see or choose to ignore the consequences of their liberal inheritance.

Marshall on Human Nature

It was pointed out at the beginning of this book that anarchism is something of a hybrid of liberalism and socialism.[18] If it shares many of the concerns of liberalism, then it was born from the same reaction to capitalism as socialism. Both socialism and anarchist-communism, as Bertrand Russell has remarked, 'have risen from the perception that private capital is a source of tyranny by certain individuals over others'.[19] Indeed, for Bakunin, one would be unthinkable without the other. As the opening and famous epigraph of Dolgoff's collection of Bakunin's writings reminds us: 'Liberty without socialism is privilege, injustice; socialism without liberty is slavery and brutality.'[20]

Although it is commonly recognized that anarchism has its origins in both liberalism and socialism, less thought has been given to the consequences of this twin ideological inheritance. One scholar of anarchism who attempts to trace the debt of anarchism to both liberalism and socialism is Peter Marshall.[21] His recent history of anarchism outlines this inheritance and in so doing provides a stimulating and provocative account of the anarchist conception of human nature.

His analysis of the anarchist conception of human nature is studious but flawed. For whilst Marshall provides an arresting and sometimes persuasive argument, it is imperative that his description of anarchism as 'a creative synthesis' of liberalism and socialism is rejected. Anarchism is not the 'synthesis' of these two outstanding political traditions as Marshall suggests. Rather, its double inheritance forces anarchism into an irresolvable stalemate over the question of human nature. Indeed, it is because of the nature of its origins that anarchism is dismissed as a tradition of political thought without shape or continuity; because it hovers between liberalism and socialism, it emits a sense of incoherence and inconsistency that is seized upon by its ideological rivals.

Having said that the consequences of its double inheritance are less well appreciated, anarchism's disagreement with socialism, or Marxist-Leninism to be more accurate, is well known. The two ideologies part company over the means and ends of the revolutionary struggle.[22] However, the roots of this discord lie deeper than the simple manifestation of varying revolutionary strategies would suggest. The rationale behind the anarchist objection is, to put it very simply, that Marxist-Leninists have misunderstood human nature. There is, anarchists caution, a lust for power in humankind that will jeopardize the very outcome of the revolutionary process itself. As Bakunin advised: 'No one should be entrusted with power, inasmuch as anyone invested with authority must, through the force of an immutable social law, become an oppressor and exploiter of society.'[23] History seems to have vindicated the anarchists' account. Aside from the dispute with the Marxist-Leninists, anarchists, in general, have also frowned upon the endeavours of those socialists who have invested their faith in parliamentary mechanisms and procedures as a means to bring about a new kind of society.

There is, however, an obvious common thread that runs through both socialism and anarchism. Most undergraduate students of political theory are broadly aware that there is little to differentiate between the goals or objectives of anarchism and communism.[24] Each ideology works towards a stateless, propertyless, moneyless society in which individual freedom is finally released from the alienation and exploitation that have constituted the benchmarks of capitalist society and its philosophy of free-market economics. The analysis may be crude and may gloss over one or two moot points of interpretation, but it is in essence correct.[25]

Whereas anarchism's sometimes stormy relationship with socialism has been well documented, the similarities and contrasts with liberalism are less likely to be appreciated. Perhaps this is because anarchism has often been viewed as a cousin of socialism, rising in reaction to liberal democratic institutions and values which are commonly perceived to be the lifeblood upon which capitalism depends. But as Peter Marshall has noted there is much that might be regarded as common ground between liberalism and anarchism. Both liberals and anarchists have a healthy suspicion of the state. The fact that anarchists want to abolish it, whilst liberals would be satisfied with a formal set of restraints (and, in some cases, minimizing the extent of its activity) to bridle its power, does not detract from the underlying unity of distrust that marks the attitude of both ideologies toward this concept.

Both are also highly sceptical of centralized bureaucratic institutions and eschew concentrations of political authority. There are, of course, many areas of contention, not least of which is the anarchists' desire to dissolve the state. Liberals may have some sympathy with this position, but they exercise a more cautious and more consistent approach than that which it is advanced by the social anarchists. This is the crux of the differences between the ideologies. But why and how can these differences be maintained?

Marshall believes that one way to appreciate the dissimilarities between liberalism and anarchism over the state is to examine the ideas of John Locke, the seventeenth-century physician and philosopher, whose *Two Treatises of Government* has been regarded as the finest statement of liberal political theory. Consequently, Locke is often employed as a pivotal figure in providing a justification for a minimal state.[26] But why does Locke suggest that individuals should leave the state of nature in preference for civil society and place themselves under the rule of government? The standard reply is that in making this transition individuals secure the preservation of their property, which when conceived in the wide sense of the term means that individuals seek to protect their natural rights to life, liberty and property.[27]

This in itself does not amount to a convincing explanation as to why individuals should abandon the freedom and equality that characterizes the state of nature.[28] To understand why it is that individuals are considered to be better off in a political society, Locke draws attention to the inconveniences that beset the state of nature. The first of these is the lack of an established and settled law upon which controversies may be resolved. The second is the want of an impartial and common judge with authority to determine differences according to the law. The third and final inconvenience is the lack of power to enforce a given sentence when right.[29] It is for these reasons that Locke advises that civil society is better able to defend people's property. As Peter Marshall asserts, Locke 'only differed from the anarchists in thinking that life in a state of nature could be uncertain and inconvenient without known laws and a limited government to protect the natural rights to life, liberty and property. Anarchists agree with Locke that humanity has always lived in society, but argue that government simply exasperates potential social conflict rather than offering a cure for it.'[30]

In so far as Marshall wants to elicit the fundamental disagreement between Locke, as a representative of liberalism, and anarchism he is right to point out this difference. But one has to ask whether Marshall has fully understood the implications of his statement? In particular, Marshall seems unaware of the underlying reasons for Locke's insistence on limited government. The inevitability of government, for Locke, is a consequence of the conception of human nature that he works with. As such, government amounts to a reflection of his thinking on human nature and how that can be best accommodated outside the state of nature. Of the three inconveniences noted by Locke, it is the second which is crucial to his argument for individuals placing themselves under the authority of laws and government. In the state of nature individuals may avail themselves of the power to execute the law of nature. In effect, this is a power to punish the offender who commits a crime against the law of nature. The difficulty, for Locke, is that those offended against are hardly likely to remain disinterested in the punishment that they mete out. As Locke describes it, as everyone in the state of nature is 'both Judge and Executioner of the Law of Nature, Men being partial to themselves, Passion and Revenge is very apt to carry them too far, and with too much heat, in their own Cases; as well as negligence and unconcernedness, to make them too remiss, in other Mens'.[31]

Possessing a power to execute the law of nature, individuals, in Locke's opinion, are too likely to be biased and judge in accordance with self-interest when the transgression affects them personally, and are unlikely to show any interest at all when they are not personally or directly involved. Quintessentially, this is an observation or judgment on human nature. Individuals are self-interested, and when given power are prone to abuse it. Within the state of nature the power to execute the law of nature is shared by all; hence the abuse of power is associated with individual disputes. From the analysis contained in Locke's state of nature argument it is but one short step to assume that the abuse of power in the hands of one in absolute authority in civil society can be many times greater than the abuse of power in the state of nature.[32] Government, then, must be limited, for human nature can and does lead to an abuse of power if individuals are provided with that opportunity.

Locke's anxiety about the inconveniences of the state of nature originates from his understanding of human nature. But this point seems to be lost on Marshall. Whilst there may be differences between Locke and the anarchists, the initial comparison with Locke, understood in terms of a commentary upon human nature, reveals that the social anarchists have more in common with Locke than

Marshall appears to be aware of or cares to admit. As Locke's concern to limit the powers of government, to minimize the dangers of an abuse of power, derives from a particular set of assumptions about human nature, so the social anarchists are cognizant of, and respond to, the potential problems that are generated by the endurance of egoism in human nature.

Whereas the mechanisms or practices for dealing with the problems caused by human nature may vary between liberalism and anarchism, the two ideologies are responding to and reflecting a shared appreciation of the egoism that is present in human nature. One way that Locke reacts to this, is to build into his theory of political obligation a right to resistance. Alternatively, one could consider the anxiety about human nature and a possible abuse of power that underwrites the constitutional strategy of the Founding Fathers of the American Revolution, very much influenced by Locke, in establishing a formal separation of powers as a means to avoid an excessive concentration of power in any one institution of state.[33] Responding to the same concerns, social anarchists have cautioned Marxists about the dangers inherent in their revolutionary strategy of the 'dictatorship of the proletariat'. More importantly, some social anarchists (notably Proudhon), seem to attempt to obviate the dangers of egoism by retreating to a position that corresponds so closely to a state that it becomes increasingly difficult to justify this portrait of future society as anarchy.

Given the shared concern or anxiety about the potential dangers that egoism presents, the question that Marshall ought to be addressing is not how Locke and the anarchists differ, but why it is that they do not agree. What is it that separates liberalism from anarchism? Some explanation is required to explain why it is that the social anarchists, unlike Locke, appear, as Marshall thinks, to be 'confident that the natural solidarity of interests and the advantages of a free and communal life will be enough to maintain social order, and with the principal causes of strife – imposed authority and unequal property – eradicated, social harmony will prevail'.[34]

The answer, for Marshall, resides in his belief that anarchists offer a contextual conception of human nature. Whilst Marshall may not always be aware of the latent assumptions about human nature that underpin some of his observations on anarchism, he is conscious of the overlap between anarchism and liberalism on the subject of power and its possible abuse. He refers, for instance, to the fact that anarchism shares with liberalism a recognition of Acton's caveat 'that power corrupts and absolute power corrupts absolutely'.[35] He concedes, further, that anarchists subscribe to the view of a will to power in humankind. This has been noted in his assessment of Kropotkin above, but it also underscores his comprehension of anarchism as a whole. Accordingly, he writes that anarchists 'recognise with Hobbes and Adler that the will to power over others is a common tendency amongst human beings. They are aware that, given the opportunity, not only do ex-slaves often try to become masters, but oppressed men try to find weaker beings to lord it over.'[36] 'But,' he continues, 'anarchists do not see that this tendency is intrinsic in human nature, but rather a product of our authoritarian and hierarchical society.'[37]

In suggesting that anarchists concur with the liberals on the subject of power and its abuses, Marshall is claiming that the two ideologies arrive at a common conclusion from different directions. The liberal insistence on minimal government reflects their assumption that egoism is an ineradicable and therefore permanent feature of human nature that has to be accounted for in any society. The anarchists, according to Marshall, do not support such a view. In their opinion, the problems of egoism are endemic to authoritarian and hierarchical societies alone. This, then, is the difference, for Marshall, between Locke and the anarchists. The two ideologies are operating separate conceptions of human nature. For the anarchists, a change of environment will lead to a change in human nature, or so Marshall informs us; whereas for the liberal, human nature will remain unaltered but will be kept in check after the transition from a state of nature to civil society.

To the extent that Marshall prosecutes this line of reasoning he has formulated a relatively coherent and defensible argument. As such it would account for the manner in which the social anarchists transcend the caution exhibited by liberals in their endeavours to establish a working basis for the good society. But Marshall's analysis does not stop here. He goes on to suggest that a complementary or additional reason for the anarchists' conviction in a future stateless society is to be found in their unbridled optimism. As he describes it, shortly after his passage on Locke, anarchism's 'confidence in the advantages of freedom, of letting alone, is thus grounded in a kind of cosmic optimism. Without the interference of human beings, natural laws will ensure that spontaneous order will emerge.'[38]

The question that has to be raised here, though, is whether this optimism bears any relation to the anarchists' conception of human nature. The quotation just cited would appear to indicate that the optimism displayed by anarchists has little to do with human nature.

Evidently, it descends from a rather metaphysical design that orders society according to the laws of nature. Presumably these are not the laws of nature that Locke refers to. So what are they? Marshall, not surprisingly, is rather reticent on this issue. Further analysis reveals that human nature may indeed have a part to play in the optimistic outlook that identifies the anarchist approach. Later in his mammoth-sized text Marshall reiterates his earlier point about optimism, but at the same time acknowledges that human nature may be partly responsible for the anarchists' confidence in a future society without a state. 'Anarchists are,' he writes, 'unashamedly optimistic. Many base their optimism on the existence of self-regulation in nature, on the spontaneous harmony of interests in society, and on the potential goodwill of humanity.'[39]

Apparently, human nature does contribute to the anarchists' optimistic assessment about the possibility of a future stateless society, but this position is difficult to reconcile with the judgment Marshall makes earlier in his text that anarchists generally doubt the existence of any natural goodness in humankind. Although Marshall acknowledges that 'Kropotkin came closest to a notion of "natural goodness"', he admits that few 'anarchists believe in natural goodness'. On the contrary, 'it could be argued that the anarchists have not only a realistic, but even a pessimistic view of human nature'.[40]

What, then, is one to make of Marshall's argument? On the one hand he seems to be suggesting that anarchists invest their faith in future society because they believe that the transformation in circumstances and environment brought about by the change from capitalist society to anarchist society will release the potential for goodwill or sociability in human nature. For this to happen, though, human beings must already possess the ability for sociability or goodwill in capitalist society. If goodwill is to be considered a potentiality of human nature, then the capacity for goodwill cannot have been eradicated by capitalist society, for surely that is the nature of any phenomenon described as potential – it is there just waiting to blossom in the right environment. Presumably, this is simply suppressed by the environment that individuals find themselves in under capitalist rule. If this analysis is right, and I can see no other obvious explanation, then Marshall is not saying that anarchists assume that human nature is entirely dependent on environmental circumstances, that it is completely malleable; rather he is implying that the conception of human nature that anarchists employ contains an assumption that there is something given or intrinsic about human nature, notably goodwill. On the other hand, it appears that whatever it is that is innate in human nature, most anarchists do not think that it is natural goodness. The deeper one dives the murkier the water becomes.

Perhaps it would be fairer to Marshall to say that his confusion arises from the difficulty he experiences in arranging his argument. It seems that, whilst he is in possession of the necessary pieces of the puzzle, the pattern or picture of the jigsaw eludes him. For example, in pronouncing that the optimism displayed by the anarchists is dependent, in part, on an assumption about human nature, Marshall seems to be saying, in something of a surreptitious whisper, that sociability or goodwill is intrinsic in human nature and it is this which provides the grounds for anarchism's optimism. At the same time, he is forced to recognize that most anarchists refrain from affirming this. Moreover, the emphasis on innateness threatens the very success of the transition from capitalist society to anarchist society. This is why Marshall wants to argue that the anarchists consider egoism to be peculiar to capitalism alone. For in proposing that sociability or goodwill is inherent in human nature, Marshall will have to advance very important and convincing reasons to explain why egoism is not innate. Obviously he cannot do this, and hence attempts to usher in the sociability argument through the back door.

A better strategy would be to announce that anarchists do believe that human nature has intrinsic properties and these include both egoism and sociability. Recognition of the former is something they have in common with liberalism. Acknowledgement of the latter is indicative of their shared heritage with socialism. It explains why anarchists observe with a persuasive measure of accuracy the corrupting effects of power. It explains further why they counsel against the dictatorship of the proletariat or a workers' state. Likewise, it accounts for their belief in the ultimate attainability of a peaceful, harmonious society that is devoid of the oppressive structures that demarcate capitalist society.[41] More importantly, it clarifies the inconsistency or ambivalence inherent in anarchist ideological theory.

It is this double inheritance that illuminates the anarchist philosophy of history; the conviction that there are two distinctly identifiable trends in human history: libertarianism and authoritarianism. That history may unfurl its consequences in either direction amounts to a confirmation of the doctrine that human nature may at one time be subject to the influences of either egoism or sociability. By ascribing to human nature the capacities of both egoism and sociability, the social anarchists are able to explain why it is that the modern state developed in the first place, and are forced to concede that any future historical developments may either reinforce or reject the predominating historical trend.[42]

Of course much of the optimism present in anarchist writings was fuelled by the general ambience of the late eighteenth and nineteenth centuries. As April Carter remarks, the utopian dimension of revolutionary political movements had its origins in 'the historical optimism of the nineteenth century'.[43] Science too was contributing to this climate of optimism. As Kelly observes, Bakunin's caveat about the dangers of a scientific élite becoming a new ruling class was significant, if only because his warnings were made at a time when scientific advances instilled the hope that science would remedy society's ills.[44]

This is undoubtedly true, but it is only a partial explanation for the anarchists' faith in future society. Like all other ideologists, anarchists have little reservation in selecting evidence that supports their conclusions or political preferences; and, in keeping with the times, anarchists were not reluctant about engaging in apocalyptical rhetoric, or of announcing the imminence of revolution. Such activities were an integral part of the broad socialist milieu, which included revolutionary anarchists like Bakunin and Kropotkin, and were representative of the climate of revolutionary fervour that swept across much of Europe during the nineteenth century.[45] But a deeper analysis of the relationship between human nature and history commands the conclusion that anarchists have no good reason to suppose that history will favour their preferred social outcome.

A Utopia Too Far?

A conception of human nature is a necessary condition of the anarchists' belief in the possibility of a future stateless society. It is a tool for criticizing present social and economic relations, and, thereby, also a means for providing a moral justification for future society; and it serves as a foundation for constructing the edifice of a stateless society. Without that basis anarchism would be devoid of one of its major weapons in its attempt to prove the viability of an anarchist society. However, anarchists have also to provide convincing historical reasons to account for their belief that a future stateless society is possible. By itself, human nature may be a necessary condition; but it is not in itself a sufficient condition in attempting to argue the possibility of a stateless society. In other words, anarchists cannot rely solely on human nature to explain why it is that a stateless society will come about in the future. Something above and beyond a conception of human nature is required to explain the optimism of the anarchists that a social revolution is imminent.

To avoid the charge of utopianism, anarchism has to draw on historical evidence to support its belief that an anarchist society will one day emerge from the mists of history. Traditionally, this optimism and the evidence for that has been drawn from the anarchists' socialist inheritance. As Kelly has noted, both 'German left Hegelians and French utopian socialists were united in the optimistic belief in the inexorable movement of history from slavery to freedom'.[46] It is this kind of belief in the progress of history toward anarchy or freedom that leads commentators like Daniel Guérin to argue that anarchism employs 'the historical method in an attempt to prove that the society of the future is not an anarchist invention, but the actual product of the hidden effects of past events'.[47]

History, however, may not assume a unilinear direction toward a society that is blessed with an ever increasing degree of freedom. This work has revealed that the social anarchists perceive history as a kind of Manichean battle between the forces of liberty and the forces of authority. Later anarchists, such as Emma Goldman, support this view, believing that historical progress results in 'an enlargement of the liberties of the individual with a corresponding decrease of authority wielded over him by external forces'.[48] The result of this philosophy of history is that anarchists have to abandon any pretence that anarchism is historically inevitable. Thus Avrich comments that Bakunin 'refused to recognize any preordained laws of history. He rejected the view that social change depends on the gradual unfolding of "objective" historical conditions. He believed, on the contrary, that individuals shape their own destinies, that their lives cannot be squeezed into a Procrustean bed of abstract sociological formulas.'[49]

There is, then, no historical guarantee that anarchy will ever be reached, and in this sense anarchism should be regarded as a utopian political ideology. Anarchism's philosophy of history reveals that the revolutionary rhetoric that anarchists engaged in during the nineteenth century was essentially optimistic. Revolution, if it is not inevitable, is a matter of will; and the best means for assisting the revolutionary will of the masses is to inspire them with an insurrectionary demagoguery that convinces them of the proximity of revolution. Likewise, human nature can only offer hope. Creating a social environment that is designed to foster the principles of sociability in humanity is no guarantee that human nature will respond in this direction (although it could – hence the hope.). Neither history nor human nature can afford a bond that will deliver an anarchist society at the time of asking.

Both history and human nature are involved in setting out what is possible in politics. The nature of the relationship between history and human nature in a political ideology is responsible for defining the parameters of possibility. The real criticism of an ideology, then, lies not in comparing its vision of the good life with existing reality, but in determining the extent to which it differs 'from how things must be'.[50] The interplay between anarchism's philosophy of history and its conception of human nature results in the very possibility of an anarchy being questioned on grounds of both history and human nature. Accordingly, it is not in a position to meet its self-incurred obligation of a stateless society. Anarchism should be classified as a utopian ideology, because contrary to Kropotkin's protestations it does convey 'the idea of something that *cannot* be realised'.[51] Marshall's point, then, about the ideology of anarchism as a creative synthesis of liberalism and socialism is not entirely accurate. As Paul Thomas recognized, the combination of liberalism and socialism 'is bound to be tense and unsteady'.[52] If anything Thomas has understated the strength of the tension. Rather than resulting in a creative synthesis, as Marshall maintains, anarchism's double inheritance has left it caught between desiring a stateless society and realizing the unlikelihood of its ever getting there. Consequently, it might be better to think of liberalism and socialism as the thesis and antithesis of anarchism, an ideology that is still searching for a successful synthesis of its ideological progenitors.

Notes

1. See, for example, D.E. Apter 'The Old Anarchism and the New – Some Comments', in David E. Apter and James Joll (eds) *Anarchism Today* (Macmillan, London, 1971) pp. 4–6.

2. See M.B. Hamilton 'The Elements of the Concept of Ideology', *Political Studies* 35, 1 (1987) p. 38.

3. G. Duncan, 'Understanding Ideology', *Political Studies* 35, 4 (1987) p. 651.

4. Robert J. McShea, 'Human Nature Theory and Political Philosophy', *American Journal of Political Science* 22, 3, (1978) p. 677.

5. G. Duncan, 'Political Theory and Human Nature', in I. Forbes and S. Smith (eds) *Politics and Human*

Nature (Pinter, London, 1983) p. 11.

6. A. Vincent, 'British Conservatism and the Problem of Ideology', *Political Studies* 42, 2 (1994) p. 206.

7. Given the recent developments in conservative practice and theory, both in the United Kingdom and America, the identity of conservatism is now a matter of some dispute. Such problems, however, are of little concern to this work. So, for argument's sake, I will assume that to be a conservative is to be devoid of what Scruton regards as an excessive dependence on economic matters. See, for example, his chapter on property in R. Scruton, *The Meaning of Conservatism* (Penguin, Harmondsworth, 1980).

8. Although rather different from traditionalist conservatism in many ways, the neo-conservatism of Thatcher continued the commitment to the basic law and order programme by investing heavily in defence and policing, despite its declared aim of reducing public expenditure. See, for example, A. Gamble, 'The Politics of Thatcherism', *Parliamentary Affairs* 42, 3, (1989) p. 357.

9. A recent and convincing argument against this is provided by Vincent, *op. cit.*

10. This philosophy of imperfection is manifested quite openly by Edmund Burke, who is often regarded as the father of modern conservatism. See E. Burke, *Reflections on the Revolution in France*, (Penguin, Harmondsworth, 1982) pp. 171 and 193. For a general appreciation of conservatism as a philosophy of imperfection, see A. Quinton, *The Politics of Imperfection* (Faber & Faber, London, 1978).

11. This description of the relationship between the id and the ego is to be found in 'The Ego and the Id', in S. Freud, *On Metapsychology: The Theory of Psychoanalysis*, trans. J. Strachey (Penguin, Harmondsworth, 1984) pp. 363–4. Evidence that conservatives seek justification of humankind's moral imperfections outside religion is provided by Quinton, *op. cit.*, p. 14.

12. This classic quotation is drawn from T. Hobbes, *Leviathan* (Penguin, Harmondsworth, 1981) p. 186.

13. If conservatism displays inconsistency in its belief that the ruling classes are exempt from the imperfections of human nature, Marxists, in establishing the 'dictatorship of the proletariat', proffer what is, to the anarchist, an argument that is devoid of any appreciation of a notion of a will to power.

14. D. Miller, *Anarchism* (Dent, London, 1984) p. 93.

15. M. Bakunin, *Revolutionary Catechism* (1866), in S. Dolgoff (ed.), *Bakunin on Anarchy* (George Allen & Unwin, London, 1973) p. 91.

16. Quoted in D. Guérin, *Anarchism: From Theory to Practice*, (Monthly Review Press, New York, 1970) p. 22.

17. A. Heywood, *Political Ideas and Concepts: An Introduction*, (Macmillan, London, 1994) p. 317.

18. Peter Marshall, *Demanding the Impossible: A History of Anarchism*, (HarperCollins, London, 1992) is in keeping with this view. He argues that anarchism 'combines ideas and values from both liberalism and socialism and may be considered a creative synthesis of the two great currents of thought' (p. 639). A similar assumption about the

coherent combination of liberalism and socialism in Bakunin's collectivist anarchism is made by B. Morris, *Bakunin: The Philosophy of Freedom*, (Black Rose Books, Montréal, 1993) p. 152.

19. B. Russell, *Roads to Freedom*, (Unwin, London, 1977) p. 46.

20. The quotation is drawn from Bakunin's *Federalism, Socialism and Anti-Theologism*, (1867), in Dolgoff, *op. cit.*, p. 127.

21. Marshall has some useful observations on the relationship of anarchism to both liberalism and socialism. See Marshall, *op. cit.*, pp. 639–42.

22. As P. Thomas, *Marx and the Anarchists*, (Routledge & Kegan Paul, London, 1985) pp. 13–14 points out, neither Marx nor the anarchists separated means from ends in an absolute sense. 'Both Marx and Bakunin', he writes, 'saw the International not only as the embodiment of the revolutionary movement as it then existed, but also as a presentiment – quite possibly the presentiment – of future society which, like all societies, would be stamped by its origins.' In this sense, the means are the ends.

23. G.P. Maximoff, *The Political Philosophy of Bakunin: Scientific Anarchism*, (Free Press, Glencoe, 1964) p. 249.

24. Within this context I consider the terms socialism and communism to be interchangeable.

25. As John Clark indicates, there are a number of disagreements between anarchism and Marxism in particular. See his *The Anarchist Moment* (Black Rose Books, Montréal, 1984). A short but useful survey of the nature of the differences is provided in chapter 13 of Morris, *op. cit.*

26. One of the better known examples of this is the work of R. Nozick,

Anarchy, State, and Utopia, (Blackwell, Oxford, 1974). Thomas, *op. cit.*, p. 8 provides a brief but illuminating comparison of Locke and anarchism.

27. See J. Locke, *Two Treatises of Government*, (New American Library, New York, 1965) pp. 395–9.

28. For an expression of the state of nature in these terms, see ibid., p. 309.

29. All three inconveniences are described by Locke in ibid., pp. 396–7.

30. Marshall, *op. cit.*, p. 14.

31. Locke, *op. cit.*, p. 396.

32. This seems to be a recognized understanding of Locke's interpretation. See, for example, I. Hampsher-Monk, *A History of Modern Political Thought* (Blackwell, Oxford, 1992) p. 98.

33. Of course it should be noted that Montesquieu was probably the source upon which the Founding Fathers drew when deciding to institute a separation of powers, rather than Locke.

34. Marshall, *op. cit.*, p. 629.

35. Ibid., p. 640.

36. Ibid., pp. 46–7.

37. Ibid., p. 47.

38. Ibid., p. 14.

39. Ibid., p. 664.

40. Ibid., p. 643.

41. The similarity of Marx and Bakunin on this issue is noted by A. Kelly, *Mikhail Bakunin: A Study in the Psychology and Politics of Utopianism*, (Clarendon Press, Oxford, 1982) p. 195.

42. Marshall is understandably reluctant to get into a debate about the anarchist philosophy of history; because as he comments, in relation to Proudhon, by 'arguing that authority and liberty presuppose each other, Proudhon crosses the

boundary from anarchism to liberalism with his belief in a minimal State to ensure contracts are kept.' (Marshall, *op. cit.*, p. 253.) What Marshall seems unwilling to admit is that as both Bakunin and Kropotkin follow Proudhon's philosophy of history (see Kelly, *op. cit.*, p. 121) his argument is germane to all of the nineteenth-century social anarchists.

43. A. Carter, *The Political Theory of Anarchism*, (Routledge & Kegan Paul, London, 1971) p. 84.

44. See Kelly, *op. cit.*, pp. 203–4.

45. Bakunin's hopes of imminent revolution are detailed in ibid, pp. 184–5. Evidence of Kropotkin's belief in impending revolution has been outlined in the previous chapter.

46. Kelly, *op. cit.*, p. 286. It is worth noting that Bakunin was greatly influenced by left Hegelian thinkers, and by Hegel. Bakunin first translated Hegel's *Gymnasium Lectures* into Russian in 1838. As A. Lehning, (ed.) *Michael Bakunin: Selected Writings* (Cape, London, 1973) p. 11 notes, this 'was the first of Hegel's works to appear in Russian.'

47. Guérin, *op. cit.*, p. 41. See also ibid., pp. 153–4.

48. E. Goldman, 'The Individual, Society and the State', in A.K. Shulman (ed.) *Red Emma Speaks: Selected Writings and Speeches by Emma Goldman* (Wildwood House, London, 1979) p. 87. Cf. ibid., p. 97.

49. P. Avrich, *Anarchist Portraits*, (Princeton University Press, New Jersey, 1988) p. 6.

50. G. Duncan, 'Political Theory and Human Nature', in Forbes and Smith, *op. cit.*, p. 15.

51. P. Kropotkin, *Modern Science and Anarchism*, (Freedom Press, London, 1923) p. 46. Emphasis in the original.

52. Thomas, *op. cit.*, p. 7.

7

Epilogue

To Abandon Human Nature?

The difficulties associated with the concept of human nature have led some to suggest that the concept should be jettisoned. 'It is my view,' Marshall writes, 'that we should abandon the use of the term "human nature" since it implies that there is a fixed essence within us which requires certain conditions to express itself, or some inherent force which directs us outside the influence of history or culture.'[1] Initially, this may seem like an apostasy of a conception of human nature in favour of existentialism. However, Marshall stops short of adopting a fully-fledged existentialism. Instead he opts for what he terms a 'soft determinism'. Whilst Marshall acknowledges that 'there are causes which influence us', he qualifies this admission by suggesting that 'all causes [are] incomplete and open-ended. Such causes dispose but do not determine.'[2] Furthermore, as for the search for an unmistakable identity or essence of human nature, whether it be good or evil, we should leave well alone. 'We have,' he acknowledges, 'innate tendencies for both types of behaviour; it is our circumstances which encourage or check them. While our present authoritarian and hierarchical society encourages egoism, competition and aggression, there is good reason to think that a free society without authority and coercion would encourage our benevolent and sympathetic tendencies.'[3]

By enunciating such arguments Marshall is placing himself very firmly within the social anarchist framework of the nineteenth century. For whatever reason though, Marshall is either unable or unwilling to recognize the similarity of his own views and the assumptions that underpin the social anarchists' conception of human nature. However, in following their paradigm of human nature he countenances the accepted view of the social anarchists that there 'is no pre-ordained pattern to history, no iron law of capitalist development, no straight railroad which we have to follow. Although it is always made on prior circumstances, history is what we make it; and the future, as the past, can be either authoritarian or libertarian depending on our choices and actions.'[4]

There are two very good reasons for not rejecting the notion of human nature. First, because ideologies are in the business of proselytism it is human nature which serves as the linchpin when endeavouring to persuade prospective converts to throw their lot in with any political creed. A conception of human nature, then, is at the heart of justifications for this or that ideology. Accordingly, to attempt to persuade a sceptic of the merits of one's cause without recourse to a conception of human nature would render that task exceptionally difficult. The absence of any understanding of what constitutes the well-being of humankind, or of how individuals are to find fulfilment of their potentialities, leaves one in a position devoid of meaningful criteria by which to arbitrate between alternative forms of social, political and economic organization. Indeed, it is difficult to imagine what an ideology without a conception of human nature would look like.

Secondly, there are sound philosophical reasons for maintaining a conception of human nature within the anarchist ideological narrative. Social anarchism embodies a humanist perspective. It is not that it argues that human nature is truly inexplicable by reference to nature alone, but that the value of any future anarchy is conceived in terms that plainly benefit the human individual above all others. Social anarchism is unashamedly human-centred and anarchy promotes the flourishing of human nature. It is as though we owe it to ourselves to strive for anarchy. By releasing ourselves from the yoke of capitalism and its dehumanizing practices, anarchy enables individuals to become truly free, to fulfil their true nature by discarding the profit motive as the *modus operandi* of society.

Much of this is inspired by anarchism's socialist inheritance. But whatever its origins, such reasoning is becoming increasingly out of place in a world awakening to the tocsin of environmental degradation. Many people now believe that capitalism is not solely to blame for our current environmental problems, but that technology and industrialization themselves are as equally if not more guilty.[5] People are nowadays not only conscious of the legacy of environmental difficulties that arise from industrial production, but are becoming increasingly aware that the old models of politics, the old division between capital and labour, between capitalism and socialism, can no longer properly explain or offer viable solutions to our present environmental predicament. But it is precisely at this juncture that anarchism holds an advantage over its political rivals. Kropotkin was clearly aware of the need to achieve balanced communities and maintain a blend of industrial and agricultural production, and is occasionally cited as a source of inspiration for green political thinkers.[6] And it is precisely this kind of attitude that contemporary anarchists should preserve. Amidst a growing concern about the sustainability of our contemporary lifestyles, anarchism can only hope to convince people of the validity of its epistemology by building upon the accomplishments of its most consistent and articulate theorist.

Calls to abandon human nature emasculate anarchism's ability to present a holistic ontology that encapsulates not only present-day ecological consciousness but the basic building blocks of our comprehension of what it means to be human and our relationship with nature. Ever since the advent of evolutionary theory, elaborated with notable success by Charles Darwin in his *The Origin of Species* (1859), it has become increasingly difficult to divorce human beings from nature. One of the obvious implications of Darwin's text and works like T.H. Huxley's *Evidence as to Man's Place in Nature* (1863) is that nature is now conceived as a system, as an interconnected and interrelated series of phenomena. As Huxley argued, all species are linked by a web of life. Individualism and atomism are philosophical concepts that are incommensurable with the portrait of nature, in its widest sense, as provided by Darwin and as taken up by contemporary green thinkers.

Very few now doubt the overall tenability of the evolutionary hypothesis, which rapidly displaced the Creationist argument elaborated by the Christian church. The important point, however, is that the evidence of evolution leads us inexorably toward a holistic paradigm from which to assess the nature and position of humankind. Humanity is incontestably rooted in nature; and insofar as it is, anarchism would do well to reconceptualize its conception of human nature. Kropotkin, then, was right to emphasize the evolution of humankind in his assessment of human nature. Any future attempts to jettison this concept would make a mockery of our present understanding of the nature and consequences of being part of humanity.

None of this distracts from an equally obvious factor, and that is that human beings are deeply social and cultural creatures. To assert that humankind's evolutionary inheritance is totally responsible for the behaviour of humanity would be absurdly deterministic and reductionist. Just as human beings are inextricably bound to a shared ontology with other species and nature itself, so society and culture also permeate our being. The holistic paradigm does not begin and end with nature. A truly holistic paradigm embodies both nature and culture. Humans correspond with nature through the media of society and culture. Therefore, any model that attempts to explain who we are and what we are doing would not be worth much if it failed to recognize the socio-cultural dimension of the relationship between humanity and nature.

Future Modes of Thinking

So where does this leave nineteenth-century anarchism? Insofar as it is humanist in its expression of humanity's place in the world it is intellectually unfashionable, if only because it bucks the trend of post-modernist discourse away from metanarratives. But that might not be a bad thing. Indeed, to the extent that anarchism recognizes egoism as a motivating factor in human behaviour then, arguably, it would be intellectually dishonest for it to pretend that it offers an ontology of humanity that is not humanist. Egoism dictates some form of self-interest, even an enlightened self-interest, in the way humanity's relationship with the environment is conceived. But the presence of humanism does not detract from anarchism's ability to reconceptualize human nature within a new holistic paradigm. It is possible to argue that humans reconsider their relationship with the environment without sacrificing any semblance of concern over their own fate or destiny. Indeed, ecological anti-humanism is beset by difficulties surrounding the concept of intrinsic value.[7] Intrinsic value is the notion that other life-forms, and even nature itself, have a value which means that we should regard nature as an end in itself and not merely as a means to satisfy the pursuit of our own ends. But in what or where do we invest intrinsic value? And as it is human beings that bestow the value, how is it possible to escape a charge of humanism or anthropocentrism? Such philosophical questions remain unresolved and point to the problems of attempting to exclude humanity from any conception of nature and the environment.

However, anarchism does have to begin to qualify its conception of humanism. At the heart of much anarchist thinking on human nature is the belief that humans need to labour. In itself this is a fairly innocuous assumption. But when it aligns itself with the Promethean objective of humanizing the world and transcending nature, in much the same way that Marx conceptualizes the struggle between nature and humanity, then anarchism should think seriously about jettisoning that conception of human nature and forging a new approach.[8] The dangers with this way of thinking lie in the susceptibility to divorce humanity from nature, a separation based on an assumption that humanity is somehow superior to nature, that it betters itself morally by dominating nature. In a sense this line of thought is to be found in Rousseau as well as Marx. In contending that humankind only achieves true or moral freedom when it leaves behind the state of nature, Rousseau considers that we have come to gain something superior to the mere independence that we cherished in our savage state. And inasmuch as Rousseau has influenced nineteenth-century anarchist thought, then that tradition of thought has to be re-examined and cleansed of any remnants of crude humanism. Such thinking has underpinned much political thought since, and still occupies many conceptual schemes, anarchism included. But it is precisely this which anarchism has to abandon. The tide of public opinion is turning against such reasoning as people become conscious of their responsibility to care for the planet. Contemporary anarchism will win few friends by repeating old orthodoxies. The struggle to overturn this reasoning is real and difficult. For it is not only political argument that contemporary anarchists have to deal with but the teachings of the Judaeo-Christian tradition itself. Central to this tradition is an understanding of the world as created by God. Within God's design humankind occupies a special place in the Great Chain of Being. That humankind was made in the image of God and that nature is there to serve the needs of humanity renders humanity separate and superior to nature. Whilst not without its critics and rival interpretations,[9] the message of Genesis imparts a powerful argument for the belief that humankind is lord of all it surveys and represents a philosophy which is undoubtedly responsible, if only in part, for nature's chronic depletion and degradation. It might be objected that in an increasingly secular society the task of overturning such philosophy, insofar as it is grounded in revealed religion, may not be as problematic as it at first seems. Perhaps there is some truth in that.

However, the reference to religion reflects the nature of the task ahead. Whether people's attitude toward the environment is determined by the Judaeo-Christian tradition or not, is of little significance. What is of importance is that that tradition is just one of the contributing factors to the present arrogance with which humankind perceives the environment. For whatever reason, humanity through its various practices has established an almost unbridgeable chasm between humanity and nature that has to be united if environmental problems are to be solved successfully.

For anarchism, this represents an immense problem but also a magnificent opportunity to help fashion the future direction of society. The scale of the problem is equivalent to the task confronting the Enlightenment. The objective here was the removal of a whole world view, a view perpetuated by the Church and indebted to myth, faith and superstitions. Similarly, the task now confronting ecologists and green anarchists is how to overcome the hegemony of an almost universally accepted world view imposed by the success of the Enlightenment. That view is composed of the benefits bestowed by materialism and industrialism, of the advantages afforded by science and technology, of an unparalleled belief in the power of reason and the sanctity of the individual. To achieve any lasting and sustainable change in the relationship between humanity and its environment it is these concepts that have to be challenged. Various attempts are being made, and one instance of this from within an anarchist perspective is the recent text by Todd May.[10] If anarchists can contribute to this challenge, then they may be presented with an unprecedented opportunity to mould the future. This is what is at stake, but the contest can only be entered by leaving behind some of the baggage of their nineteenth-century conception of human nature.

Notes

1. P. Marshall, *Demanding the Impossible*, (HarperCollins, London, 1992) p. 138.
2. Ibid., p. 141.
3. Ibid., p. 142.
4. Ibid., p. 144.
5. See, for example, J. Porritt, *Seeing Green: The Politics of Ecology Explained*, (Blackwell, Oxford, 1984) pp. 19–21.
6. See, for example, D. Pepper, *The Roots of Modern Environmentalism*, (Croom Helm, London, 1986) pp. 188–93.
7. For instance, see T. Hayward, *Ecological Thought: An Introduction*, (Polity Press, Cambridge, 1994) pp. 62–71.
8. It has already been demonstrated that both Proudhon and Bakunin adopt this line of reasoning about labour and humanity.
9. A useful introduction to the Christian position on nature is provided in D. Pepper, *Modern Environmentalism: An Introduction*, (Routledge, London, 1996) pp. 148–55.
10. T. May, *The Political Philosophy of Poststructuralist Anarchism*, (Pennsylvania State University Press, Philadelphia, 1995).

Index

SOVEREIGNTY AT THE MILLENNIUM